Secrets of the Lodge

Origins, practices and beliefs of Freemasonry

Secrets of the Lodge

Origins, practices and beliefs of Freemasonry

TUBAL CAIN

Delphi Publishing

First published in Great Britain in 1999
by Delphi Publishing.

A catalogue record for this book is available from the British Library.

ISBN 0 9535155 0 8

Printed in Great Britain

DELPHI PUBLISHING
PO Box 33, Prestatyn,
Denbighshire,
LL19 9ZP
Wales

To my friends, family and Thanos and to those who endeavour to expand mans understanding of the unknown.

CONTENTS

Part Two
BELIEFS OF FREEMASONRY

List of Plates

1. Poussin *Shepherds of Arcadia* Louvre (copyright - Bulloz, 21 Rue Bonaparte, Paris)

2. Giza Pyramids, Giza, Egypt

3. Piri Reis Map Istanbul (Copyright - The Department of Navigation, Hydrography and Oceanography of Turkish Navy)

4. Sphinx, Giza, Egypt

5. The Great Pyramid, Giza, Egypt

6. Entrance to Karnak, Luxor, Egypt

7. Lower section of Giza pyramid

8. Quarry at Aswan, Aswan, Egypt

9. Cleopatras Kneedle, London

10. Al Asqa Mosque, Jerusalem, Israel

11, Temple Mount, Jerusalem, Israel

12. Chartes Cathedral, Chartes, France

13. Templar Graves, Kilmory, Lock Sween, Argyll, Scotland

14. Inside Rosslyn Chapel, Roslin, Midlothian, Scotland (copyright - Rosslyn Chapel Trust)

15. Arial view of castle at Montsegur, France (Copyright - Network Photography)

16. First Degree sign, annonymous

17. Second Degree sign, annonymous

18. Third Degree sign, annonymous

19. Qumran, Dead Sea, Israel

20. Nazca lines, Nazca Plain, Peru

List of Illustrations

Diagram 1 showing Precession of the Earth

Diagram 2 demonstrating the angles inside a pentogram

Diagram 3 the symbol used in Masonry to denote a Grand Inspector General

Diagram 4 of John Dee's symbol uesd in *Monas Heiroglyphica*

Introduction

Approaching the elusive and controversial topic of Freemasonry has not been a straightforward task. First of all I am not a Freemason, and am therefore free from the constraints and oaths to which all Freemasons are bound and are obliged to swear upon. Being outside the 'brotherhood of men' (Freemasonry) has made it difficult at times to obtain immediate access to knowledge concerning Freemasonry, however it has also enabled me to examine it objectively and to gain a perspective which, it is hoped, the average reader will be able to comprehend and which this book will be able to communicate effectively to the reader.

When I first started my research into Freemasonry, I began reading the existing books on the market. Unfortunately this only served to generate more questions in my mind than

I had before I began. For instance, after reading parts of the Masonic rituals (which at first sounded ludicrous to me), I could not understand how many eminent and seemingly level-headed people, that I knew to be masons, took them so seriously. On the other hand many books gave me the impression that Masonry was in some way an academic pursuit which again I couldn't reconcile with the lack of learning exhibited by some Freemasons I knew. Within this whirlwind of confusion I remained convinced that there was an aspect or aspects to masonry which I had not yet understood or grasped and which could answer my proliferating array of questions.

Since this period of confusion I have subsequently gained an insight into Masonry which explains why men of vastly different disciplines and personalities are prepared to consider themselves collectively as a brotherhood and to acknowledge each other as brothers. Such terms of endearment, even bestowed upon perfect strangers within the craft (another term for masonry), would seem nonsensical to the average person. Even their methods of mutual recognition are guarded, by their obscurity, from the auspices of the population at large. In most cases this would be confirmed with a handshake, or even orally, e.g. "Are you a travelling man?" in which case another mason should answer "Yes, from east to west." Masons may also ask, "Are you the son of a widow?" or "Are you on the square?". It is hoped that this book will clarify the true nature of Freemasonry to the reader, and go some way to explain Freemasons' actions towards each other and the ways in which they endeavour to protect the privacy of their practices and beliefs, and in some cases even their identities as Freemasons.

Much of the information published in this book comes from first hand knowledge from Freemasons themselves, and from numerous publications, many of which are not freely accessible to the public. I am also indebted to those people who have helped me while writing this book. Throughout my research I have been fortunate to discover and decode numerous Masonic documents, which enabled me to form a much clearer picture of Freemasonry than I could ever have anticipated at the book's inception.

This book has been designed to inform the reader about the history of Freemasonry, and the secrets and beliefs which they hold so dear, a factor resulting from their turbulent history and the nature of their rituals. The terminology used in the book has been kept as basic as possible, however, the reader must become accustomed to the term 'esotericism' and the meaning of the term conveyed in the book. The term 'esoteric' is described in the dictionary, as 'with meaning that is understood only by those who have received the necessary instruction or training.' This definition can be applied very broadly, however, the words 'esoteric' and 'esoterism', as they are applied through this book, refer to the secret mystical knowledge held by the initiates of such organisations as the Rosicrucians, Orange Order, Ordo Templis Orientis (Alister Crowley Groups), the Buffaloes, the Illuminati and of course the Freemasons. These organisations are classified as esoteric, not merely because they have developed specific ways of communication only understood among themselves, but also because they are connected by underlying beliefs, the extent of which comprises the content of this book. However, much of this knowledge can only be fully grasped by those who have been initiated. To many readers esoterism will seem very alien, displaying facets beyond their imagination. But, acknowledging concepts such as spiritual rebirth and the immortality of the soul are paramount in understanding the basis upon which the beliefs of Freemasonry ultimately revolve.

As many readers will have already have noticed, Tubal Cain is a pseudonym, the significance of which will become evident to the reader in the course of the book. It was decided that the book should be published under a pseudonym as the majority of Freemasons are passionate about their secrets and beliefs. For instance, under the Freemasons' Constitutions IV(4) it instructs Masons to be:

. . . cautious in your words and carriage, that the most penetrating stranger shall not be able to discover or find out what is not proper to be intimated; and sometimes you shall divert a discourse, and manage it prudently for the honour of the worshipful faternity.[1]

However, according to a leaflet, produced by the Grand Lodge, entitled 'What is Freemasonry':

The secrets of Freemasonry are concerned with its traditional modes of recognition. It is not a secret society, since all members are free to acknowledge their membership and will do so in response to inquiries for respectable reasons. Its constitutions and rules are available to the public. There is no secret about its aims and principles. Like many other societies, it regards some of its internal affairs as private matters for its members.

From the above statement all that can be understood is that the only thing secret about freemasonry are its 'modes of recognition' and that all the other aspects of freemasonry such as their rituals and beliefs are simply private matters. But, are we talking about something which is private (by definition belonging to a particular group and not shared with others) or secret (by definition - something which is kept from the knowledge of others). I refer the reader to Constitution IV(4) above, for him or her to decide what is 'proper to be intimated'. Freemasons are also encouraged to quote, "We are not a secret society, but a society with secrets.". To my knowledge freemasons have no plans to modify this quotation.

It is hoped that the reader will consider this book a fair representation of Freemasonry's origins, practices and beliefs. Contrary to some peoples' two dimensional views on

1. Grand Lodge, United Grand Lodge of England　Constitutions, p.10

Freemasonry, this book is neither an endorsement of Freemasonry nor anti-Masonic. Throughout the book I have attempted to uncover the true nature and essence of Freemasonry and convey it to the reader in a form capable of being understood by most people. Whatever the repercussions which may emerge from this publication, I must add that what I have done I believe to be right and justified.

PART ONE

ORIGINS AND PRACTICES OF FREEMASONRY

Chapter One

What is Freemasonry?

If the Grand Master should abuse his power and render himself unworthy of the obedience of the Lodges, he shall be subjected to some new regulation, to be dictated by the occasion; because, hitherto, the Ancient Fraternity have had no reason to provide for an event which they have presumed would never happen. (Article 15. General Laws and Regulations of Freemasonry) .[1]

For those people outside the realm of Masonry (the institute to which Freemasons belong) or other esoteric societies, knowledge of what Freemasons stand for, practise and believe is a very closely guarded secret. Freemasonry is unique with respect to its large membership in Britain and throughout the world and in its ability throughout the previous couple of centuries to have sustained such secrecy and ambiguity. The Grand Lodge of England was officially founded in 1717 and

1. Grand Lodge, United Grand Lodge of England Constitutions, p.23

with this came the public acknowledgement of Masonry's existence, but, as will be demonstrated later, the roots and the foundation of Freemasons practices and beliefs are ingrained in deepest antiquity. Many Masonic Lodges claim to have been in existence since medieval times and their association with stonemasonry and medieval guilds would to some extent seem to endorse this view. Some Lodges even claim descent from as far back as the Egyptian pharaohs. But how has such an ancient society, shrouded in secrecy, maintained such a tight lid upon their beliefs and activities? What other kind of organisation could have persuaded its members through the centuries not to reveal its secrets and to keep their knowledge out of the public limelight and firmly in the realms of mystique and obscurity. It is the author's intention to explain not only the impetus behind Masonry's secrecy, but also to reveal the enigmas of Masonry and to explain its true nature, upon which a clear understanding of Masonry can be gained.

From the 280,000 (approximately) Masons in Britain, some people will surely have seen either members of their family or people they know, dressed up in a dinner jacket with briefcase in hand either going to or returning from a lodge (meeting place of the Freemasons) meeting. Lodges are scattered throughout Britain, totalling over 3,000 at the present time.[2] Most members disclose very little even to their nearest and dearest and questions about what they do within lodge meetings are quickly brushed aside by comments such as, " it's all an excuse for a group of men to get together and have a drink", or "the masons are a charitable organisation but we never talk about the good work we do." Inside their briefcases (as some people may have witnessed) they keep their Masonic literature, paraphernalia and apron, which they use in their rituals and ceremonies; it is strange, for those outside Masonry, to imagine how or even why such items are used. It is also difficult for people to fathom how many intelligent and eminent men can take such a society so seriously. Masonry is not only widespread in Britain (where it

2. Wilmshurst, Walter, The Meaning of Masonry, p.9

originated), but has spread its wings all over the world even into countries such as Saudi Arabia, Russia, Mexico and China. What is it that motivates men from all walks of life to become so secretive and protective, and to believe that they are somehow privileged to have been initiated into, and become part of the Masonic order?

Some Freemasons regard themselves as society's elite who have been introduced into a divine and highly dignified organisation and who practise certain rituals, ceremonies and guard a knowledge which they believe is too highly regarded for the auspices of the population at large. Much of the eminence and respect associated with Masons and Masonry in the past, has all but withered away. Instead the modern public's perception of Freemasons rests upon suspicion, scandal, and the ever-present conspiracy theories. Some maintain that this view has emerged from scaremongers, intent on destroying Masonry; or that it is simply a reflection of a changing society. Whatever the causes, it is evident from assessing general attitudes towards Masonry, that publicly it has lost its way in recent years, and that much of the cause of this must lie with the Masons themselves; rather than solely with the imaginations of those outside the order. The Grand Lodge now produces leaflets on Freemasonry in an attempt to dispel what they regard as people's misconceptions about freemasonry. For example in one leaflet titled Freemasonry and Society a comment is made on the use of membership:

> A Freemason must not use his membership to promote his own or anyone else's business, professional or personal interests. This is made clear directly or by inference several times during a Freemason's early career so that no Freemason can pretend to be ignorant of it. A Freemason who transgresses this rule may be suspended from Masonic activities or even expelled.

The leaflet also sets out the principles of Masonry:

> The principles of Freemasonry do not in any way conflict with its members' duties as citizens, whether at work or at home or in public life, but on the contrary should strengthen them in fulfilling their public and private responsibilities. Thus there is no conflict of interest between a Freemason's obligation and his public duty. If an actual or potential conflict of duties or interests is known to exist or is foreseen, a declaration to that effect should be made. It may on occasion be prudent to disclose membership to avoid what others mistakenly imagine to be potential conflict or bias, but this must be a matter for individual judgement.

It could be argued that if every single Freemason adhered to these principles, then the public's perception of Freemasonry would be much more favourable. Indeed people's perceptions of Masonry range from the innocent to the fantastic, but before entering further into the realms of controversy and debate, the fundamental beliefs of Masonry must be understood.

The Essence of Masonry

It is believed by Masons all over the world that Atlantis did once exist and that these Atlantean people were highly advanced - maybe not as technologically advanced as we are today - but advanced with regard to their knowledge and evolution.   The essence of Masonry is the belief that they, the Masons, are the keepers or guardians of this archaic knowledge from Atlantis (whether Atlantis did actually exist or not is discussed further on in chapter two). Schwaller de Lubicz (a prolific esoteric writer) maintains and freemasons are taught, that we as human beings have regressed spiritually throughout the thousands of years since Atlantis. It is also believed that the highly advanced knowledge of the Atlantean's was not lost after the Atlantis calamity, but was carried into the ancient cultures of the past, most notably that of the Egyptians where its possessors built the Sphinx and three great Pyramids at Giza. The knowledge possessed by the Atlanteans was only known to the high priests and pharaohs of Egypt and remained a closely guarded secret from all but the initiated. This secret knowledge was then taken out of Egypt by Moses and was then passed on through successive generations of Jewish kings and their initiates. This knowledge, Masons believe, was used in the building of Solomon's Temple, which is a central feature of Masonic lodges and their rituals performed within them. Inside all Masonic Lodges there are generally two main rooms - one is a function room, where the masons dine and have access to refreshments, and the other and most important one, is referred to as the Temple. This is supposed to represent and mirror the layout of the Temple of Solomon, and it is within this room that the Masonic rituals take place.

In spite of the destruction of the Temple of Solomon in 587 BC, the secret knowledge of the Atlanteans was still passed through the Davidic line of kings, and it is believed by Masons that Jesus was a Grand Master of his time, meaning that he was the head of an esoteric group of which his twelve disciples were part. Although this knowledge still existed after Jesus' time amongst small groups capable of withstanding the advent of Christianity and then Islam, it was not until the twelfth century that esoterism achieved prominence again - this time under the Knights Templar. Their excavations and discoveries under Solomon's Temple marked a significant turning point in esoteric history. Official accounts of the Templars maintain that they were all arrested in 1307 (many being put to death) and that after this time they simply ceased to exist. However, as will be shown later, the existence of

Freemasons testifies to the Templars' existence and their knowledge post 1307. Many Masons also claim that they inherited the majority of their esoteric knowledge from the Templars. Throughout the centuries many esoteric organisations have sprung into existence: Rosicrucians, Orangemen of Northern Ireland, Klu Klux Klan, Gesellshaft, the Buffaloes and Ordo Templis Orientis (Alister Crowley groups) to name a few. The freemasons believe they are the cream of all these other esoteric societies, and that some of these groups, which are politically motivated, have adopted obscured esoteric doctrines in order to perpetuate the cohesion amongst their members. This view is endorsed in the Grand Lodge Constitutions under Aims and Relationships of the Craft:

> 8. The Grand Lodge is aware that there do exist Bodies, styling themselves Freemasons, which do not adhere to these principles, and while that attitude exists the Grand Lodge of England refuses absolutely to have any relations with such Bodies, or to regard them as Freemasons. [3]

Freemasonry on the other hand has always presented itself as an apolitical organisation and has a:

> policy of standing aloof from every question affecting the relations between one government and another, or between political parties, or questions as to the rival theories of government. [4]

However, of these other esoteric societies, the Freemasons concede that the ones closest to the legacy of Atlantis are the Templars - a tradition which carries on to this day. However, membership to the Templar order is limited, and the privilege of becoming a Templar is normally only accessible to the kin of existing Templars usually from Grail descent (this is explained in chapter six).

3. Grand Lodge, United Grand Lodge of England Constitutions, p.x
4. Grand Lodge, United Grand Lodge of England Constitutions, No.7, p.x

There are many aspects to this archaic knowledge which Freemasons believe they have inherited from the Templars, and was the lost knowledge of the Atlanteans. This knowledge, which is entirely in a dimension of its own, cannot be communicated through words or language, but is regarded as so deeply meaningful and subconsciously linked that it can only be communicated through rituals and symbolism. It is they believe a way of communication and a knowledge which surpasses mere conscious thought and is the key to accessing a person both emotionally and spiritually into a new dimension and realization which is elevated from mere mortal and material considerations. Evidence that such spiritual practices and traditions were prevalent in ancient times has emerged recently in Graham Hancock's and Santha Faiia's *Heaven's Mirror*, which endorses Masonic beliefs that their traditions were present in, and emanated, from ancient times:

> Such correspondences lead us to suspect that the lineaments of an ancient rebirth ritual - wrapped up in sophisticated astronomical observations and descended from a world-wide cosmological system that also left its legacy in Egypt and in south -east Asia - lie scattered and fragmented throughout the land of Mexico. This system, which taught the duality and interpretation of ground and sky, earth and heaven - matter and spirit - urged the initiate to shed attachments to the sense-world (as he might drop broken flutes) and to ascend upwards, through self-sacrifice and the quest for knowledge, to the celestial realms.[5]

In today's world many people are turning to all forms of cults and religion in an attempt to find some meaning in their lives. It is not enough any more simply to satisfy the need for material wants and there always remains something irrational and inexplicable which seems to elude westerners from realising their full quality of life. The need for purpose and meaning in most peoples lives is absolute, and purpose

5. Hancock, Graham and Faiia, Santha, Heavens Mirror, p.37

is in most cases inextricably linked to the spiritual and emotional nature of a person's being. This many masons believe, is one of the fundamental flaws of today's society. It has lost sight of the subconscious or spiritual nature of mans being and has missed the fundamental lessons of a society which had advanced, many thousands of years ago, along more fulfilling lines - Atlantis.

This view is also endorsed by learned Masons who believe that glimpses of this Atlantean knowledge and the realisation it brings is evident in many ancient cultures around the world. For instance aborigines exhibit many features completely alien to western culture. They believe themselves to be telepathic and to be able to engineer out of body experiences, while such beliefs only produce scepticism, for most, in the western world. The North American Indians also claim the ability to project their spirits beyond the boundaries of time and space, as do Buddhists. They also believe in an underlying theme central to their lives, of the world being in harmony and everything being in perfect balance, which is a belief held by most ancient cultures of the world. This belief also endorses that everything occurs according to a certain type of order, a sort of perpetual pattern. One exponent of the importance of these ancient beliefs and their connection to modern science is Fritjof Capra. In his book *The Tao of Physics*, he makes startling connections between ancient eastern cultures, such as Buddhism, Taoism and Hinduism, and the development and beliefs held by modern physicists. Such beliefs, as the reader will later ascertain, are not new to esoteric thinking or the Freemasons, who maintain that the ancient cultures of the world which still exist in many places throughout the world today possess forms of this ancient but supreme Atlantean knowledge.

The depth of this knowledge is similar to and can be understood through the way people perceive art; imagine spending half an hour looking at a great painting such as a Rembrant or a Van Gogh. Most people would simply look at the colours, its accuracy and merely how well it depicts a certain scene, like that of a photograph. However, by applying a more emotional and subconscious perspective to the painting, it would be looked upon very differently. How well the painting depicts anything would not be an issue anymore, but the painting would be seen as a whole portraying a deeper meaning through its symbolism and proportions. It must be emphasised here that this ancient type of Atlantean knowledge is believed to be inherited by the Freemasons, which is inherent in amongst other things, in aspects of the arts, through painting, acting and almost all forms of expression which are free from the constraints of mere conscious thought. As Schwaller de Lubicz notes, to develop this ancient way of thinking a person must shed his simplistic conscious nature and pass beyond the purely analytical and see what each symbol expresses to him on a more emotional, subconscious and subsequent higher level. This is also the way in which a true artist would look at a painting as opposed to a lay person, and it is precisely this type of knowledge of the subconscious which the Masons believed was once possessed by the Atlanteans and is now capable of being grasped by them. Communicating on this higher level of thought and its development is central to the whole institution and purpose of Masonry. It is appreciated that the reader may at first find this a difficult concept to grasp, however its clarity will become evident as the reader advances through the book. However, it may help the reader to reflect upon the words of John R. Bennett:

> The truth (that is the truth Freemasons seek through their practices) lies concealed in its symbols, and these, constituting, as they do, a picture language, or art speech, are made to carry a complete philosophy of the existence and relations of Deity, nature and man. [6]

It is not widely known that Adolf Hitler and Wagner were both esotericists, that is, they were believers and followers of

6. Bennet, J., Origin of Freemasonry and Knights Templar, p.109

esoteric wisdom. Hitler once explained, in esoteric terms, the effect that Wagner's music had upon him:

> When I hear Wagner, it seems to me that I hear rhythms of a bygone world. I imagine to myself that one day science will discover, in the waves set in motion by The Rhinegold (an opera), the secret mutual relations connected with the order of the world. The observation of the world perceived by the senses precedes the knowledge given by the exact science as well as by philosophy. [7]

The bygone world Hitler mentions is in all probability a reference to Atlantis. He then he talks of secret mutual relations connected with the order of the world; as will be explained later this idea of mutual relations relates to Einstein's relativity theory and is ingrained in many ancient cultures throughout the world. However, the last sentence is of importance to the reader trying to grapple with the concept of Masonry or esoterism. 'Senses precedes the knowledge given by exact science . . .' , meaning that within our subconscious and through our intuition we can advance beyond the boundaries of conscious thought to which esoterists believe society today has limited its perception. This view is at the heart of esoteric and masonic thinking and is the basis upon which their beliefs ultimately stand and it is further emphasised, they believe, in Wagner's Faust. Max Heindel explains in his *Mysteries of the Great Operas*:

> A lifetime of study has brought Faust no real knowledge. The conventional sources of learning prove barren in the end . . . But the deeper he delves into matter, the greater the mysteries that beset his path, and at last he will be forced to abandon further research or believe in God as a Spirit whose life invests every atom of matter. Faust has come to that point. He says that he has not worked for gold 'nor

7. Baigent, Leigh and Lincon, The Messianic Legacy, p.179

treasure, nor worldly honour, rank, nor pleasure.' He has striven from love of research and has come to the point where he sees that a spirit world is about us all; and through this world, through magic, he now aspires to a higher, more real knowledge than that contained in books. [8]

Another example of this higher knowledge is evident, the Masons believe, through music itself. All types of music have the ability to bring out some type of feeling or emotion within a person. Why do some melodies, especially those in minor keys sound melancholic, while others sound soothing to the ear or exhilarating? Esotericists maintain that the whole concept of creating music which is pleasing to the ear, is to finely balance harmony with a certain amount of discord. As the reader will later discover, this is a further concept of duality which the more learned Masons will recognise as being at the heart of Masonic ideology. Pythagoreans (the followers and advocates of Pythagorean thought which many believe to be esoteric) believe that there is a hidden mathematical reason why a certain order of notes strikes us as harmonious. They believe, as Isaac Newton (past Grand Master) and many other esoterists, that the series of notes which comprise the musical octave, mirror the distances of the planets from the earth. Part of this higher knowledge (originally possessed by the Atlanteans) has to do with the appreciation of the effects of different music and sounds. Music, for everyone is seen as a form of expression, it is not as rigid as many of man's pursuits have become today. Therefore, it may be no coincidence that Freemasons have excelled in the field of music: John Philip Sousa, Sullivan (from Gilbert and Sullivan), Wolfgang Amadeus Mozart, Sibelius, Haydn and Claude Debussy who was a Templar Grand Master. It may have been through the application of their esoteric knowledge, as esoterists endorse, that these composers were able to produce some of the greatest classical music ever. The creation of music is an instinctive expression accessing much deeper

8. Heindel, Max, Mysteries of the Great Operas, p.14

insights than exist on a purely conscious level. It is in this respect that Masons believe that humankind has regressed since the days of Atlantis, since the ability to access this knowledge, which the masons believe is within everyone, is severely curtailed by the type of society we have made today. Masons would argue that mankind's emphasis on conscious thought has made society rigid, in this respect, and the result has been the stagnation of our spiritual evolution.

Within the past century at least there has been a massive divergence between the arts and the sciences. There is even scant convergence, in the academic world, between the subjects within arts or within sciences, which has produced a high degree of specialisation in most fields today. The Masons believe, because of their knowledge, supposedly derived from Atlantis, that this divergence is unfortunate because for mankind to fully evolve both the arts and the sciences or religion and science, must be appreciated and considered concurrently. This is reflected by Manly P. Hall (a 33 degree Freemason) in the *The Lost Keys of Freemasonry*:

> Science and theology are two ends of a single truth, but the world will never receive the full benefit of their investigations until they have made peace with each other, and labour hand in hand for the accomplishment of the great work- the liberation of spirit and intelligence from the three- dimensional prison-house of ignorance, superstition, and fear. [9]

An example of convergence between art and science can be demonstrated through the works of a well known esoteric painter Leonardo da Vinci. His depiction of the Last Supper, at first glance, seems at first to be simply a painting of Jesus and his disciples sitting at a long table, however, many esotericists believe that the painting displays elements of precision geometry, which to them testify to its esoteric undertones. Similarly, Henry Lincon co-author of the best-selling *The Holy Blood and the Holy Grail* discovered that Poussin's

9. Hall, Manly p., The Lost Keys of Freemasonry, p. xvi

Shepherds of Arcadia, as shown in Plate 1, exhibits pentagonal geometry. Although many art historians dismiss this finding as purely coincidental, Lincon has also discovered that certain places when linked up on the map surrounding the area which the painting supposedly depicts, also exhibit the geometry of the pentagram; the details of which are discussed in chapter six.

Masons are taught that a type of precision exists within art, and scientists could now be beginning to discover that there may be justification for such a belief ; through the 'Chaos Theory' . The chaos theory states that every random occurrence is not random at all, but occurs in accordance with a definite pattern. Such a pattern is only evident after thousands and thousands of random events. This theory applies right across the board from the dripping of water from a tap, to the number of persons infected over time during a measles epidemic. The Masons go further in their beliefs maintaining that these patterns are governed by numerology and celestial or astrological forces. The basis of this higher knowledge is that by accessing our powerful subconscious we will then be able to see things as a whole, rather than seeing everything at purely face value, a consequence which masons, and esoterists believe is a product of our conditioning.

Masonry touches upon many broad and diverse subjects such as : numerology, astrology (celestial harmony), the existence of extraterrestrials, Egyptology, the Bloodline of Jesus and even spiritual resurrection. Much of the previous statement is qualified in the Fellowcraft or second degree of Freemasonry, where the candidate is required to answer certain questions put to him:

Q. What do the seven steps allude to?

A.   The seven sabbatical years; seven years of famine; seven years in building the temple; seven golden candlesticks; seven wonders of the world; seven planets; but more especially the seven liberal arts and sciences; which are, grammar, rhetoric, logic, arithmetic, geometry, music, and astronomy. For these and many other reasons, the number seven has ever been held in high estimation among Masons."

Although these beliefs seem to be an array of seemingly unconnected subjects and may be difficult for the reader to acknowledge, through this jungle of diversity there exists an underlying theme in the way that freemasons think and approach their beliefs disguised in symbolism and allegory.

Masons also profess to be the inheritors of the esoteric knowledge of the Templars, who display an impressive acumen in their Grand Masters. Below is shown the Grand Masters of the Prieure de Sion (the names of which correlate closely to the Templar Grand Masters), which have existed through the centuries taken from Beignt, Leigh and Lincon's *The Holy Blood and the Holy Grail* [10]; information which initially appeared in the *Dossiers Secrets* by H.Lobineau.

Grand Masters of the Prieure' de Sion

Jean de Gisors	1188-1220
Marie de Saint-Clair	1220-1266
Guillaume de Gisors	1266-1307
Edouard de Bar	1307-1336
Jeanne de Bar	1336-1351
Jean de Saint- Clair	1351-1366
Blanche d'Evreux	1366-1398
Nicolas Flamel	1398-1418
Rene d'Anjou	1418-1480
Iolande de Bar	1480-1483
Sandro Filipepi	1483-1510
Leonard de Vinci	1510-1519
Connetable de Bourbon	1519-1527
Ferdinand de Gonzague	1527-1575

10. Baigent, Leigh and Lincon, The Holy Blood and the Holy Grail, p.133

Louis de Nevers	1575-1595
Robert Fludd	1595-1637
J.Valentin Andrea	1637-1654
Robert Boyle	1654-1691
Isaac Newton	1691-1727
Charles Radclyffe	1727-1746
Charles de Lorraine	1746-1780
Maximilian de Lorraine	1780-1801
Charles Nodier	1801-1844
Victor Hugo	1844-1885
Claude Debussy	1885-1918
Jean Cocteau	1918-

Although these names appear as the Grand Masters of the Prieure' de Sion, which is closely affiliated with the Templar Order, many believe that some of these men were also Grand Masters of the Templar Order. As the reader will acknowledge these men have been highly influential in placing their mark upon and shaping history through their particular insights and discoveries. But, is it mere coincidence that these men who have advanced the boundaries of both art and science, all happen to be Grand Masters? Or is it the case that these men somehow applied their esoteric knowledge and as such their amazing contribution to history and the advancement of knowledge was a consequence of this? Whatever the answer may be, it will be obvious to the reader where the Masons' answer will lie. Furthermore many of the men that have made an indelible mark on history were Masons: Sir Winston S. Churchill, Lawrence of Arabia, General Douglas MacArthur, Oscar Wilde, Robert Burns, Mark Twain, Sir Arthur Conan Doyle. Here are just a few names which demonstrate how widespread masonry is and the immense contribution that these men have made in shaping events and influencing society into what it has become today. It is possible that the way these great men conducted themselves throughout their lives, may be attributed to their esoteric teachings. For instance Lawrence of Arabia, after his secondment to the Arab Bureau, made the decision to cross the Sinai and attack Aqaba. He did this in the belief that the symbolism of such a feat would unite the Arab people behind him; the significance of symbolism in communicating esoteric knowledge will become apparent later. As he stated in his book *The Seven Pillars of Wisdom*:

> The Sheriffs rebellion had been unsatisfactory for the last few months: (standing still, which, with an irregular war, was the prelude to disaster): and my suspicion was that its lack was leadership: not intellect, nor judgement, nor political wisdom, but the flame of enthusiasm, that would set the desert on fire. [11]

The application of esoteric knowledge through the use of symbolism might also possibly apply in Douglas MacArthur's case. He insisted on being filmed wading through the water with his men, onto the islands which he intended to capture. This symbolism proved highly beneficial in the hearts and minds of his soldiers and for their morale. Sir Winston Churchill may also have applied his esoteric indoctrination through his speeches, in the form of short effective phrases which could easily be recalled and became a symbol of Britain's defiance during the Second World War. On the other side was another prominent esotericist - Adolf Hitler. He was critical of freemasonry and although he outlawed its practices, was a strong advocate of esoteric wisdom and practice:

> Their hierarchical organisation (the Freemasons) and the initiation through symbolic rites, that is to say without bothering with the brains but by working on the imagination through magic and the symbols of a cult - all this is the dangerous element and the element which I have taken over. Don't you see that our party (the Nazis) must be of this character? [12]

11. Lawrence, T.E., The Seven Pillars of Wisdom, p.67
12. Baigent, Leigh and Lincon, The Messianic Legacy, p.196

Before invading Russia, Hitler boasted, "All we have to do is kick in the door, and the whole rotten edifice will come crushing down before us." Little did he know it, but he would have to deal with another leader, who in it is widely believed was trained in esoteric doctrines. During his younger years, Stalin is known to have lived with a highly influential eso-terist, whose endeavours still, in some ways, shape the direc-tion of esoteric thought today - G. I. Gurdjieff. The high level of symbolism used by both Hitler and Stalin during the War, was aimed at brainwashing their nations into a stupor of fanat-ical zeal. They knew that the War would not be dependent upon the size of the opposing forces alone, but also upon the need to be victorious. For this people would have to believe they were going to win, and both leaders knew from their esoteric backgrounds, that the only way of producing such beliefs was to appeal to their nations subconscious - thus the need for such powerful symbolism. Hitler's oratorical skills, even to this day, are considered impressive by many politicians, although justifiably not his speeches' content. His speeches not only swept the average German off his feet, but they also had a huge effect on the country's intelligensia. Today many politicians would agree that achieving a compa-rable effect through oratory would be an unrealistic, if not an impossible supposition. As Lawrence of Arabia succinctly puts it, ' . . . the dreamers of the day are dangerous men, for they may act out their dreams with open eyes to make it possible . . . this I did.' [13]

Masonic influence is particularly prevalent in America (this will be explained later), and nearly all the American presidents have been Masons; they include : Andrew Jackson, James K. Polk, James Buchanan, Andrew Johnson, James A. Garfield, Theodore Roosevelt, William Howard Taft, Warren Harding, Franklin D. Roosevelt, Harry Truman, Lyndon Johnson, Gerald Ford, and Ronald Regan.

Apart from the obvious avenue the Masons use for communicating their beliefs i.e. stonemasons' tools, Masonry or esoterism places great emphasis upon art, occult mathematics

13. Lawrence, T.E., The Seven Pillars of Wisdom, p.23

and often literature as a way of communicating their secrets to other initiates and also as a form of expression and an outlet for their esoteric beliefs. This expression can be seen throughout history often subtly hidden from the attentions of the public at large, while at the same time being incredibly meaningful to Masons themselves. Thanks to Robert Bauval and Graham Hancock (of whom more will be discussed later) people's attention is finally being turned to the geometrical language of the pyramids and the messages which emanate from their geometry and celestial alignments. Further on through history another great expression emerged in the form of cathedrals - in particular Chartres. It still remains a mystery why the red and blue pigments inside this cathedral's windows have failed to be identified by chemists. It is believed that it would probably take someone a lifetime to fully encode the hidden esoteric meanings of this most magnificent cathedral. Not only is it full of precision geometry, but the high standard of craftsmanship demonstrates a knowledge of building which was not supposed even to exist at its time of construction. Throughout the centuries countless works of art and literature have emerged which, although only displaying a superficial meaning to the population at large, held and still hold a deeper meaning to the esoteric initiates of each age.

Having previously mentioned the existence of pentagonal geometry in Poussin's Shepherds of Arcadia the painting of the particular tomb, some believe situated near Rennes le Chateau in southern France (although now destroyed by treasure hunters), is of great importance. As Baigent, Leigh and Lincon explain, the inscription on the tomb reads: 'Et in arcadia Ego' (In arcadia I dwell) - which in fact is a clever anagram for: 'I Tego Arcana Dei' (Begone! I conceal the secrets of God)[14]. Another esoteric painting known as the 'Isenheim altarpiece' by Matthias Grunewald is housed in Colmar Museum in Alsace. The painting depicts Jesus on the cross, with John the Baptist (supposedly murdered many years earlier) pointing at him, and his mother and Mary Magdalene kneeling next

14. Baigent, Leigh and Lincon, The Holy Blood and the Holy Grail, p.40

to each other. It also shows a stream of blood flowing from Jesus and into a chalice. The symbolism enunciated from this piece of work will be confusing to the reader who has not been introduced into the concept of symbolism or the scenario which it implies. In the Russian Church of St Mary Magdalene, Jerusalem, Mary is depicted holding a red egg in her hands, symbolising fertility. Such symbolism would simply be dismissed by many, however, to Masons and esoteric organisations alike, these symbols represent a fundamental part of their beliefs. Many legends such as the story of King Arthur, the Holy Grail and Jason and the Argonauts (to name a few) have much more meaning to Freemasons than to the average person. Music and Opera have also served as other avenues of esoteric expression. Mozart's Magic Flute is filled with Masonic undertones; it has been suggested by some that the opera was too revealing and that Mozart was murdered because of it. Wagner's operas also exhibit esoteric meaning and history:

> Contrary to popular supposition the characters and events portrayed in the 'Ring' are not all mythical. Certainly the deeds of Gods and heroes described there are the stuff of myth, but human beings who later came to be given names like Siegfried, Gunther and Gutrune actually existed in the first millennium of the Christian era, even if it is not always clear with which individuals the characters are to be identified." [15]

In fact esoterists believe Wagner's operas refer to Knights of the Grail, which relates to one of the fundamental beliefs of Masonry and is explained in chapter six.

Also literature such as the Shakespearean plays, which esoterists believe have much more meaning to them as they believe that they were written by Francis Bacon, and are esoteric archetypes. Similarly the ancient Greek and Egyptian myths are meant to be full of archetypes, and in many cases

15. Millington, B., Wagner, p.191

celestial knowledge, which although were understood by certain initiates at that time, were to the population at large considered as true accounts of the existence of omnipotent gods. Here are only some of a whole catalogue of examples of esoteric symbolism, expression and archetypes which it is hoped the reader will be able to understand after discovering the insights of this book. This is explained in Max Heindel's *Mysteries of the Great Operas* :

> As previously said, all myths are vehicles of spiritual truths veiled under allegory, symbol, and picture, and, therefore, capable of comprehension without reason. As fairy stories are a means of enlightenment to children, so these great myths were used to convey spiritual truth to infant humanity. [16]

Up until now, these hidden meanings have only been accessible to esoteric initiates simply because of the fact that they have been made aware of them through what they have learnt, and the way in which they apply this knowledge. It is hoped that the reader will gain enough insight from the revelations of this book to be in a position to make his or her own synergies and discover the many other forms of esoteric expression which have emerged throughout history and which exhibit esoteric meanings and signification.

Although freemasons are immensely secretive about their beliefs and practices, this is not the overriding factor in explaining Masonry's covert nature. The disguise of esoterism to the public at large has been esoterism's very nature. It is not a question of deciphering a certain code or studying esoteric books. As Schwaller de Lubicz succinctly puts it :The tool must be of the same nature as the objective to be worked upon. Spirit is found only with spirit, and esoterism is the spiritual aspect of the world, inaccessible to cerebral intelligence.' [17] It is submitted that this is the true secret of masonry and other esoteric societies, because all secrets emanate from understanding and applying its nature.

16. Heindel, M., Mysteries of the Great Operas, p. 72
17. Lubicz, Schwaller de, Esoterism and Symbol, p.3

During the course of this book many of the secrets of Masonry are revealed, however simply knowing the secrets of Masonry is not enough to fully understand Masonry's true nature. This is why many books professing to deal with Masonry usually end up as far from discovering it as when they first started. An effort has been made in this book to grasp the essence of Masonry so that it can be understood to the reader in its true context. To understand Freemasonry properly, it is necessary to realise its basis, from the very beginning, from which its members believe their knowledge first emanated - Atlantis.

Chapter Two

Atlantis - source of Egypt

" . . . if there was such a recurrent, cyclical geological phenomenon as earth-crust displacement, and if the last displacement had shifted the enormous land mass we call Antarctica
out of temperate latitudes and into the Antarctic Circle, it was
possible that the substantial remains of a lost civilisation of
remote antiquity might today be lying under two miles of ice
at the South Pole." [1]

Most books which deal with the background of Masonry
invariably begin with a brief history of the Templar Knights.
Although the Templars feature prominently in Masonic history,
knowledge of the Templars alone only provides a glimpse of
esoteric and therefore Masonic history as a whole. Therefore
for the reader to effectively grasp how Masonry come about
as an organisation and the purposes behind its existence, it
is necessary to start at the very beginning so that the

1. Hancock, G., Fingerprints of the Gods, p.495

reader may see esotericism as a continuum as it has developed, or in some people's opinions, been re-discovered through the centuries.

The story of Atlantis has fuelled the imagination of millions for centuries. More than two thousand books have already been written on Atlantis, but most people dismiss it as a mere myth. However, every few years some well respected academic or explorer brings out a new theory about the location of Atlantis. If Atlantis is merely a myth, then how has it kept coming back to haunt our 'realistic perceptions' about the history of man upon this earth. As previously mentioned, Freemasons take the story of Atlantis very seriously and believe that the archaic knowledge which they posses and practise came from the Atlanteans via Egypt. The archaic knowledge referred to here forms the cornerstone of esoteric and Masonic beliefs. But, what evidence is there that Atlantis did or even might have existed?

The first mention of Atlantis appeared in two of Plato's dialogues, the Timaeus and Critias written in 360 and 350 BC respectively. He spoke of a land rich in natural resources and an almost perfect natural paradise for its inhabitants. He said that the people of Atlantis were descendants of the God Poseidon, who wedded a mortal woman named Cleito. They had ten sons and divided Atlantis into ten kingdoms, with the eldest Atlas presiding over the capital - of the same name. Plato claimed that Poseidon and Cleito lived in a Temple of pure gold, three times the size of the Parthenon. The Atlanteans, he said, were technologically and intellectually highly advanced, but eventually greed overtook them and Atlantis was punished by the gods with its eventual destruction by earthquakes and a great flood. Plato's description of Atlantis and especially Atlas are very detailed. Such a story would be too remarkable for most to take literally or at face value. However, Plato's reputation for honesty and frankness, coupled with the fact that he claimed the story was told to him by a very eminent statesman at that time called Solon, has added authenticity to the story thus, for many, keeping it out of the realms of pure mythology.

Subsequent writers have added to the debate upon the possibility of the existence of Atlantis. Francis Bacon (Templar Grand Master), was known to have researched Plato and the Atlantis story, which led him to write, *The New Atlantis* in 1600, in which he described an advanced society existing on a remote island which by choice remained unknown to the rest of the habitable world. In 1870, English copies of Jules Verne's science fiction classic, *Twenty Thousand Leagues under the Sea*, could not be produced quickly enough for the demand it created. However, the biggest surge in interest regarding Plato's Atlantis began in 1882 with the publication of Ignatius Donnelley's *Atlantis - The Antediluvian World*. Donnelley was once described as the cleverest man to have sat in the American Senate. He also believed, as do many esotericists, that Francis Bacon wrote the Shakespearean plays, and devoted much time and effort in attempting to decipher, what he believed, were the cryptically coded messages hidden in the plays but, his attention became distracted from this task by the story of Atlantis. At the time, the evidence which Donnelley presented for the existence of Atlantis would have been very convincing to the average reader, however many of his arguments have not stood up to today's scientific and academic scrutiny.

Donnelley believed, as do many Freemasons and Atlantologists, that Atlantis, as the name suggests, existed in the Atlantic ocean. Plato stated that Atlantis was beyond the 'Pillars of Hercules', which Donnelley identified with the Gibraltar strait. He also attributes certain place names such as the Atlas mountains near the west African coast, and the Aztecs reference to a place in the east called Aztlan, as evidence of Atlantis; and expounds synergies in how the transatlantic cultures, such as the Egyptian and the ancient South American civilisations developed. Some of the evidence Donnelley presents is unmistakable and does point to a transatlantic contact in ancient times, either between developing cultures themselves, or that they were in some way influenced by the same culture - possibly Atlantis. He also points to the similarity in pyramidal structures built by the Olmecs, Mayas and Egyptians, and their sudden leap in advancement of building techniques, which he states could only have come from Atlantis. Graham Hancock's *Fingerprints of the Gods* is a great endorsement of this theory, that ancient cultures were influenced either by each other, or by one particular civilisation - which might have been Atlantis. His book demonstrates the synergies which exist between cultures in terms of their building techniques, the sizes and types of buildings which they built, and their celestial inclinations (which can be gleaned from the alignment of their temples to various astral bodies and equinoxes). Hancock develops this theory even further in *Heaven's Mirror*, in which he brings to light some startling revelations which he argues connect many of the ancient structures and civilisations of the world (these discoveries are considered later in this chapter).

It is sad in a way that Donnelley's theories do not hold up to the geological and geographical scrutiny demanded by science today. Most scientists today believe in the plate tectonics or continental drift theory - that millions of years ago the land masses of the Americas (North and South), were connected to Europe and Africa, and that they broke away and gradually moved apart to produce the earth as it looks today. The existence of the transatlantic ridge (running from North to South under the Atlantic ocean) and evidence of its past volcanic activity, together with the fact that the Americas fit into Africa and Europe is a very convincing endorsement of the continental drift theory.

Some argue that the ancient Thera (now Santorini) may have been Atlantis. In 1470 BC a massive volcanic eruption completely destroyed much of Thera, and it is argued that Plato's dates were mistakenly interpreted and he actually meant that the destruction of Atlantis occurred in 1470 BC instead of 9600 BC. It is evident that some of Thera's' history fits in well to Plato's criteria for Atlantis - destruction by earthquake, the sophisticated culture, and the circular form of the island before its destruction. It is unlikely though that Plato's Atlantis was Thera because the ancient Greek method of listing dates provides no room for error i.e. the date that the ancient Greeks give as the time that Thera existed as a civilisation is far too late in history to be Atlantis. The ancient Greeks are unlikely to have made an error with this date, because mistakes such as adding a nought or taking one away couldn't happen; each unit of calculation (e.g. hundreds or thousands) was specifically denoted by a different sign.

Considering the different theories upon the location of Atlantis, Hancock argues that it is precisely the continental drift theory, coupled with the Piri Reis map which proves that Atlantis could have existed. If the continental drift theory (also known as plate tectonics) is applied to the land-masses of the world then, as Hancock endorses, the land-mass which we know as Antarctica would have been positioned further north than it is today. The Piri Reis map (as shown in Plate 3) is a further endorsement of this theory, but as Hancock argues, it in fact goes beyond this, by demonstrating that Antarctica was at one time capable of being mapped, and therefore must in all probability have been capable of being inhabited. Today Antarctica is under one mile of ice and scientists do not agree on the date that the continent became glacial - estimates range from 5 million to 4000 years BC. However, Hancock also presented the map to some leading American cartographers who stated that the map is quite an accurate representation of Antarctica's landmass (at least the part which appears in the map), furthermore some were even willing to state their reputations that it was Antarctica which appears on the Piri Reis map. The Piri Reis map also draws the immediate inference that at some time in the distant past there must have been a civilisation which possessed a highly developed knowledge of navigation and cartography. Erich von Daniken's view that this map was originally made by extraterrestrials cannot be supported here although, as chapter seven explains, the belief in extraterrestrial beings is an important part of Masonry. There is simply too much evidence of a highly advanced knowledge existing in antiquity to say that these people were not capable of circumnavigating the globe. Some of these ancient navigation techniques are believed by masons to be contained in the 'Royal Arch Mariners' degree of Freemasonry. Furthermore, in Bacon's *New Atlantis*, he claims that the inhabitants of this ancient island civilisation, which existed in remote antiquity, were highly accomplished sailors and navigators.

The Piri Reis map was copied in the 16th century from a very ancient map, by a Turkish Admiral (Piri Reis). It was only in 1818 over 300 years later that Antarctica was dis-covered. Although unknown to Piri Reis at the time, this map was to prove more accurate than the subsequent maps made by the Spanish as late as the 18th century. No one can say for certain where the ancient map from which it was copied originated, and its source has baffled archaeologists and sci-entists alike but, so conventional history tells us, there were no advanced cultures or peoples who possessed advanced nav-igation skills existing in ancient times. The Piri Reis map is a highly accurate world map, suggesting that the culture which devised it must have accurately navigated the lands and oceans of the planet. Such a supposition implies some remark-able feats - first, that whoever made the map must have had tremendous resources with which to conduct such a study, and must have travelled extensively around the world. Second, the ancient people who devised the map must have been highly skilled sailors. Third, they must have been accomplished navigators who had discovered a method of navigation which was precise in measuring both longitude and latitude. Although latitude can be measured by the angle of the pole star above the horizon, measuring longitude involves a much more com-plex process, which some would argue, requires instruments which did not even exist in ancient antiquity. The Piri Reis map shows the position of Antarctica which in relation to the other continents of the world shown is further north than it is today. Furthermore, as aforementioned, geological surveys of Antarctica have demonstrated remarkable similarities between their positions of land-mass under the ice and those contained in the Piri Reis map. Many Masons believe that Plato's Atlantis was Antarctica and that the navigational expertise and knowledge which it took to create the Piri Reis map still exist today in closed esoteric circles; as noted earlier, some of these techniques are believed to be contained in the 'Royal Arch Mariners' degree.

Whenever Atlantis existed, whether it existed at all, or whatever its contribution (if any) to mankind's development, it is an immensely important part of Masonic tradition, as from the very beginning, new Masons are instilled with the Atlantis story as the source from which their knowledge and traditions have derived. Not only do we hear Plato refer to a Temple existing on Atlantis of gargantuan size, but Freemasons are taught that the highly advanced ancient civilisations of the past did not just come about in a vacuum, but learnt their great architectural skills of construction, and celestial insights from the Atlanteans. Ancient South American traditions also endorse this, with numerous accounts of bearded men of caucasian complexion arriving on their shores in ships. These men, known by various names by different peoples such as Viracocha and Quetzalcoatl, brought with them incredible wisdom and insight which they passed on to these ancient people in an attempt to educate them, and as accounts testify, to mould them into a more integrated and advanced society. These strange men then left as they had arrived via the sea, and it is widely believed that this was the reason the Aztecs welcomed the Spanish invaders upon their arrival and paid a heavy price for their perceptions, initiated by their ancestors in ancient times by these philanthropic bearded men.

Further evidence of highly advanced knowledge existing in ancient times was found in Lubaantum, British Honduras in 1927, and what has become known as the 'Skull of Doom'. It was found inside a thousand year old Mayan temple, and it still baffles scientists and archaeologists alike. It is carved from a single piece of rare quartz crystal, is about five inches in height and weighs over eleven and a half pounds. It is not remarkable that such a skull has been carved from such a rare piece of quartz, but what is remarkable is the precision of the carving and the knowledge which it implies the carver possessed. Scientists agree that it could not have been made by any known tool in existence at the time it was created. The intricacy of its carving produces a vast array of prisms to produce incredible luminescence. Some archaeologists claim the Mayas were much more advanced than people are led to believe through conventional history, however there is no evidence of any tools to suggest the Maya ever possessed the technology to make such a skull. It cannot be said that the skull came from or was made (assuming their existence) by the Atlanteans, but such a remarkable knowledge of optics must imply that a civilisation once existed which had gained a vast insight into optics and the behaviour of prisms.

There are countless enigmas associated with the ancient world which cannot simply be explained away. As Alan Alford explains in his book *Gods of the New Millennium* :

> It is as if - all around the world - there is a shadowy prehistory that precedes the official history of civilised man. Out of this history, a legacy has passed down to us - a legacy in stone, a legacy in mythology, a legacy in technology, which can only now be recognised in the twentieth century. [2]

For instance, archaeological evidence supports the view that the ancient societies on both sides of the Atlantic knew about the earth's precession. This is the process by which the earth wobbles upon its axis - a cycle which is completed once every 25,500 years (approximately), as shown below.

2. Alford, A., Gods of the New Millennium, p.135

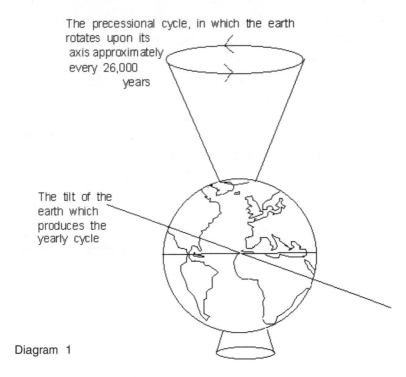

The precessional cycle, in which the earth rotates upon its axis approximately every 26,000 years

The tilt of the earth which produces the yearly cycle

Diagram 1

Ancient sites such as Stonehenge in Britain, Machu Piccu (Peru), the Pyramids at Giza (Egypt), Chichen Itza (Mexico), to name a few, all demonstrate a knowledge of astronomy far too advanced to have existed at that time, or so we are meant to believe. Great feats of architecture, precision engineering and the movement of gargantuan sized obelisks positioned neatly into place cannot simply be explained nor compartmentalised into some neat academic framework - no matter how convenient it may be.

Masonic tradition has always maintained that the highly advanced skills which the ancients acquired (as mentioned above), came from Atlantis. It is remnants of this knowledge, from the Atlanteans, of which the Masons and other esoteric societies profess to be the guardians to this day. Within the chain of guardians of this knowledge, which originated in ancient times, are the Egyptians. They, the masons believe, like many other ancient civilisations, inherited the knowledge of the Atlanteans, and it is from the Egyptians that the Masons believe their knowledge was inherited. Some lodges in Britain even profess to being directly descended from the Egyptians, but this is probably an analogy of their belief that within the subconscious lies the knowledge of past generations spanning back to ancient times. They further believe that under the paws of the Sphinx lies a chamber, in which are contained the ancient records of the Atlanteans detailing the history of the earth and mankind. So, it is to Egypt that we must first turn in order to attempt to find the clues of man's past and the extent of the knowledge which the Masons believe they have inherited.

Egypt

According to Masonic tradition, the Sphinx and the three pyramids at Giza were built well before the time that Egyptologists believe they were constructed. Masons and esotericists alike believe that the three pyramids at Giza were subsequently adopted by the Egyptian pharaohs as burial chambers. The smaller pyramids built upon the Giza necropolis, as shown in Plate 2 (showing the three larger pyramids behind them), although momentous, are by comparison amateur and these esotericists say, were built after the Sphinx and the three great Giza pyramids. As Alan Alford explains in his *Gods of the New Millennium* :

> I would now like to put forward a much more plausible theory - that the Giza pyramids preceded all of the other pyramids in Egypt and they acted as a model for them. I would like to suggest that someone was once privy to the knowledge of the empty coffer which was hidden in the sealed upper section of the Great Pyramid. The later pharaohs then copied the empty boxes, which they believed to be symbolically important.[3]

3. Alford, A., Gods of the New Millennium, p.132

Masons believe that the original purpose for which the three larger Giza pyramids were built was functional not simply for burial chambers. The fact that many of the pyramids were so accessible to thieves and treasure hunters testifies to this. For centuries the Templars through to the modern Masons and esotericists of today have maintained that there is a geometric and astrological language which emanates from the pyramids. The Masons claim to being the recipients of this knowledge and believe that they must guard the secrets, to which only the initiated can be enlightened. Many of these secrets have been lost through the ages, but many others are still known and handed down in Masonry through the Chapter degree and other higher degrees within Masonry. These concepts are now being brought to light through authors such as Graham Hancock, Adrian Gilbert, Robert Bauval, Alan Alford and Colin Wilson. Furthermore such concepts are now finally being accepted as an important part of Egyptology by the archaeological world.

The age of the Pyramids has for the most part of the last century, remained an unquestioned issue; however, re-evaluation of previous archaeological techniques has revealed that the evidence used to construe the time of construction of ancient Egyptian megaliths is scanty to say the least. For example, the building of the Sphinx has been attributed to a Fourth Dynasty king named Khafre, simply because the letters KAHF appear in mid sentence on a piece of granite directly in front of it. It may seem surprising to the reader to learn that neither the Sphinx, as shown in Plate 4, nor its builder are mentioned in any Egyptian ancient text, yet the contention that Khafre built it has remained authentic and unquestioned by the archaeological and most of the academic world for almost the whole of the past century.

It was R. A. Schwaller and J. A. West who first proposed a theory that the Sphinx was much older than Egyptologists believed, and proof of this, they said, lay in the erosion marks which can be seen around the Sphinx's body and neck. The erosion marks were first thought by West to be evidence of the Great Flood, which would push the date of the Sphinx construction back to before the Ice Age to at least 10,000 BC. Further analysis by Schwaller supported the view that the Sphinx is much older than has previously been suggested and could not have been constructed as late as the Fourth dynasty period. However, in his opinion, the erosion lines around the Sphinx are not consistent with a tide mark, but with intense weathering i.e. the precipitation induced by heavy rainfall. In Schwaller's view the only rainfall which could have caused such erosion occurred 10,000 BC or before, and as such the Sphinx could not have been built in Khafre's time.

Authority has also been added to this theory by Dobecki - a geophysicist asked by West to asses the Sphinx and give his expert opinion whether or not the Sphinx is much older than Egyptologists have been led to believe. Not only did Dobecki confirm West's belief about the age of the Sphinx, but he also carried out seismic tests around the Sphinx and found a definite rectangular shaped structure, about five metres below ground level, directly under the paws of the Sphinx. Dolbecki's endeavours add credence (but cannot be relied upon as hard evidence) to the Masonic belief that their exists a chamber under the Sphinx, known to them as the 'Hall of Records', which contains the ancient texts of Atlantis. Excavations to uncover what lies under the paws of the Sphinx have been refused by the Egyptian authorities, and as Graham Hancock explains, the grounds of their refusal would seem to support the notion that a deliberate attempt is being made to prevent the excavation of this chamber, either for fear of what it might contain, or that it is not quite the right time yet for the discovery.

The evidence presented by archaeologists and academics as proof that Khafre built the Sphinx, is as flimsy as the proof which they present to qualify that Khufu, Khafre and Menkaure (three pharaohs from the Fourth Dynasty), built the three biggest pyramids at the Giza necropolis. To rely on some crude graffiti above the roof of the King's Chamber in the Great Pyramid, which has no signs of being original to the pyramid's construction, surely flies in the face of basic common sense. However what has probably happened here happened with the Sphinx also; when the perceptions of eminent archaeologists are repeated through time, they become authenticated and enter the realms of reality within that particular profession. Although the evidence presented to confirm that the three pyramids of Giza were built by three pharaohs from the Fourth Dynasty is certainly not conclusive, there is no written evidence to prove otherwise; however, this theory can be rebutted by the celestial or astrological evidence which has now come to light.

It was Robert Bauval and Adrian Gilbert, in their blockbuster *The Orion Mystery*, who first made known (for those outside the realms of Masonic teaching), the astrological positioning of the pyramids. They found that the three pyramids, although almost next to each other, were slightly off line from each other and wondered why, when such precision was used in building them, was there such an absence of it in their positioning. They first found that the three pyramids at Giza resembled the positions of the three stars which represent Orion's belt. By then simulating computer images of the positions of these stars through the centuries they found that the position of the three stars which comprise Orion's belt together with the Milky Way (represented by the Nile), mirrored the position of the three pyramids at Giza and the Nile (represented by the Milky Way) around 10,500 BC.

Even though the above points are capable of withstanding much academic scrutiny, a connection can also be made between the Great Pyramid and the period about 2,500 BC - which would be during the time of the Fourth Dynasty. Within the Great Pyramid, there are what was believed to be ventilation shafts, two emanating from the Kings chamber and two which were deliberately unfinished emanating from the Queens chamber. It has subsequently been discovered that these shafts (measuring approximately 22cm by 23cm (width x height) and extending through the pyramid), are not ventilation shafts at all. And it has been found that in 2,500 BC the shafts would have been aligned to the stars Sirius and Zeta Orionis to the south, and Beta Ursa minor and Alpha Draconis to the north. What is remarkable about the alignment is that it marks a very significant event in the history of these stars - the time at which they were all on the meridian line (this is an imaginary line running through the sky which intersects the sky from north to south, or vice versa, in equal halves). It is probably the case that these shafts were not in alignment with these stars at the time of the pyramids' construction, but were designed to mark a significant epoch in celestial history. The reader will later understand the significance of the Meridian to Masons, as it appears in their passing ceremony from the first to second degree : 'it necessarily follows that the sun must always be at its Meridian with respect to Freemasonry.' The positioning of these four stars on the meridian line would have been a great event to the esotericists at that time. Furthermore in 10,500 BC both Orion's belt and the constellation Draco would have been on the meridian - the significance of this is described later.

Within Masonry, great emphasis is placed upon celestial movements; not merely the movements themselves, but in the emerging patterns and alignments that occur. They believe that mankind's history - past, present and future - is governed by the stars and planetary movements. As the reader will discover this concept, known as dualism, rests upon the premise that what occurs above (in the sky), occurs below (upon the earth) - as above so below. This belief is not an extension of the astrology contained in tabloid newspapers. It is instead a different form of astrology which can, esotericists believe, predict major events in history, together with divine births. The fact that these shafts in the Great Pyramid were aligned on the meridian support the ideas of Masonic proponents who believe the Egyptians were once the guardians of esoteric knowledge which they have inherited. So, although some may construe the alignment of the shafts as sufficient evidence on which to base an assumption that the pyramids

of Giza were built in 2,500 BC, the fact that the three pyramids of Giza and the Nile map the positions of Orion's belt
and the Milky Way at 10,500 BC cannot simply be explained
away. According to Egyptologists there was not anything which
resembled a civilised society existing at this time.

In addition to the above points, the stars which comprise the Orion constellation together with the star Sirius have
very special significance to modern masons in the resurrection
or rebirth of their soul (the reader will understand the theory and workings behind this after reading about the third
degree ceremony contained in chapter four), and they were
obviously significant to the pyramid builders. As Hancock and
Faiia note:

> What is most striking however, is the extent to which
> both systems of initiation (those in Egypt and Central
> America) focused on astronomy, particularly on an eso-
> teric knowledge of the cycles of the heavens, and
> aspired to immortality amongst the stars. [4]

The burden of evidence, in favour of the pyramids being built
before 2,500 BC and which accords with Masonic beliefs, is
further endorsed by Hancock and Bauval, who point out that
the Sphinx faces directly east, and is therefore precisely
aligned with the spring and autumn equinoxes. It also has a
particular shape and clearly depicts a lion, which if zodiac
constellations were under consideration would clearly indicate
the star sign Leo. At present the ecliptic path of the sun on
the horizon passes through the constellation of Pisces, at 2,500
BC the ecliptic path of the sun on the horizon passed through
the constellation of Taurus. However, the last time the constellation Leo marked the spring equinox was at 10,500 BC[5];
this accords with the date represented by the pattern of the
Giza pyramids. Such synergies can hardly be coincidental and
point to the possibility that the Freemasons may indeed be
correct in their beliefs, almost certainly that the Sphinx and
the Giza pyramids were earlier constructions than the

4. Hancock, G., and Faiia, S., Heavens Mirror, p.23
5. Bauval, R., and Hancock, G., Keeper fo Genesis, p.83

archaeological world has led us to believe. Furthermore there is evidence, a theory first expounded by Carl Jung (a keen esotericist), that the Egyptians knew about the precession of the earth. That is that every 25,920 years the earth completes a cycle, by which it wobbles on its axis. As it wobbles on its axis the ecliptic path of the sun on the horizon passes through the constellations of the zodiac (a diagram demonstrating the precessional cycle has been shown previously on page 48). It takes approximately 2,100 years for the sun to pass through a particular constellation. For instance, the sun's ecliptic path on the horizon was in Taurus from 4,360 to 2,200 BC and then passed into Aries from 2,200 to 120 BC. Is it mere coincidence that within these different eras, the Egyptians worshipped a Bull in the era of Taurus, and a Ram in the era of Aries (as demonstrated in Plate 6 by the entrance to the Karnak Temple, Luxor). These facts prove to some, beyond doubt, that the Egyptians must have known about precession, and therefore assuming this to be the case, this would support the belief that the Giza necropolis was constructed when the constellation, on the horizon, Leo was in the ecliptic path of the sun - 10,500 BC.

Furthermore, the recent revelations in Hancock and Faiia's *Heaven's Mirror*, also present evidence linking ancient sites with the year 10,500 BC. In 1996 John Grigsby discovered that the positioning of certain temples on the ancient site of Angkor, Cambodia, closely resembled the constellation Draco. Further analysis by Hancock and Faiia discovered that the only time in history where the constellation Draco would have mirrored the temples at Angkor would have been 10,500 BC. They also point out that at 10,500 BC the constellations of Draco (positioned due north) and Orion (positioned due south) would have been on the meridian (as noted earlier); with the constellation Leo directly east on the spring equinox denoted by the Sphinx. It is curious that such seemingly unconnected places not only show high degrees of precessional alignments in mapping these constellations, but both are astronomical markers of the time 10,500 BC. Although it is indisputable that the temples at Angkor were built by Khmer monarchs from 802 AD to 1220 AD[6] these structures may have been built upon a much earlier site, or their positioning may have been copied from knowledge passed down from ancient times. Whatever the true state of affairs may be, we are still left with these enigmatic markings constructed in stone pointing to the time 10,500 BC.

But Hancock and Faiia do not stop there. They have gone on to demonstrate that there is also a link between Angkor, Giza and other ancient sites, known as Navels of the World' within their global longitudinal positioning. For example, that Giza is 72 degrees longitude from Angkor, Giza and Angkor are approximately 144 degrees from Easter Island, Pohnpei is 54 degrees from Angkor, Angkor is 72 degrees from Kiribati, Kiribati is 18 degrees from Pohnpei, Paracas is 108 degrees from Giza and 36 degrees from Easter Island.[7] The revelations in *Heaven's Mirror* show beyond doubt that the ancients must have been capable of measuring longitude, known about precession, and been capable of accurately mapping the stars (in the cases of Angkor and Giza are reference markers to 10,500 BC). But the most remarkable revelation is that these sites have been positioned with reference to other ancient sites implying knowledge communicated between their constructors. These sites are also connected numerologically because adding the digits of the angles of longitude of these sites always results in the number nine. For example: 3+6, 5 + 4, 1 + 8, 7 + 2, 1 + 0 + 8. Such a harmonious numerological connection may be difficult to attribute to coincidence. Furthermore all these angles of longitude between the ancient sites aforementioned are connected with pentagonal geometry, as shown below.

6. Hancock, G., and Faiia, S., Heavens Mirror, p.128
7. Hancock, G., and Faiia, S., Heavens Mirror, p.254

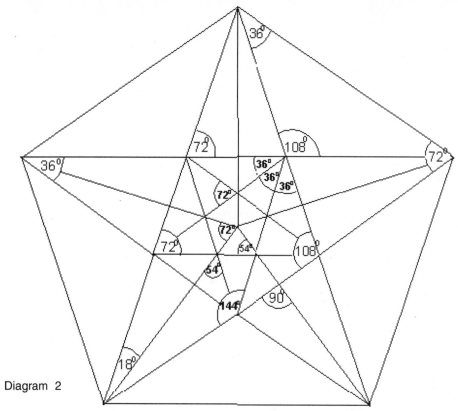

Diagram 2

This could prove to be a very important link between the ancient world and Henry Lincon's discoveries into the esoteric pentagonal geometry present in Poussin's *Shepherds of Arcadia* and the positioning of villages in the Rennes le Chateau region of southern France (discussed further in chapter six).

It is generally accepted that whoever did build the immense structures of the ancient world, were a highly skilled people, not only in their astrological positioning (e.g. the three pyramids at Giza), but also in the enormity of the blocks which were used, and also in their incredible precision. For example the variation in length from measuring the four sides which comprise the Great Pyramid's base is less than 0.1 %. The Giza pyramid's alignment to the North, East, South and West directions are near perfect. The dimensions of the Great Pyramid almost match precisely the dimensions of the earth on a scale of 1:43,200 (with the pole representing the top of the pyramid and with the four edges of the pyramid intersecting the equator). Furthermore, this proves that the

Egyptians knew the values of Pi (they would have had to have known this to calculate the height of the pyramid from its base); it may also prove, or may be mere coincidence (which is doubtful), that they knew the dimensions of the earth. Hancock and Faiia's discoveries on the longitudinal positioning of numerous ancient sites would seem to support this view, that such a knowledge did exist. An ancient knowledge of the earth's dimensions and structure is not uncommon - for instance in Constantinople in the 16th century a copy was made of an ancient map, the resulting map has already been discussed - the 'Piri Reis' (Plate 3). It is of importance historically, not for the fact that someone had attempted to make a map of the world, but that the map shows Europe, West Africa, and the Eastern coast of South America, and was found to be more accurate than the maps that the Spanish were producing as late as the 18th century. Also of interest, with regard to knowledge of precision is the Mayan calendar, which has proved itself to be more accurate in its calculation than the modern Gregorian calendar. [8]

The precision of the dimensions of the pyramids is remarkable to say the least, it would take much more than a book or two to explain the intricacies of geometry and mathematics which emanate from the pyramids' structure. Such precision would have been time consuming for the pyramid builders, but does not only demonstrate the obvious - that they were meticulous in their work - but also that they were part of a highly knowledgeable and advanced society which was capable of great feats of precision. From the evidence presented so far, it seems that the picture emerging is one which is more in tune with Masonic beliefs than with contemporary Egyptology - that a highly skilled society existed before the days of the pharaohs; however whether such a knowledge was indeed inherited from the Atlanteans is a moot point. Although Hancock's and Faiia's evidence of connections between ancient civilisations of the past would seem to be irrefutable, maybe an excavation of the so called 'Hall of Records' will provide a more substantive answer to enig-

8. Hancock, G., and Faiia, S., Heavens Mirror, p.38

mas such as these.

Precision is a skill in any form, and even the immense size of the pyramids at Giza have withstood some of the most demanding architectural scrutiny. These blocks fit perfectly together, in most places not even a razor blade can penetrate the joints. These blocks are connected by a very thin layer of cement between them. Archaeologists are at a loss to explain how the pyramid builders could have applied such a thin and perfectly even layer of cement to these blocks. To date, no conclusive theory has emerged which comprehensibly explains how the blocks were shaped so precisely, or the precision with which they were moved into place. Plate 7, shows the precision fit of the granite blocks which once covered the three great Giza pyramids - these blocks being removed over the centuries to build Cairo.

The shaping of the blocks is an amazing facet of these pyramid builders. How is it that they were able to shape such large pieces of sandstone and granite into near perfect rectangles? Each edge at almost perfect right angles, and surfaces so flat and smooth that any flaws lie beyond the scope of human visual perception. They must have been aided by tools or devices which could accurately measure and assess the sculpting of these blocks. In Graham Hancock's *Fingerprints of the Gods*, he points out that on the inner surface of a sarcophagus found in the Great Pyramid there exist spiral engravings, like those which are produced from circular drilling machines. Engineers have concluded (judging by the distances between each swivel), that the type of machine which produced the engravings must have been operating at an extremely high speed (with regard to revolutions per second), furthermore, the sarcophagus is made of diorite, which apart from diamond is the hardest rock substance known to man; and it is believed that not even a diamond edged drill would have been able to penetrate through diorite at such a speed. Conventional wisdom cannot explain such a phenomenon. However, Christopher Dunn (an expert in machine tools) has studied these feats and proposed an ingenious solution - that ultrasonic sound was involved in the drilling technique.

He bases his theory on the fact that the distances between the revolutions or swivel marks, made by whatever drill the pyramid builders used, are wider in the quartz sections of rock than the granite. But, quartz is harder than granite, and what is clearly demonstrated is that the drill used has penetrated the quartz more easily than the granite. Dunn proposes that since quartz is susceptible to high pitched vibrations, much more than granite, the pyramid builders must have used some sort of ultrasonic drill. The Masons believe that there were tools around at that time which were capable of such feats. One of these tools was known as the 'shamir'. According to Masonic tradition, this device was housed in one of the bronze pillars in Solomon's Temple together with valuable texts pertaining to the inherited Legacy of the Egyptians (further on in the book the reader will become accustomed to idea that the Israelites (as depicted in the Old Testament) were instrumental in preserving the secrets and Masonic legacy of the Egyptians). The shamir, which was also believed to be passed down from the Egyptians, was stored in a lead basket, and it was said that it could not be stored in a vessel of any other metal as it would burst it apart. Unfortunately, the shamir vanished with the destruction of Solomon's Temple, however (and as the reader will understand later), is it not curious that it could only be stored in a lead basket? It begs the question, if such a device did exist at all, was it in some way connected with radioactivity?

Masons are taught that in ancient Egypt the quarrying process involved boring holes into the rock at certain distances from each other, and then hammering cedar wood into the holes which they had bored. Water was subsequently added into the holes containing the cedar wood, and the subsequent expansion caused by the swelling of the wood was enough to split the rock apart. From Plate 8 (from the quarry at Aswan), the reader will be able to acknowledge that the holes (only about six inches deep), are uniform, with respect to the size of each one. This would endorse the theory that the ancient Egyptians may have used drills, as such uniformity between the holes would be untypical of man especially as these were only used for the quarrying process. After quarrying the stone they were then shaped into blocks and floated down the Nile from Aswan to Giza. In 1878 this knowledge of floating rocks of such size was put into practice again with the help of the Freemasons' knowledge (they themselves believe), with the floating of Cleopatras Kneedle (as shown in Plate 9), a 200 ton obelisk from Heliopolis (Egypt) to the Thames Embankment in London.

The immense size of the blocks used to build the pyramids, certainly brings more questions to light. There are few cranes in this technologically advanced day and age capable of lifting 200 tons or more, and yet by looking at the blocks which make up the pyramids, one would swear that each block was put together with ease - almost like a lego set. The most plausible theory to date concerning the movement of the blocks is that they were pulled into position via ramps made of earth. This theory is all well and good, but the logistics of such a venture are rather daunting. For a start, to drag a block weighing 200 tons would (it is estimated) require between 2000 and 2500 men all synchronised and pulling at the same time. It is then estimated that the maximum gradient to allow for such a block to be pulled up a ramp would be one in ten; which would mean that the length of the ramp would necessarily have to be 10 times longer than the height to which it was to be pulled up to. Furthermore, it would require even more men to pull one of these blocks up such a gradient. Even if the pyramid builders could have synchronised such a large number of men, and managed to get it up such a ramp, it would still be very difficult to move that stone into the exact position they required. How indeed, were such weights lifted or dragged up to the different levels of the pyramids structure? No evidence exists of there being any machinery, capable of completing such a task, then or possibly even now; but just because no evidence has been found, it does not preclude the possibility of such machines existing in the past, or maybe even being discovered in the future. The size of the Great Pyramid can be appreciated in Plate 5.

The possibility of machines or a machine capable of building a pyramid thousands of years ago, is a difficult concept to swallow. However not as hard to swallow as the Masons' belief or explanation of how the pyramids were built. The Masons do not believe that the blocks weighing 200 tons were actually lifted by the pyramid builders at all. They believe that the pyramid builders or the Egyptians had learnt from the Atlanteans a method of harnessing the immense magnetic forces which run along lay lines. This power was not, they believe, used as a source of energy for any machine, but it was harnessed in such a way as to considerably reduce the gravitational effects upon the blocks used in the pyramids' construction - therefore reducing their mass.

In his book *The Pattern of the Past*, Underwood describes lay lines as being 'generated within the Earth; to involve wave motion; have great penetrative power; to form a network on the face of the Earth, to affect the germination and manner of growth of certain trees and plants; to be perceived and used by animals; to affect opposite sides of the animal body and to form spiral patterns.' The ancient Egyptians, Celts, Aztecs and many other ancient people were obsessed with lay lines. The Celts, believing that the power of the lay lines could be harnessed, built all their dolmens and stone circles upon lay lines - as the Egyptians built their pyramids upon them too. The reader may also recall (from chapter one), that the Templars always built their Gothic churches on lay lines, it has been said that they were mapping them out; these connections linking lay lines with ancient cultures throughout history is unlikely to be merely coincidental. Masonic opinion endorses that the numerous synergies which exist between ancient civilisations in terms of their constructions, alignments of those constructions, and beliefs, are all echoes of a previous knowledge which originated from Atlantis.

Underwood explains that lay lines are controlled by the number 3 in their construction and the number 7 in their spiral patterns. As aforementioned numerology is an important constituent of Masonic and esoteric ideology, they believe that certain numbers have sacred mystical significance. John Mitchell in his *The View over Atlantis* believed that celestial energy could be harnessed from lay lines and this energy could in turn be used for flight. He adds that it is this connection or fusion (as he calls it) of terrestrial and celestial forces and the power created from it that made possible the construction of the pyramids (as has already been noted), Mitchell maintains that the cabalistic number for this fusion is 1746 (known to Freemasons as the celestial number of fusion) and can, they say, be discovered in the dimensions of the Great Pyramid. There are numerous Celtic legends which refer to magical flights on stones, which were made possible by harnessing the power of lay lines. Also, is it merely coincidental that claims of UFO sightings and their flight paths invariably follow the paths of the lay lines below? Assuming that UFO's do exist, are they possibly harnessing the power of these mystical lay lines?

A recent discovery involving the spinning of magnetic fields at very high speeds, has been proved to reduce the gravitational force acting upon it. Although this experiment has only been performed on a very small scale, it opens up the possibility of the effects of the experiment being amplified if it was conducted on a larger scale. Were such effects utilised as the Masons believe - to allow the pyramid builders to lift such large stones to such heights? Further research is currently continuing into the effects of magnetism upon gravity, but isn't it indeed plausible that whoever built the pyramids was in possession of some ancient archaic knowledge, which allowed them to spin the magnetic forces within the Earth (these could possibly be the spiral patterns Underwood was referring to), and thus negate to a large extent the effects of gravity? It seems yet again that another Masonic belief has been shown, to some extent, to be at least a possibility, and cannot simply be dismissed out of hand as a scientific impossibility. Lay lines also feature prominently, the Masons believe, behind the purpose for which the great Giza pyramids were constructed.

Why were the Pyramids Built?

There are various theories in existence today attempting to explain why the pyramids were built. For the past century at least, it has been Egyptologists who have determined the pyramids dates of construction and reasons for their construction. Thus, up until recently, almost the whole world firmly believed that all the pyramids were built as burial chambers for the pharaohs. However, the shortfalls of this theory have already been explained, especially with respect to the Great Pyramid. It is believed by some esotericists that the three largest Pyramids at Giza were not even built by the pharaohs, but were subsequently adopted by them for the purposes of burial.

The three pyramids at Giza representing Orion's belt are in marked contrast to the pyramids surrounding them. They are larger, built of larger blocks and steeper then the other pyramids at Giza. Alan Alford believes that the pyramids representing Orion's belt were built long before the others and that the other pyramids, which he believes were built after these, show a marked decline in building skills. Masonic beliefs support this view, and the considerable differences between the size of the three main Giza pyramids, and the others, can be seen in figures 3 and 5. The celestial evidence would seem to support this too (i.e. the pyramids mirroring Orion's belt at 10,500 BC). It is accepted that many of the pyramids were built as burial chambers for the pharaohs, but surely such a theory cannot be attributed to the three at Giza.

The Giza pyramids demonstrate an incredible knowledge of precision geometry and Masons believe that each angle, measurement and dimension has meaning, that it speaks a mathematical language, which only the initiated can understand. Some aspects of the mathematical meaning of the pyramids have been explained previously, but esotericists believe that the pyramids go beyond this; that there are certain numbers which hold great mystical significance encoded into the pyramids at Giza. For instance they believe that within the Great Pyramid's dimensions is encoded the number 1746, which represents the celestial number of fusion. Maybe those studying the dimensions of the pyramids should measure in cubits, rather than feet, as John Dee advocates in his *Monas Hieroglyphica*. However, although the pyramid emanates a numerological and mathematical language and Masons attribute great importance to these mystical numbers (as a way of enhancing themselves spiritually), they do not believe this was the only reason the three largest pyramids at Giza were built. One of the underlying similarities between nearly all the ancient civilisations from the Sumerians, Egyptians, Olmecs, Mayan to the Greeks and Romans (to name a few), was the precision which is evident in everything they built; and although Masons appreciate this and the meaning behind it, they also believe the Great Pyramid had, as aforementioned, a functional purpose too.

Another exponent of this functional theory is Alan Alford, whose conclusions are based on years of study and scientific appreciation of the Great Pyramid. He believes that the Great Pyramid was used at one time to produce water fission. It is believed by numerous scientists around the world, that by splitting a water molecule into its component parts, hydrogen and oxygen, one hundred times more energy can be produced from burning these products than the energy used to initiate the water split or fission. This theory has scientists very excited as it could be an answer to the fuel crisis which scientists say is imminent in the next 30 to 40 years. Alford's examination of water fission and its application to the Great Pyramid is quite convincing, but at the same time he attributes the pyramids construction and use to extraterrestrials. Extraterrestrials have, according to Masons, played an important role in history, and encompass a large part of Masonic beliefs, however, Masons do not attribute the pyramid's construction or use to them.

The masons belief about the Great Pyramid is also that it was built as a functional device, however, their beliefs are very different from Alford's. In contrast, as previously mentioned, they maintain that the Great Pyramid is in fact two pyramids; one directing itself into the ground, and the other resting on top - the pyramid which can be seen. Masons are taught that the Great Pyramid is a beacon, the top pyramid representing the higher astral world, to which Freemasons profess to belong - as will be explained in chapter four. The other pyramid underneath representing our material world. They believe that the Great Pyramid's power is generated by lay lines, and that at some time after the year 2000 the top pyramid will turn 45 degrees. This event they maintain, will be triggered by certain celestial forces which will make the pyramid operable, creating a link between this world and others which are part of this higher astral understanding. To foster such beliefs, some would argue, is totally unreasonable. There is no evidence to suggest that such an event is going to occur, but such a belief is very much part of Masonic teachings and tradition, marking (if it does actually happen) a new epoch in time to Freemasons and esotericists alike. However, what can be said about the Great Pyramid are that its dimensions, when applied to the construction of other pyramids of any size, bring to light some totally inexplicable phenomenon.

While making some tests upon the dimensions of the Great Pyramid, Karel Drbal, a Czechoslovakian radio engineer, found that when he placed a razor blade one third of the way up to the top of his small pyramid replicas, they became sharp again. To add to his enlightening discovery he also found that the razors became immune to rusting. He subsequently went into business producing these small replicas of pyramids naming his product 'The Cheops Razor Sharpener'. But this was not the only inexplicable phenomenon discovered, as A. and S. Landsburg explain:

Alert entrepreneurs picked up Drbal's concept in France and Italy, producing pyramid shaped milk and yoghurt cartons that definitely retarded spoilage. Nobody can explain how or why these pyramidal structures have this effect. Apparently the ancient Egyptians knew something we don't. [9]

There are even fridges available based upon this same structure. Such enigmas would accord with the pyramid being an active and functional device as the Masons believe. However, whether these strange facets of the pyramid are to do with it generating the power of lay lines remains to be seen.

If the Giza Pyramids were the first to be built, with the smaller pyramids being built afterwards, then this is an endorsement of the Masonic belief, (mentioned in chapter one), of the decline of mankind's knowledge which he possessed in ancient times and the subsequent loss of many of the secrets man once held. Although, many of the secrets were retained by the Egyptian pharaohs, it is evident by comparing the smaller pyramids to the three larger ones which represent Orion's belt, that some of the secrets of the ancients did not stand the test of time.

After Egypt

As aforementioned, Masons maintain that their esoteric knowledge was possessed and handed down to them indirectly through the Egyptians. As Albert G. Mackey explains:

> Egypt has always been considered as the birth place of the mysteries. It was there that the ceremonies of initiation were first established. It was there that truth was first veiled in allegory, and the dogmas of religion were first imparted under symbolic forms. [10]

9. Landsberg A. and S., In Search of Ancient Mysteries, p.101
10. Mackey, A. G., Encyclopedia of Freemasonry, Vol. 1, p.270

But what chain of events led to this knowledge falling into the hands of the Freemasons of today?

Firstly, if we accept as esotericists believe, that the pharaohs were the keepers of this knowledge, and they, by their divine descent from the gods, were the guardians of esotericism; then we are left with two distinct possibilities. Either that the Masons or their esoteric ancestors, the Templars, found this knowledge and brought it directly from Egypt. Or that someone, who by divine right had been initiated into the esoteric wisdom of the pharaohs, brought it out of Egypt in ancient times and handed it down in some way to the esotericists of today. It is the latter theory to which esotericists adhere. However, some Masons believe that some of their knowledge came directly from Egypt. A passage from the Chapter degree, which masons are required to recite from memory during the ritual, testifies to this:

> We cleared away more of the loose earth and rubbish, when we found that instead of a solid rock there was a series of stones in the form of an arch, and being aware that the architect of the previous structure had designed no part of it in vain, we determined to examine it, for which purpose we removed two of the stones, when we discovered a vault of considerable magnitude, and immediately cast lots who should descend.
>
> The lot fell on me; when, lest any noxious vapours or other causes should render my situation unsafe, my companions fastened this cord of life line round my body, and I was duly lowered into the vault. On arriving at the bottom, I gave a preconcerted signal, and my companions gave me more line, which enabled me to traverse the vault; I then discovered something in the form of a pedestal and felt certain marks or characters thereon, but from the want of light I was unable to ascertain what they were. I also found this scroll, but from the same cause I was

unable to read its contents. I therefore gave another preconcerted signal, and was drawn out of the vault bringing the scroll with me. We then discovered from the first sentence that it contained the records of the Most Holy Law, which had been promulgated by our God at the foot of Mount Sinai.

The last sentence is obviously a reference to Moses, who as will be explained, is of immense importance to Masons and their esoteric history. It is not known how true this story is, or indeed how true any of the stories contained in the degrees of Freemasonry are, the authenticity of some is dubious to say the least; this is probably due to the lack of literature connected with them, and also the allegorical design in which their knowledge is contained which is meant to be applied through rituals. Having said this the Masonic degrees are designed for two principal purposes - the first, being to give the candidate an insight into the type of knowledge about to be imparted to him, to set the scene as it were; but more importantly, to bring the candidate onto a new level spiritually i.e. to bring him to a higher level of consciousness advancing him through the astral planes. In this respect, the Masonic degrees are effective. However, the Masonic degrees (notwithstanding the secrets imparted during and after the degree ceremony) cannot be relied upon as authentic accounts of what once actually occurred, because authenticity is incidental to the purpose and nature of the degree ceremonies (this is explained fully in chapter four).

According to Masons, the strongest case for the way in which their knowledge was brought out of Egypt, is that a divine figurehead, initiated into this knowledge, brought it out. To Freemasons and esotericists alike, this event could not be more clearly documented, as they believe the story is contained in the Old Testament Book of Exodus, and they believe, the figure who, brought this knowledge out was undoubtedly Moses:

Later when the child was old enough, she took him to the king's daughter, who adopted him as her own son. She said to herself, 'I pulled him out of the water, and so I name him Moses.' [11]

Then Moses, who at some point realised his own identity as an Israelite, took his people out of Egypt:

Moses said to the people, 'Remember this day on which you left Egypt, the place where you were slaves. This is the day the Lord brought you out by his great power . . .' [12]

As was briefly mentioned previously, Masons maintain that the Old Testament is a true account, not a bunch of exaggerated stories, of what actually occurred written in the only way these ancient people could explain, in certain instances, the involvement of an extraterrestrial or extraterrestrials in their lives. This concept of the Old Testament containing possible accounts of extraterrestrial involvement is discussed further in chapter seven.

It is also important to note that Freemasons attach great importance to the Book of Enoch. They believe Enoch was the first to discover the zodiac and gained great knowledge in planetary movements. The fact that Enoch lived for 365 years is also significant to Freemasons, as it represents the number of days in a year. Masons also believe that he was the first to characterise the rite of initiation. It was through Moses and the successive generations of Israelite kings documented in the Old Testament, that (Masons believe) the esoteric knowledge of the Egyptian pharaoh's was kept alive. In M. F. Carey's *Freemasonry in All Ages* he describes how:

'The knowledge contained in the mysteries were imparted by God to Adam, and by him to Seth, and so on through the antediluvian patriarchs through

11. Old Testament, Exodus 2:10
12. Old Testament, Exodus 13:3

Enoch to Noah, and then transmitted by them to Abraham, who communicated them to Isaac, Isaac to Jacob, and thus on to Solomon.' [13]

Although this esoteric continuum was once again interrupted by the defeat of the Israelites and the destruction of Solomon's Temple this knowledge continued within small Israelite circles after this, and esotericists believe that Jesus, Mary Magdalene and John the Baptist were notable advocates of this knowledge and actively followed its teachings. These beliefs will be considered in turn, but let us first turn to the next glory years where esotericism again achieved such prominence, heralded by none other than the enigmatic and elusive Knights Templar.

13. Carey, M. F., Freemasonry in All Ages, p.70

Chapter Three

The Knights Templar

We are already certain, and have said so in previous books, that there has been at least one major forgotten episode in human history - a lost civilisation destroyed in the great cataclysms at the end of the last Ice Age. Much connects that civilisation to the epoch of 10,500 BC. But the possibilities we are considering here are even more remarkable: the possibility that a system of knowledge once practised by that civilisation may have been salvaged from its wreckage by survivors and the possibility that ways may have been devised to distribute the knowledge around the world and transmit it to the future, down through the generations, perhaps even into modern times. [1]

Almost all literature which deals in one way or another with matters concerning masonry will have some reference to the Templar Knights or Knights Templar. Some people believed them to be sorcerers, alchemists, or keepers of a secret

1. Hancock, G., and Faiia, S., Heavens Mirror, p.236

knowledge. This sometimes elusive order sprung from almost nowhere to become "powerful beyond the scope of most kings" [2]. So what was it that induced the creation, produced its rapid expansion of wealth and political prowess, and caused the sudden demise of this most mysterious of orders? And indeed, how do they fit into this esoteric continuum through the centuries? How did their defiance and their ability to conceal their knowledge ultimately lead to the Masonic guilds of Freemasons?

Origins of the Knights Templar

The story of the Templars begins with the journey of two men to the Holy Land in 1104. These men, Hugh de Paynes and the Count of Champagne, both from the province of Champagne in France, visited the Holy Land five years after the first crusade. Many have postulated upon what actually prompted the two to undertake such a journey. Some believe it was simply curiosity, or that the two were on a pilgrimage. However, in recent years, attentions have been drawn to the connections which existed between southern France and the Holy Land via the Cathars, but, historical evidence relating to this connection is scanty and such a connection has not as yet been conclusively proven. But, what is certain is that Hugh de Paynes and the Count of Champane did find something of interest, something important enough to warrant Hugh de Paynes returning to the Holy Land in 1116. It was something which, on his return to France (after his second trip), led him to recruit eight knights (at this point they were known as 'The Poor Knights of Christ and the Temple of Solomon') and set out again with these knights for the Holy Land.

There have been numerous speculations as to exactly what prompted Hugh de Paynes to make these three trips, returning the third time with eight knights he had recruited

---

2. Knight, C. and Lomas, R., The Hiram Key, p.34

into this new order, their stay in the Holy Land lasting approximately seven years. Some say the expeditions were induced by a quest for the Holy Grail, or that they were looking for the Ark of the Covenant, or searching for the secrets of Atlantis passed down by the ancient Egyptians. However, whatever the motivation was behind these tempestuous journeys to the Holy Land by Hugh de Paynes, he must have evaluated the risks and decided his objective was worth the sacrifice of his time and devotion. Such devotion is characteristic of someone who had a preconceived notion of what he was going to find. It is interesting to speculate, but did the Cathars (before their genocide, which is discussed later,) pass on information to Hugh de Paynes concerning some hidden treasure and/or hidden knowledge? It is also of no coincidence that their name 'The Poor Knights of Christ and the Temple of Solomon' was a direct reference to Solomon's Temple, around which the Masonic degrees revolve (as the next chapter will reveal).

The nine knights (including Hugh de Paynes) set up their headquarters upon Mount Moria - on the foundations of Solomon's Temple. Even though Solomon's Temple was destroyed in 587 BC by the Babylonians, the foundations still remained intact, and it was these foundations or rather, what was underneath them, which interested the nine knights. However, in the 30th degree of Freemasonry (also known as 'Knight of Kadosh'), eleven knights are quoted as being in the Holy Land:

. . . notwithstanding which, there have been always found some faithful Masons; which is clearly proved in the brilliant manner in which the order of Masonry was received in the year 1118, when eleven Grand Elect and Perfect Masons, the most zealous, presented themselves to Garinous, Prince of Jerusalem, Patriarch and Knight Mason, and pronounced their promises between his hands.

That these knights are referred to as Masons testifies to the link between the Templars and Masons, and is not simply used as a term of endearment, but refers to those who practised the esoteric doctrines which the Masons believe they have inherited from the Templars.

At this stage certain circumstances start failing to add up. Firstly, the nine knights had disclosed their official duties in the Holy Land as protecting pilgrims on the highways around Jerusalem, but how could nine knights be expected to police around 50 miles of highways, let alone the numerous pilgrims travelling precariously upon them? Secondly, the location of their headquarters (Mount Moria) was not strategically located for this task. More importantly King Baldwin 1 of Jerusalem granted the Templars exclusive use of a large part of the Al-Aqusa Mosque (as shown in Plate 10) and its outbuildings, which he intended to keep as his own Royal Palace. Such a concession would have seemed generous at the very least to an established order at the time, but it did not make sense to grant such privileges to a then unknown order. Obviously, there must have been someone fairly influential already pulling strings, probably aware of the importance of what the expedition might find. Is it Baldwin II du Bourg who is referred to in the 30th degree as the 'Prince of Jerusalem, Patriarch and Knight Mason . . .'? If so then this implies that there was some special relationship between Baldwin II du Bourg and the knights. And if so then this necessarily implies that there must have been some forward planning before the knights arrived in Jerusalem, and also that Baldwin must have attached great importance to the knights expedition. The 30th degree also seems to refer to Baldwin as a 'Knight Mason', does this mean that he had already been introduced into esoteric doctrines?

As soon as the knights set up their headquarters on Mount Moria, they began secret excavations under Solomon's Temple Mount (shown in Plate 11). These excavations were kept so secretive that they have not been documented, and the only real evidence for the excavations was left by the knights themselves, these knights soon to become known as the Knights Templar. Graham Hancock, unsatisfied with the official historical account of Templar activities in the Holy Land (protecting pilgrims), uncovered evidence that the nine knights were searching for something and did indeed tunnel under Solomon's Temple Mount. As he quotes from an Israeli Archaeological Report:

> The tunnel leads inwards for a distance of about 30 metres from the southern wall before being blocked by pieces of stone debris. We know that it continues further, but we had made it a hard and fast rule not to excavate within the bounds of the Temple Mount which is currently under Moslem jurisdiction, without first acquiring the permission of the appropriate Moslem authorities.[3]

For seven years the nine knights hardly communicated with the outside world to such an extent that it was as if they did not exist. It is not difficult to have quiet admiration for these knights who must have been fanatically dedicated to these excavations throughout the seven years they spent there, while maintaining to keep such a low profile in a strange and sometimes hostile land. Considering the extensive privileges granted to the knights and their official duties, which were evidently, being used to disguise their actual duties, a person could not be frowned upon for suggesting that the expedition to excavate the foundations of Solomon's Temple was preconceived, that they had prior knowledge of what they might or even were going to find under the Temple. Furthermore an analogy can be drawn here between the so called 'protection of pilgrims' and 'keeping the secrets of stonemasonry amongst the few'; history has demonstrated that in both these cases the explanation does not fit the practice.

In 1126 the nine Templars left Mount Moria (the site of King Solomon's Temple) and travelled back to France with, it is rumoured, large amounts of gold and some parchments

3. Hancock, G. The Sign and the Seal p.94

containing ancient esoteric texts. They may not have found what they had originally intended to, but it is certain that what was found was of immense importance and has formed the cornerstone of what we know today as Freemasonry. It is known that after his arrival, Hugh de Paynes contacted the Abbot of Citeaux to help him translate some Hebrew texts, these were obviously the ones found under the Temple of Solomon by the nine Knights.

One of the eight knights recruited by Hugh de Paynes was Andre de Montbard, and it was his uncle St Bernard of Clarivaux, who by 1126 had risen to an influential position within the church and was rumoured to have sent the nine knights to Jerusalem. In 1128, with the nine Templar knights safely back on French soil with whatever they had found, it was now time for St Bernard to perform his part in the furtherance of this order. Although the order had existed for nine years, it had no official backing or recognition from the church. This was soon remedied through the Synod of Troyes (a meeting of influential church representatives who decided on what the constitution of the Templars should be), and whose secretary was none other than St Bernard. Although decisions during meetings of this nature were normally arrived at through a consensus of opinion, this particular meeting may just as well have been attended by St Bernard himself and no one else; as he personally drew up the Templars' 'rule'. The Templar Rule consisted of seventy two articles which included every aspect concerning how a Templar should conduct himself through his daily life. Firstly they were sworn to poverty, chastity and obedience. They were to dress in a simple white cloak, forbidden to wear any firs (apart from lambs wool), and had to sleep in their underwear and were forbidden to cut their beards. They had to be completely celibate and were only allowed to kiss their mothers , sisters and aunts. In addition to these requirements they were also expected to be knights in the sense of accomplished swordsmen and expected to fight to the death if so commanded. The rigorous discipline expected of the Templars is expressed

78

in the Templar Oath:

> I swear to consecrate my discourse, my arms, my faculties, and my life, to the defence of the sacred mysteries of the faith and to that of the unity of God. I also promise to be submissive and obedient to the Grand Master of the Order . . . At all times that it will be necessary, I will cross the seas to go to battle; I will contribute succour against infidel princes; I will not turn my back on three foes; and even if I be alone, I will fight them if they are infidels." [4]

The Templars were also provided with three horses and a squire and had to share their meals with another Templar so both would eat from the same bowl. The strict adherence to this life of penance was meant to be matched by their skills of chivalry. They were renowned in their day as being the most disciplined fighting force in the world. It was as if the Templars were expected to be extreme characters, who could switch from prayer to slaughtering Muslims from one moment to the next. It would be fair to say in hindsight that the Templar order and its constitution was in fact engineered by St Bernard. It was one of St Bernard's proteges, Pope Innocent II, who declared a papal bull that the Templars should owe allegiance to the pope and no other ecclesiastical body; basically making them a law unto themselves. The large surge in membership can also be attributed to St Bernard's efforts, through his promotion of the order and his ability to influence the church. As Graham Hancock puts it: 'By late 12th century the order had become phenomenally rich, was operating a sophisticated International Banking System and owned properties throughout the known world.' [5]

It is no coincidence that Gothic architecture came on to the scene in the 1130's. It was the Templars who built some of the great Gothic churches and the near impregnable castles in the Holy Land, which were highly advanced in terms of building techniques and their incredible architecture

4. Mackey, A. G., Enclycopedia of Freemasonry, Vol.1, p.480
5. Hancock, G., The Sign and the Seal, p.98

for the middle ages. Churches throughout France and Britain lay testament to the highly advanced skills involved which were really before their time; but, was it advancement of architecture as such or the relearning of ancient building techniques which were, for instance, used previously and had been lost since ancient times. Graham Hancock puts it very succinctly:

> . . . what if these discoveries (under the Temple of Solomon), had included the lost architectural secrets of geometry, proportion, balance and harmony that had been known to the builders of the pyramids and other great monuments of Antiquity. [6]

This may at first look like a piece of far fetched speculation, but doesn't the astonishingly high craftsmanship and architecture of the Templar Knights give evidence and point to such knowledge being found. Furthermore Masons are instructed in the ancient building techniques, demonstrated in their rituals, which they believe were used by the ancient Egyptians. The Masonic degree rituals are nearly all connected in some way with building, for instance the first three degrees are meant to mirror the construction of Solomon's Temple; the symbolism of the tools, such as the square, compass and trowel; enabling the candidate to advance spiritually.

In 1932 C. N. Johns excavated the Templar fortress of Atlit south of Haifa. He concluded that even by modern standards the architecture of the Templars had been exceptional. In 1174 a German monk named Theoderic was highly impressed with the extensive arches, vaults and roofs which were built in and around the area of the Temple Mount (Mount Moria). Furthermore, is it purely coincidence that the great arches and roofs referred to by Theoderic, were also typical of Gothic architecture produced by the Templars. In the early period of Gothic architecture, St. Bernard seems to have had a major influence in its development and direction. His emphasis upon proportion, harmony and balance seems

6. Hancock, G., The Sign and the Seal, p.99

to have been the hallmark of early Templar church builders. It is highly unlikely that Gothic architecture came about in a vacuum, and the close similarities between Templar buildings around the Temple Mount (the arches and tall roofs), and the Gothic churches and cathedrals seems to confirm that a connection must have existed. This view is also endorsed by St Bernard's close involvement with the Templars and Gothic architecture, especially one building inparticular, and thought by many to be the most magnificent cathedral of all - Chartres (shown in Plate 12).

With the evidence presented so far, it is becoming particularly likely that some type of knowledge including ancient building techniques were discovered under the foundations of Solomon's Temple by the Templar knights. The Templar Order was given a constitution by St Bernard through the Synod of Troyes and then with his endorsement grew rapidly in membership and wealth. At this period also (early 1130s) highly advanced forms of architecture began to appear (known as gothic). This is obviously no coincidence because the Freemasons, who claim links from the Templars, take the word Mason in their name from the word 'stonemason'. Furthermore, as previously referred to, the Masonic rituals or rites practised by Freemasons enact the building of the Temple of Solomon and the principles of balance, harmony and proportion as expounded by St. Bernard. In fact the Masons' symbol of the square and the compass are meant to represent the building tools used by the ancients, but it must be emphasised that these are only allegories to Freemasons for the purpose of spiritual advancement.

After the Synod of Troyes the Templars' possessions and wealth became very extensive. Their activities had expanded from Jerusalem to Egypt, Constantinople and throughout the Middle East (to name a few places). By the 13th century they were becoming heavily involved in the internal politics of the countries in whose realms they resided; for instance, they were supposedly involved in the composition and signing of the Magna Carta. The Templars soon established their own fleet and owned a substantial part of Bristol, which was at that time one of their major ports. Such an extensive array of activities required funding, and this was provided for by donations of wealth and land, the rents from their numerous properties, and the interest charged through their money lending activities. By the mid 13th century the Templars had become major bankers for every throne in Europe. It has also been rumoured that a great treasure was found under the Temple of Solomon which was subsequently used to consolidate their wealth; there could be some truth in this, however it is more likely that the order which sprang from what they had found under the Temple of Solomon, would have revered the treasure found there rather than use it to consolidate their wealth.

Special privileges seemed always to be granted to the Templars, for instance they were not required to pay tax in England. Rules were imposed upon money lending, the Christians were not allowed to collect interest upon loans, and Jews only allowed to charge a maximum of 43% interest per year; whereas there were no restraints laid down for Templar financial enterprises. The Templars were also the first to devise the transfer of funds from one place to another, which did not require the physical movement of those funds. This they achieved through the use of credit notes, which were comprised of elaborate Latin codes which only the Templar banks could decipher. As the reader may have gathered from the first chapter, the Templars were accustomed to the use of codes in disguising their esoteric knowledge. The Templars were also renowned for providing their own perceptories (places where valuables could be deposited safely), and these perceptories existed all over Europe; the largest and most famous of all was the Paris perceptory. They were also involved in collecting taxes, and also acted extensively as trustees for property and funds. Baigent and Leigh attribute the creation of the financial institutions of Europe as principally down to the Templars' financial talents.

The Templars were closely connected with the Cathars, and it has been rumoured that the Templars were formed to carry on the Cathar legacy. The Cathars were a religious sect which had existed since the earliest Christian times, and believed theirs to be the only true faith. They repudiated the Catholic faith and denied that Jesus was the Son of God believing him to be a mere mortal, which as the reader will note later is also a belief engrained in Templar and Masonic traditions. They also held Mary Magdalene in very high regard which also accords with Templar and Masonic beliefs. In 1209 the Papacy began a crusade against the supposed Cathar heretics, slaughtering whole populations of Cathar towns and villages which existed mostly in southern France. The Templars did not participate in this catholic 'blood bath', and many Templars provided Cathars with a refuge while many Cathars subsequently joined the Templar Order. This connection will become relevant later, but it is enough for the reader now to appreciate that a connection between the Templars and Cathars did exist. Picknett and Prince, authors of *The Templar Revelation* approached one research group Abraxas, inquiring about possible connections between the Cathars and Templars:

> They replied that there were clear links between the two groups that went well beyond mere family ties and which are usually overlooked by historians- for example, even at the height of the Albigensian Crusade (Cathar crusade) the Templars sheltered fugitive Cathars, and there are documented examples of them also giving succour to knights who actively fought for the Cathars against the crusaders. [7]

The financial privileges granted to the Templars enabled them to command great power and influence throughout Europe. Their reputation for accepting new ideas, sciences and all types of hidden knowledge did not just happen overnight or by chance. From the beginning the Templars recruited members of society who were highly influential, were very well connected, and people regarded by society as impeccable in

7. Picknet, I., and Prince, C., The Templar Revelation, p.104

terms of character and achievement. They also connected themselves closely with royalty (the reason for this will become self evident to the reader in chapter six), however as their wealth and influence increased throughout the 12th and 13th centuries, some royal families became suspicious of their growing power - particularly King Philip of France. This prompted him to take extensive steps to gain back the power he believed he had lost to the Templars during his reign. In fact many believed at the time that in France the Templars were more powerful than the king. The culmination of King Philip's interference with the Papacy and his single minded-ness in destroying the Templars' led to a day that history has not forgotten - a day on which people even today become unnaturally suspicious fearing that some disaster or other is going to happen - Friday the 13th 1307.

The Templar dissolution

King Philip's quest to destroy the Templars had been prompt-ed earlier. First of all he must have considered it insulting not to be made an honorary member of the order at his request. Secondly, Philip had financial problems, his treasury was on the verge of bankruptcy and he must have dreamt more than once of laying his hands on the enormous wealth that the Templars had accumulated. Also, now that Jerusalem had finally succumbed to Islamic Military superiority, they became an order without a purpose for existing, and an order without a home. Philip was aware that their original purpose for existence (to protect the pilgrims in the Holy Land) had become obsolete and he was also aware of their intention of setting up a separate state for themselves in Languedoc a southern province of France - ambitions which mirrored the Teutonic Knights creation of a separate state called Ordensland which comprised the eastern Baltic area. Their attempt to set up a separate state of their own under the nose of King

84

Philip was at that time futile. Surely the Templars were too aware of Philip's growing animosity towards them due to their extensive power and wealth to attempt such an antagonistic move. Or maybe they believed that the King could be controlled. Philip at the time was not powerful enough to deal with the Templars alone - in fact his position had become precarious with the Templars extensive power and influence in French politics.

Another factor, expounded by Graham Hancock, which may have contributed to the Templars' demise, was that in 1306, an Ethiopian delegation arrived at Avignon. They were sent by Emperor Weden Ara'ad to communicate his fears regarding his country's future autonomy from Templar intervention. Evidence for Templar presence in Ethiopia exists in the architecture of many churches built by the Templars in Ethiopia which still stand to this day; and also from historical records which testify that it was white men who were the architects of the highly advanced churches built in Ethiopia. However, Templar presence in Ethiopia may not have been motivated by an urge to build churches there, but rather in the quest for the Ark of the Covenant. It has been rumoured that it was the Ark which first prompted the initial expedition of the nine knights to the Temple Mount.

The Templars' quest for the Ark of the Covenant must have continued after the excavations under the Temple Mount; the story of what happened to the Ark has been written in stone by the Templars at Chartres. It was important to them, as it once stood in the centre of Solomon's Temple (Holy of Holies). They had traced its movements from when it was stolen to the present day, and according to Graham Hancock, finally found it in Axum, Ethiopia. Abu Salih, an Armenian geographer noted that in the early part of the 13th century, the Ark was "attended and carried" by men who were "white and red in complexion, with red hair".[8] For most of its time, the Ark of the Covenant has remained at Axum, and it is around this area that Templar emblems have been found carved into stone. Graham Hancock has postulated that the

8. Hancock, G., The Sign and the Seal, p.159

Templars may have been planning to bring the Ark back to France, and that it is this which prompted Emperor Weden Ara'ad to send the delegation to Avignon in 1306. The delegation's purpose was achieved, they did reach the Pope and warned him of the possible threat the Templars posed to Ethiopia's rulers or of their possible plans to take the Ark and bring it to France. This could only have contributed to the already growing uneasiness of Templar motives, and may even have been a contributory factor in the Templar's dissolution.

To rid himself of the Templars, Philip had to recruit the aid of the Papacy, which was at first not forthcoming; so he arranged the kidnap and murder of Pope Boniface VIII , and it is rumoured, his successor Benedict XI. At this point he placed a man on the throne of the Papacy, whose obedience was guaranteed - the former Archbishop of Bordeaux - Pope Clement V. As head of the Catholic Church, Clement V was used by Philip in his plan to destroy the Templars, but it must also be emphasised that Clement V might not have needed prompting by Philip, he may well have had ambitions of his own concerning the Templars; the Ethiopian delegation visit may also have contributed to Clement V's attitude towards the Templars. However, it will also become apparent to the reader that the Templars esoteric beliefs were at odds with the Catholic Churchs' version of the life of Jesus and what he stood for, and their dissolution may have been due to the threat their knowledge posed to the foundations of Catholicism. However, from the 30th degree of Freemasonry (commonly known as Knight of Kadosh), it would appear that Philip was the sole instigator of the Templars' dissolution:

This king (Philip the Fair) having found a man fit for his purpose to be the agent of his revenge, caused him to be elected pope, and promoted to St. Peter's chair, in the year 1305, under the name of Clement V. This pope after his election established his see at the city of Lyons, where his first care was to execute the six first conditions which Philip had imposed upon him. The time of declaring the seventh being arrived, Philip did not delay in declaring to the pope, that, by his oath, he was to join him to entirely destroy and exterminate the Knights Templar, to the extent of Christendom.

Philip gathered together a string of charges against the Templars (many probably from his own imagination) and ordered his seneschals and bailiffs (through sealed orders to be opened on Friday October 13th 1307), to arrest all the Templars and strip them of their property and wealth. His intention to surprise the Templars, thereby depriving them of any opportunity to escape or carry their wealth to a place of safety, however failed. Jacques de Molay, at that time Grand Master of the Templar order had not only the opportunity to burn all of his literature relating to the Templars, but also to contact a large majority of the Templars before the arrests. The message communicated to the Templars before the arrests was to destroy all literature relating to the Order, and not to reveal any of the secrets or the rites which the order performed. As the *Catholic Encyclopedia* (1908) testifies:

> There was one feature in the organisation of the order which gave rise to suspicion, namely the secrecy with which their rites of initiation were conducted. The secrecy is explained by the fact that the receptions always took place in a chapter, and the chapters, owing to the delicate and grave questions discussed, were, and necessarily had to be, held in secret. An indiscretion in the matter of secrecy entailed expulsion from the order. [9]

Not revealing the secrets constitutes one of the fundamental aspects of Masonic law which is discussed later in this book. The evidence of the events leading up to and the subsequent

9. Catholic Encyclopedia, Vol. 14, p. 494 (Charles Moeller)

arrest of the Templars indicates that they were anticipating the arrests, and that they were informed to passively accept their arrests; although there are many reports of Templars fleeing before the arrests there is not one account of any Templar resisting arrest once apprehended.

With Philip's anticipated element of surprise being lost, his main prize (the Templar treasure and wealth), eluded him. Historical accounts tell of a treasure beyond a person's wildest imagination. This treasure and the Templar's accumulated wealth was transported (before the arrests) from Paris to the Templar port of La Rochelle in southern France. All the Templars connected with the Templar treasury escaped capture and simply disappeared; they must have left with the fleet. However, is it not suspiciously strange that more of the order were not saved or did not save themselves by fleeing, if, as is believed, a large number had a prior knowledge of their imminent arrests? Maybe it could have been that they had misjudged the deep rooted hate which Philip had fostered against them and failed to anticipate his wrath. Or it could be that they did anticipate (to some degree) the type of fate which awaited them, but on instructions from Molay reacted passively to the arrests which, when looking back through history, achieved an important purpose for the Templar Order. It also gave Masonry a clear foundation on which to establish itself; an anonymous past, and of which the explanation 'stone masons guild' would be sufficient to satisfy the curiosities of the public at large.

The ease with which the Templars were arrested meant that everyone perceived that the whole Templar order had been wiped out - it had suddenly ceased to exist. The arrest, torture and, in a large number of cases, execution of many Templars on trumped up charges, such as worshipping a god called Bahomet and spitting on the cross, carried with it the approval of the Papacy in the form of a papal bull, probably due to Philip's influence and possibly his orchestration. They were also accused of infanticide, teaching women how to abort, and denying, in Catholic ideology, Christ as the

Son of God, with respect to the Christian definition. This meant that all over Europe, Templar land and their possessions were seized, however, the harsh treatment experienced by the French Templars was not experienced with the same severity elsewhere. Many of Europe's Templars joined other orders such as the Crusader, Teutonic, Knights Hospitaller, Knights of St John and the Knights of Christ. There were a few countries where the Templars had their land seized but were not persecuted as such. Two countries inparticular interpreted the Papal bull very leniently - Portugal and Scotland. In Portugal the Templars simply carried on under a different name - The Knights or Order of Christ. Historical accounts of the Templars' presence and activity in Scotland is scanty to say the least, but as will be described later, Templar involvement was a major factor in Scotland's historical equation. After Friday the 13th October 1307, Templar activity from a historical perspective ceased; this served a very important purpose for them because they had now protected themselves from further persecution through their non-existence. Although by this time their continued activities and existence demanded absolute secrecy; echoes of which can be found in Masonic tradition with regard to the penalties laid down for revealing the secrets. Further synergies with Masonry can be expounded in the following:

> All that was required of a new member (of the Templars) was a blind obedience, as imperative in the soldier as in the monk. He had to declare himself forever 'serf et esclave de la maison' (bonded to the slaves of the dynasty). To prove his sincerity he was subjected to a secret test concerning the nature of which nothing has ever been discovered, although it gave rise to the most extraordinary allegations. [10]

It is however strange that Philip was so intent on eradicating all the Templars in Europe, even though he had found nothing through the royal sequestration of the Templar

10. Catholic Encyclopedia, Vol. 14, p. 493 (Charles Moeller)

perceptories. Could it have been that Philip believed the Templars were in possession of a treasure which was not material, but related to a certain knowledge which he may have thought he could use to enhance his power. There is no evidence that Philip believed this or that it led to his attempt to destroy systematically all the Templars of Europe. However, the Templars were supposedly in possession of such a knowledge (this is explained in chapter nine), and such a supposition would seem to fit well into the reason behind Philips obsession with the total annihilation of the Templar Order. Another possible motive, and one which will become clear to the reader in chapter six, is that he may have thought that the Templars had ambitions to replace him and put their own king on the throne; who would, for them, rule with divine right.

In England Edward II was at first reluctant to take any action against the Templars; however through pressures from the Catholic Church and Philip of France, he must have felt he had no choice. Although when Edward II finally did act against the Templars and arrested some, many more slipped through the net. Upon their arrest the English Templars did not suffer the torture and persecution of their French coun-terparts. After their arrests in England, many were simply released on bail soon afterwards. During this time Edward II controlled most of Scotland, but his order to arrest the Scottish Templars didn't really materialise, historical accounts recount that only two Templars in Scotland were arrested. King Edward II's half-hearted approach to the Papacy's papal bull and pres-sures from the French king, demonstrate that he must have been in a dilemma, not wanting to make a decision either way. In the end he settled for a compromise, on the one hand he was seen to be dealing with the Templars, but in reality he was only doing enough to maintain his relations with the church and the French King without actually perse-cuting the Templars. Many other Templars in Europe escaped King Philip's wrath, some through the bungled half-hearted attempts to arrest them, and some by fleeing in anticipation of their arrests. Of all the European countries at that time, the Templars' two greatest havens (where they were not prosecuted at all) were Ireland and Scotland. So, what actually happened to the Templar Knights of Europe who escaped persecution, and also the eighteen ships comprising the Templar fleet which left La Rochelle with, it is believed, the Templar treasure from the Paris perceptory?

There are no historical records, that indicate exactly what happened to the Templar fleet which left La Rochelle, or to the treasure it may have been carrying from the Paris perceptory. It has been speculated that the ships travelled to the Mediterranean, Scandinavia or even North America. Arguments for and against these speculations could be endless, who could possibly hope to pinpoint the motives of such a secret society? However, Masonic tradition endorses that part of the fleet went to Scotland and the other part to America. This view concurs with the evidence of Templar activity in Scotland (e.g. in the form of numerous Templar graves from that period), and Templar carvings and architecture found in America. Some writers believe that the Templars had established commercial contact with the Americas a couple of centuries before Columbus sailed.

Considering Masonic opinion, that the fleet did head for Scotland, it is evident that they would have had plenty of reasons to do so. Firstly, Scotland's leader (although at that time most of the country was under Edward II's control), Robert the Bruce, had been excommunicated by the pope. This would have made it unlikely that he would have followed any of the Popes or Rome's orders regarding the Templars. Secondly, Robert the Bruce, being at war with Edward II at that time, would certainly not have been persuaded by anything he said, and may even have done the contrary to that which Edward expected him to do. Furthermore, because Robert the Bruce was at war with England at the time, he would have been glad of any fighting men to boost and train his depleted army; especially Templars, with their reputation for discipline and fierce reputation in combat.

Of the other Templars throughout Europe who slipped through the net, many simply went undercover and continued practising their rites and ceremonies under a different name, it is not coincidental that many different esoteric organisations (in similar form to the Templars), began to spring up all over Europe. It has been suggested that a large number of knights migrated up to Scotland to consolidate their, at that time, fragmented organisation. Baigent and Leigh have concluded that:

> 'Many (Templars) however, were still at large, having successfully evaded capture by obliterating all marks of their previous profession, and some had escaped in disguise to the wild and mountainous parts of Wales, Scotland and Ireland. [11]

Masonic sources also endorse this claim and some are more specific; Baron Karl von Hund an eminent eighteenth century freemason tells of the Templar fleet first landing on the Western coast of Ireland and then proceeding to the Isle of Mull in Scotland. Baigent and Leigh, however, believe that Hund could have mistakenly believed it was the Isle of Mull where they landed, and possibly confused this with the Mull of Kintyre or the Mull of Oa; since they would probably have experienced a hostile reception on the Isle of Mull at that time. The Isle of Mull was fighting on the English side of the war with the Scots, so they would have endorsed the Papal Bull regarding the dissolution of the Templars. The indications so far, are that the Templar fleet left La Rochelle and part of it travelled to the west coast of Ireland, and then travelled north, up and around Northern Ireland to the Mull of Kintyre or the Mull of Oa. This route would have avoided King Edward II's Irish sea blockade, and also the sea further up to the north of Scotland which was patrolled by allies of the English.

From 1307, many Templars from Europe had been making their way to Scotland, where they kept their profile very

11. Baigent, M., and Leigh, R., The Temple and the Lodge, p.110

low. Evidence exists in the form of Templar graves in Argyll, which date from the early fourteenth century testifying to Templar presence in Scotland at this time (as shown in Plate 13). While in Scotland, in return for refuge and possibly their ambitions of creating a Templar sanctuary, they joined Robert the Bruce's army. By 1309 Bruce had dramatically expanded the territories under his control to what constitutes the boundaries of Scotland today. Through the years which passed from this point to 1314, Bruce and Edward fought numerous battles. Bruce was aware that he would not get the better of set pitched battles, so engaged in quick strike attacks on the English. His soldiers were lightly armoured and equipped to beat a hasty retreat after an attack, these tactics were very typical of the way the Saracens fought in the Holy Land. Baigent and Leigh believe the similarities in fighting techniques are no coincidence, i.e. that the Templars who were very much involved with training Bruce's soldiers were teaching them lessons from the Crusades. Bruce's biggest battle against Edward II was Bannockburn (1314), in which both sides agreed to fight a set pitched battle. The battle raged for two days, but on the second day when Scotland's future was hanging in the balance a fresh force appeared as if from nowhere, which consisted of knights with large banners flying before them, bearing the pattee cross (the Templar emblem). The Scots seemed unsurprised by this outcome, so it is possible it might have been part of a prearranged battleplan. However, the English, on seeing these knights (almost like ghosts being resurrected from the crusades) fled the battle and many were slaughtered as they retreated in disarray. It does not leave much to the imagination to guess who these knights were or where, years before, they had come from, but whether the English fled the battle through fear or were ordered to when the King and his generals saw the knights is unclear. It is certain that Edward, through his empathy towards the Templars, may have indeed ordered a retreat on witnessing the legendary Knights Templar.

In 1312, five years after the arrests and the Inquisition of the Templars, the order had been dissolved by the Papacy in Rome. Two years later (1314), Jacques de Molay, Grand Master of the Templars at the time of the arrests, was burned at the stake. The torture he experienced by his Inquisitors can only be described as extreme and at one point he admitted heresy, but retracted this statement before his execution. In fact immediately before his execution, he was said to have asked Philip the Fair and pope Clement V to join him within the year before the judgement of God, this is recanted in the 30th or Knight of Kadosh degree of Freemasonry:

> Good people, who see us ready to perish in the flames, you will be able to judge of our innocence, for I now summon Pope Clement V in forty days, and Philip the Fair in twelve months, to appear before the awful and tremendous throne of the ever living God, to render an account of the blood they have so wickedly shed.

It is not known for certain if these were the words actually used by Molay, however, Pope Clement V died within forty days, and Philip the Fair within the year following Molay's execution. In fact the courage and defiance shown by Molay during his years of torture have made him into a very important figure not only to the Templars but naturally to Freemasons too. He is remembered in Masonic tradition as a latter day Hiram Abiff (this is elaborated and explained more fully later on), and the way his right hand contorted when nailed to the stake is repeated in the second degree or Fellowcraft degree of Masonry.

After Bannockburn, Bruce issued a charter confirming all the Knights Hospitaller possessions in Scotland, but the charter did not refer to any Templar properties which had been handed back to them by the Hospitallers. The charter should have included such details after the papal dissolution of the order. The fact that in Scotland the Templars retained control of their existing properties after their dissolution, seems at the time, to have been deliberately concealed from those who were outside the Scottish kingdom. Although there are no explicit sources of reference upon Templar activity in Scotland, there are many references to the merger between the Knights Hospitaller and the Templars into the 'Order of the Knights of St John and the Temple'. So, in reality the Knights Hospitaller through the formation of this joint order and the fact they were holding many properties in trust for the Templars, facilitated the Templars' anonymity and the retention of their properties. Whatever was going on in Scotland after the Templars dissolution was in many ways essential to the Templars' survival in so far as the Templars had a safe haven and were only restricted in their activities by the fact that they had to maintain people's existing perceptions about their non-existence to those outside Scotland.

As the reader will recall, the Templars also had a safe haven in Portugal. It is considered unlikely that a Templar fleet carrying, it is believed, treasure from the Paris perceptory, and the hopes of the Templars' continued existence, would have risked placing all their eggs in one basket by sending the whole fleet to Scotland. It would have been much more likely that the fleet which left La Rochelle on the morning of the arrests, split up to limit the risk of the whole fleet being captured or destroyed. If this were the case and if part of the Templar fleet's destination was Portugal, as many believe, then it would explain why Portugal has become, as will be explained, such an important place in Templar history.

In Portugal, the Knights Templar were tried and found not guilty of the charges put forward by the Papacy by Dennis I (King of Portugal). This meant that they were not persecuted, unlike elsewhere in Europe, however, Portugal had to yield to their dissolution in 1312. Two years later, the Knights of Christ (or more commonly referred to as the Order of Christ) suddenly appeared, and were granted approval by Rome. The confiscated Templar property and possessions in the Portuguese realm were subsequently given to this order - in actuality given back to the Templars themselves. It has already been argued that the Templars were organised, industrious, and highly proficient architecturally and militarily. However, many people may not have realised that they were also highly accomplished sailors and navigators.

As Graham Hancock explains, the Templars' 'maritime explorations left an indelible mark on history'.[12] When Columbus sailed to America in 1492, his ships sailed under the familiar Templar emblem the red pattiee cross. It may be no coincidence that Columbus reached the Americas soon after he had promised his crew that if they did not reach land within three days they had his permission to decapitate him. Did Columbus know exactly where he was going? It is possible that he had access to the charts and diaries of his father in law, a former Grand Master of the Order. Furthermore Columbus' three ships, the Pinta, Nina and Santa Maria, sailed under the Templar flag - the Pattiee cross. His father-in-law may have travelled to the Americas himself or may just have been in possession of the Templar maps and charts, presuming they had been to the Americas before. It may seem a strange concept for the reader to grasp, but there is evidence which points to the possibility that the Templars had travelled to the Americas at least 190 years before Columbus. Without access to the original charts which Columbus may have used in his expedition his father-in-law's position as a Templar Grand Master cannot be proved significant to his endeavours, but isn't it at least curious that the man granted the accolade of discovering the America's, had a Grand Master as a father-in-law. It is now claimed that specific carvings and architecture in Scotland and America do give sufficient evidence to support the theory that the Templars had discovered the American continent before Columbus.

In fact it is due to two Freemasons that such evidence has entered the public spotlight : Knight and Lomas. Much of their evidence is derived from Rosslyn chapel, approximately three miles south of Edinburgh. Rosslyn chapel (the inside of

12. Hancock, G., The Sign and the Seal, p.88

which is shown in Plate 14) was completed in 1486; and, as will be noted by the reader later, is a place of special significance to Templars and Freemasons. The archways and ceiling decoration depict Indian maize, which is only native to America. The relevance of the completion date of the chapel is fundamental because it predates Columbus 's discovery of America (1492). In fact it was only in the 16th century that explorers began bringing back this type of maize from America to Europe. However it may be possible that the decorations in the chapel are merely a design which the Templars invented and decided to carve into the chapel's structure. The Templar depiction of the maize is quite an accurate representation of its leaf structure, although there are many other shaped decorations within the chapel which would lend itself to the notion that this may be simply coincidental. On the other hand the Templars throughout history, especially through their architecture, could never be accused of constructing designs which were just meaningless decorations; these preceding points may be evidence that the architects of Rosslyn chapel, the Templars, may have had knowledge of the Indian maize plant. To have had a knowledge of the maize; it necessarily follows that the Templars must have travelled to America, and because Rosslyn chapel predates Columbus's trip they therefore, assuming that the evidence is valid, must have been there before him.

Knight and Lomas also bring forth further evidence to support their contention that the Templars were in America long before Columbus. In Westford, Massachusetts (America), an image of a knight has been punched out of rock which depicts a knight from the 14th century. More importantly, this depiction shows a ship sailing towards a star which decorates the knights shield. To most readers the significance of this will not be recognised, but the picture becomes much clearer because the Nasreen Scrolls (similar documents to which some believe the Templars had access), refers to a vast country called Merica which was denoted by a star. French Templars used to call this land, far to the west, La Merica.

Knight and Lomas also cite a puzzling tower built in the style of the Templar round churches at Newport on Rhode Island; its architecture indicates its date of construction about the time the Templar fleet disappeared.

The evidence would seem to suggest that the Templar fleet which left La Rochelle did split up, with one group going to Scotland and another part of the fleet which may have gone to America. But what of the Templars, did they just disappear? This is what they obviously wanted everyone to believe. However, their main aim must have been to ensure that their esoteric knowledge would not simply be lost in time and to ensure it's continued existence through the centuries. The true Templars (as opposed to the Freemasons who by the completion of a degree are given the priviledge of calling themselves Templars) today are few and far between and their membership, as well as being a closely guarded secret, is almost in all cases restricted to 'Grail' families (the meaning of this terminology will be explained in chapter six). It is known that some time after the perceived Templar dissolution, stonemasons guilds began appearing in Britain. But, before turning to Freemasonry, there is also another important esoteric group which sprung up in Europe from the ashes of the Templars. What emerged was an esoteric society which inherited much of the Templars esoteric knowledge. Rosicrucianism has always had strong links with Freemasonry in terms of their practices and beliefs, and its creation comprises an important part of esoteric history.

The Rosicrucians

Few people understand the significance of the Rosicrucian Order, and its purpose for existing. The Order appeared early on in the seventeenth century. The members of the Order, as individuals, kept a surprisingly low profile, however a profusion of literature was published about these mysterious

Rosicrucians. Many through history have wondered who they were, what their motivations were, and what their connections with other orders were, and whether or not they did actually exist in a vacuum?

Many books attribute the existence of the Order to two manifestos one published in Germany, one in 1614 and the other a year later. The first called the Fama was in effect a story about the Rosicrucian order: its purpose for existing, how members should conduct themselves, and the story of its hero Christian Rosencreuz (from whom the order is supposed to derive its name). Although the order may not have been in existence when the manifesto first appeared, it soon was afterwards and rapidly grew in membership. Both manifestos, the Fama and the Confessio, are in effect a plea to those people interested in the order to declare themselves and join up. They are basically an invitation to people who were in possession of esoteric knowledge, such as the Templars, to join the organisation; while being worded in such a way only to be understood by esotericists. It is unclear who the author/s of the manifestos were, but their real intention was not to establish a new order; this, it is believed by masons, was simply a circumstance of achieving their aim. They believe that the manifestos' aim was to make contact with specific people who continued the Templar tradition and were in possession of certain information which related to a much wider message, which is known to them as the 'plan'. If this is true, then the Rosicrucians' reason for existing and its purpose all relate to the 'plan'. It is not considered wise to elaborate on the 'plan' here for it warrants a chapter to itself; however it is enough for the reader to acknowledge the Masonic belief that the Rosicrucian Order came about through a search for the people (Templars and other esotericists) who carried on Templar traditions and were in possession of certain parts of this so called 'plan'.

As mentioned earlier, the Templar tradition survived Philip's megalomania, although in a much more secretive way and under different names such as the Order of Christ and

the Order of the Golden Fleece. The engineers of the manifestos and the Rosicrucian Order were overwhelmed with
sheer amount of people wanting to join. It is granted that
many were intrigued by its air of mysticism, however the
large majority of people who came forward had some sort of
connection with the Templar Order (people who were either
Templars or members of other Orders which continued the
Templar tradition). The Fama and Confessio were very cleverly constructed, and although they do not mention the
Templars expressly, it is not difficult for someone who knows
the history and tradition of the Templars, to see that these
manifestos refer to them and their traditions.

The Fama for instance, talks of the travels of its hero
to the Holy Land (Jerusalem), Cyprus and to Egypt. These are
all particularly relevant to the Templars: Jerusalem speaks for
itself, Cyprus was a Templar stronghold, and the Templars
made numerous expeditions to Egypt during the 12th and 13th
centuries; the connections with the Templars and ancient Egypt
have already been explained. The hero, Christian Rosencreuz,
became acquainted with the Arabs and studied their philoso-
phies, as it is widely rumoured the Templars did. Statements
like, 'Our Philosophy is not a new invention, but as Adam
after his fall hath received it, and as Moses and Solomon
used it.' This is a direct reference to the source of the
Templars' religious inclinations, which will become more relevant to the reader later in the book. The Fama also states,
'we confess to have the knowledge of Jesus Christ', this is
another statement of particular relevance to the Templars and
all those esoteric groups which are descended from them.
The Fama also talks of the Rosicrucian members being brothers, which is how modern Freemasons acknowledge themselves. Both manifestos are also critical and quite detrimen-
tal towards the Catholic church and in particular, the Pope.
The Confessio (the second manifesto) refers to him as a 'blas-
phemer against our Lord Jesus Christ'. The gravity and relevance of this statement will become clear to the reader in
chapter five. The numerous synergies which exist between the

manifestos, the Templars, and the Freemasons, are surely beyond the realms of mere coincidence.

The most striking references that the manifestos offer are to a succession of Templars and the secrets which are passed on from one generation to the next. The reader will later appreciate that these types of references do hint at the 'plan', however, these references have much more meaning to esotericists than the lay person. If the manifestos were intelligently interpreted by someone who had no knowledge of the plan, it is quite probable that that person's understanding would be that some kind of plan existed. This it is believed is why there was immense interest in this new order, and would explain how it grew so quickly. Another reason for its rapid expansion must have been the atmosphere in Germany at this time.

In 1613 a marriage had taken place between Frederick V, Elector Palatine of the Rhine, and Princess Elisabeth, daughter of James I. The importance of the wedding was not so much to do with the individuals who got married, but the symbolism that the marriage presented across Europe. England was at this point Protestant as too was most of Germany , while almost the whole of the rest of Europe remained staunchly Catholic. The wedding was seen as a consolidation of Protestant forces, and seen as a unity which could compete with the ever threatening Catholic Habsburg empire. Under a Protestant ruler people could practise their different faiths much more freely, different faiths were tolerated and accepted. This was an ideal environment for the Rosicrucian Order to suddenly emerge and indeed flourish. They would not have dared be so public had the Habsburg empire, which was staunchly Catholic, encompassed Germany, indeed many who still kept up the Templar traditions would have feared a repeat of Friday 13th 1307. However, they felt safe enough to bring out many pieces of literature, which would certainly have been labelled 'heresy' by the Papacy. It is fitting that the manifestos (which were, it is believed, designed to bring forward a few German Templars who had access to parts of a message) came out at a time when a Protestant ruler was not only in power, but was perceived to be in a very powerful position through his marriage to King James' daughter Elisabeth. This may seem like just a coincidence to the reader, however some believe that the situation was carefully orchestrated by certain people who were followers of John Dee and his aspirations (this is explained fully in chapter nine).

The wedding between Frederick and Elisabeth was celebrated throughout Germany, England and other Protestant parts. Frederick arrived at the wedding in a large carriage made to look like a boat, depicting Jason of the Argonauts - this was an obvious reference to the neo-Templar Order of the Golden Fleece, and the story itself has special allegorical significance to esotericists. Some years after the wedding Frederick was admitted into the Order of the Garter - another neo-Templar order. From 1613 to 1620 people in Germany, who were members of neo-Templar organisations or esoteric societies, were allowed the privilege of freedom to practice their beliefs, without the threat of being branded as heretics. However, this atmosphere of tolerance was soon to be destroyed.

In 1619, Frederick became King of Bohemia; this meant that his influence in Europe was magnified. This prompted the Catholic Habsburgs to declare war on Frederick. The military support that Frederick expected from James I (through the marriage of his daughter), never materialised; and Frederick was finally defeated on November 8th 1620 near Prague in the Battle of the White Mountain. It was a sad end, not only for Frederick and Elisabeth who spent the rest of their days in exile in The Hague, but for the people who lived within Frederick's empire who had to suffer the wrath of the catholic inquisitors. The flourish of neo-Templar traditions and activities in Germany and Bohemia, was at an end. The neo-Templar traditionalists, again had to go underground and again dream of a time when their beliefs would be tolerated by all. The resolute attitude by Freemasons to their secrets remaining amongst themselves could be explained by what has happened to other esoteric orders when they became more public about their practices and exposed their beliefs to the interpretation of Catholic inquisitors.

The Rosicrucian movement continues to this day throughout all parts of the world, as do numerous other esoteric societies which spawned from its traditions. Even though a greater analysis of Rosicrucianism would probably reveal some interesting concepts and information, for the purposes of this book the Rosicrucian movement is only of relevance in so far as it touches upon masonry and its development throughout the ages.

The Freemasons

It is of no coincidence that Freemasonry began in the 14th century. It is a widely held perception that it had its origins in the protection of medieval British guilds of stonemasons, a type of closed shop trade union. Many people still perceive Masonry as having originated from a need to preserve the secrets of stonemasonry amongst its members. The principle being that if everyone had access to the secrets of stonemasonry, their time honoured profession would cease to exist. It seems incredible that such beliefs, and an explanation which came from the Freemasons themselves, has remained a valid reason for Masonry's unreasonably high level of secrecy, in the general public perception for so long. An analogy could be made here with the speech George Bush made after the Gulf War, saying the reason American troops went to war was to re-establish democracy in Kuwait. What people now realise is that the closest Kuwait came to democracy, before the Gulf War, was through the members of its Royal Family - the sum total of which did not enter into double figures. After the war the term 'democracy' seemed to the American public to justify conveniently the reason for the war - hiding its true motive - oil. Similarly, it was and still is convenient for Masons to disguise themselves innocently under the profession of stonemasons. This would have allowed the medieval Freemasons to legitimately carry around their tools, apron and paraphernalia for use in their rituals and ceremonies, thus allowing them to carry on their rituals and beliefs with no questions being asked. The general public were none the wiser, their suspicions were diverted as they believed their secrecy was to protect their profession; but, this was in fact what the purpose was, to protect their true profession - Freemasonry.

After the official declaration of the existence of four Lodges in London, with the formation of the Grand Lodge in 1717, many other lodges decided to declare themselves as well. In fact some of the oldest lodges in Britain still carry the name 'Temple Lodge' - signifying that the lodge was orig- inally a Templar lodge. After the formation of the Grand Lodge masons believed it was finally safe enough for them to be recognised as belonging to a Masonic Lodge and the existence of Lodges became known all over the British Isles. However, it can be argued that such a concession upon their anonymity was premature. In 1738, Pope Clement XII issued a papal bull, Eminenti Aprostolatus Specula. This bull basical- ly included a condemnation of Freemasonry and incited action from the inquisition against them. Other papal bulls of simi- lar content followed, and as John J. Robinson explains:

> Where the Inquisition had power to do so, Freemasons
> in Catholic countries were imprisoned, deported, and
> even tortured. In Portugal one man was tortured and
> then sentenced to four years chained to a bench of
> a galley for the crime of being a mason. [13]

The Holy Roman Inquisition has no place in the tolerant and less barbaric society of today. The power of the Church has greatly diminished in the last couple of decades, with revivals

13. Robinson, John J., Born in Blood, p.183

in some churches who seem to be becoming more and more distant from the traditionalist Catholic values and beliefs. In the late 1980s the Church of England stated quite categorically and unequivocally that none of their clergy should join any Masonic lodge, and those who were already Masons should discontinue their membership. But, such opinions are merely blowing hot air compared with the Church's power and influence in centuries gone by. It would seem that the balance of power between the Church and the Freemasons has switched. The rift or incompatibility between Freemasonry and the Church (especially the Catholic Church) will be explained later, but before delving into these issues of controversy, it is first necessary for the reader to gain an insight into what actually goes on within Masonic lodges and the purpose behind their gatherings, and structure of their rituals.

Chapter Four

Rites and Rituals of Freemasonry

Looking back into the remotest days of recorded history, we find a priesthood on the banks of the Nile, thousands of years before the light of Christianity dawned upon the world, teaching the existence in a future life by symbols and legends, which convey the lesson in a peculiar mode. And now, after thousands of years have elapsed, we find the same symbolic and legendary method of instruction for the same purpose preserved in the depository of what is comparatively a modern institution (Freemasonry)" [1]

Many people will have heard, from one time or another, mention of someone who is in the lodge and occasionally how high up these people are in their lodge's hierarchy. As noted earlier lodges are the places where Freemasons meet, usually once a month throughout the year, but excluding part of the

1. Bennett, J., Origin of Freemasonry and Knight Templar, p.74

summer. They come in all shapes and sizes from converted community centres and converted chapels to especially designed buildings. But regardless of their outward appearances, lodges invariably take the same basic form on the inside, one room comprising the Temple (used in rituals), and another for social gatherings. The mere fact that a person has been a member of the Masonic order for a long period of time is not necessarily an indication of how advanced they are in the Masonic order of merit. This order of merit is comprised of the number of degrees a Mason has completed, and also his position within the lodge, which should reflect his achievements and level of seniority. These positions include: Worshipful Master (overall head of the lodge - this position lasts for one year only), Tyler, Junior and Senior Deacons, Junior and Senior Wardens, Steward, and the Secretary of the lodge. The reason so many different positions are required within the lodge reflects their need to facilitate the organisation and to perform the different roles required during the enactment of the degree rituals. Within Freemasonry there are a possible thirty - three degrees which may be completed over a period of time, however many Freemasons only complete the first three, which they are required to do in order to become fully fledged masons, known as 'master masons'. After these three degrees they may choose to do other degrees for instance: Mark Mason, Royal Arch Mariners, Perfect Prince Mason, Rose Croix, Knights Templar and so on. It is only after the first three degrees have been completed that a candidate may be able to call himself a mason, and duly proceed to study and perform the rituals and rites of higher degrees.

All Masonic lodges in England and Wales are ultimately answerable to the United Grand Lodge of England, which regulate and control each individual lodge attempting to ensure equality and conformity throughout. The Grand Lodge was formed on June 24th on John the Baptist's Day (he is also patron saint of Masonry) 1717, when four London Lodges decided to join together in an attempt to standardise and regulate the direction of Masonry. It has already been stated in the previous chapter that Lodges were in existence before this date; some Masons claim that Masonry began in medieval times during the building of the Gothic cathedrals, or that it began in Biblical times or Egyptian times, however, it is not known for certain how far Freemasonry as an institution goes back in the annals of time. Although from the previous chapters the reader will acknowledge that esoteric practice has its roots in ancient times and possibly before records were made of man's activities upon this earth. The four lodges which initiated the forming of the Grand Lodge met at the Apple Tree Tavern, Covent Garden, London,[2] other lodges decided to amalgamate and eventually the Grand Lodge became known as the United Grand Lodge of England. The United Grand Lodge not only regulates Lodges throughout Britain, but also has a powerful influence over lodges in other countries as well.

The United Grand Lodge hierarchy is shown below:

GRAND MASTER	The Duke of Kent
Provincial Grand Master	Rt. Hon. Lord Farnham
Deputy Grand Master	Ian Ross Bryce
Assistant Grand Master	Marquess of Northampton

Apart from organising the annual gatherings and festivals for the Masonic hierarchy, the United Grand Lodge decides the direction, stance and image of Masonry which they wish to portray to the public at large. For instance, they will decide what Masons can and cannot disclose to the public about the craft. They also give directions to lodges upon the criteria and suitability of prospective candidates wishing to join the lodge. It is indeed a fact that many of the public are disillusioned with masonry and especially with some of the activities of its members. It could be argued that a tighter control of those joining a lodge by the Grand Lodge, may have averted the creation of such perceptions.

2. Robinson, John, J., Born in Blood, 179

The United Grand Lodge also decide upon how to approach difficult issues such as the allegations of freemasonry being inconsistent with Christianity and the control of disclosure of information from Masonic institutions. The question of disclosure was brought out publicly with the resignation of Mr Michael Higham (Chief Executive of the United Grand Lodge). The Mail on Sunday reported:-

> One source said: ' Michael Higham spoke his mind and sometimes extended policy beyond his brief. That was considered to some to be arrogance and led him into conflict with the powers that be.' [3]

The report also mentions how Mr Higham was regarded as too "outspoken". The Grand Lodge was in all probability worried about the issue of disclosure, and also of having someone very high up in the Grand lodge hierarchy which they felt they were unable to control. If Mr Higham was ousted for his outspoken attitude towards Freemasonry, then it would explain why no reason had been given to him by the Grand Lodge for requesting his resignation. The policy which has been advocated by the Grand Lodge in recent years is that Masonry has no secrets, it is simply a charitable society based on the brotherhood of men. However, how could Mr Higham's outspoken views have conflicted with Freemasonry - an organisation which maintain they have no secrets? If Masonry has no secrets then why is it not recruiting more people like Mr Higham to help its public image?

Becoming a Freemason - The Three Degrees

A person wishing to join the Freemasons must fulfil certain criteria or preconditions. Probably the most important of these is the belief in a 'Supreme Being'; this does not necessarily mean a belief in a Christian or any other type of God, only a belief in a Supreme Being or an acknowledgement that

3. Mail on Sunday (1/2/98)

everything is governed by some exterior force. The person wishing to join must also be a free man born of a free mother, over 21 years of age, and be a member of the community held in high regard. This is emphasized in the Constitutions of Freemasonry :

> The persons made masons or admitted members of a lodge must be true and good men, free-born, and of mature and discreet age and sound judgement, no bondmen, no women, no immoral or scandalous men, but of good report. [4]

In this respect whether or not the candidate has a criminal record is taken into account and also his general suitability to becoming a mason. For instance, a candidate would probably not gain admission into a lodge if he was a very strong advocate of Catholicism and a risk to revealing the secrets of Masonry (the reasons for this will become evident later), or if there were rumours of financial irregularities in his business transactions, even though these rumours might be unsubstantiated.

When a person is deemed suitable to join the Brotherhood of Freemasons, he may be invited to join a lodge. It is necessary that this person be invited by at least two members of the particular lodge in question, and that they do the inviting, and not the other way around. (The situation has changed somewhat in recent years - much of the integrity emanating from Masonry in the past has been gradually chipped away, and today it is quite common for people to be accepted into a lodge by requesting other Masons to put them forward). Once the candidate's name has been forwarded by two members of a lodge, inviting him to join, the lodge's hierarchy then decide whether or not to accept the candidate into their lodge. A candidate may be refused entry into a lodge for the most trivial of reasons, as reasons for rejection need not be given. Therefore, there is no guarantee of entry into any lodge, and the candidate's

4. Grand Lodge, United Grand Lodge of England Constitutions, p.5

future as a mason is at the mercy, discretion and subjectivity of eight members which make up the lodge committee. This selection process is done by passing a small bag around the lodge committee's table; a member of the committee may place either a white or black ball in the bag (this is done under the table so that other members cannot see which colour ball another member puts in). If all the balls are white then the candidate will be accepted into that lodge, however if there is one or more black ball present in the bag the candidate's admission into the lodge will be barred (this is what is known as being 'black balled').

In order to become a fully fledged Mason (Master Mason), a candidate must complete the first three degrees; these are known as Entered Apprentice, Fellowcraft and Master Mason. They are intended to mirror the three stages of life through which man progresses - youth, manhood and old age. In order to complete these degrees, which are completed in succession, the candidate is required to recite large passages of Masonic literature from memory, and to enact certain rituals which relate to the building of Solomon's Temple (3000 years ago) and other rituals which are ingrained in Masonic ideology and history. The candidate does not perform these rituals alone, but is guided through them by the Lodge hierarchy. These include the Worshipful Master (who is in ultimate control of the proceedings), Tylers, Stewards, Wardens, Deacons and Guards who act themselves in the degree rituals. The rituals are performed very seriously with Masonic prayers and hymns sung at the end. Such rituals, although performed physically have no physical significance, but are purely a means of communicating through symbolism messages to the candidate's subconscious to facilitate his spiritual evolution. This is emphasised in W. L. Wilmshurst's *The Meaning of Masonry*:

> The regenerated man, the man who not merely in ceremonial form but in vital experience, has passed through the phases of which the Masonic degrees are

the faint symbol, is alone worthy of the title of Master Mason in the building of the Temple that is not made with hands but that is being built invisibly out of the souls of just men made perfect. [5]

The degrees are designed to free the candidate's soul or spirit from the purely material world and facilitate its interaction and release into the metaphysical world above. The symbolism and the enactment of Masonic stories through rituals serve as keys to unlocking his subconscious. The degrees provide the trigger which enable the candidate to transcend the physical realm. As W. L. Wilmshurst explains:

> The human organism is the true Lodge that must be opened and wherein the great Mysteries are to be found, and our Lodgerooms are so built and furnished as to typify the human organism. The lower and physical part of us is animal and earthy, and rests, like the base of Jacob's ladder, upon the earth; whilst our higher portion is spiritual and reaches to the heavens. [6]

Without actually performing such esoteric rituals the reader will find these concepts difficult to grasp. However, imagine that a young heron is adopted into a family of emus. As he grows he does not attempt to fly, believing it something beyond his capabilities. Then one day he meets up with a group of herons and sees how he is not too dissimilar to them. Suddenly he is enlightened from his perceived circumstance and finds that the capability has always been within him to fly. Such a dramatic realisation is not too dissimilar to what some Masons experience when they pass through the three degrees. They believe they become enlightened, in terms of their spirit being brought out of the purely physical dimension and into the realisation that their souls are not limited to the physical or material dimension of this world, but can interact and exist in a spiritual dimension. Masons believe this

5. Wilmshurst, W. L., The Meaning of Masonry, p.82
6. Wilmshurst, W. L., The Meaning of Masonry, p.81

transformation is achieved through the enactment of the first three degree rituals, usually the transformation (which many masons profess to experience) is realised by most Masons in the third degree or soon afterwards. This realisation is referred to in Masonic terms as the resurrection or being raised.

The Masonic rituals also emphasise the attachment of the candidate to his lodge and to his fellow brothers i.e. the concept of brotherhood. The concept of brotherhood and the swearing of oaths and loyalty to fellow brothers has come about over the centuries, through the Church's repression of the Templars and Masons alike. Over the past millennium the church has held considerable power over the populace and where it deemed necessary it unleashed its brutal suppression of groups such as the Templars, or even of a whole region where certain people such as the Cathars held beliefs which were not quite in accord with the Church's view. So, it will not be difficult for the reader to appreciate how, the need for stealth and secrecy amongst the members of esoteric groups came about during medieval times. It was against this background that Masonry came about, and since such times these practices of absolute secrecy have been maintained as part of Masonry and continue to the present day. Masons also vow to help brother masons in times of need as well as, obviously, to keep the secrets of the lodge. But, why is the element of secrecy so paramount in Masonic ideology? There is a considerable difference of opinion amongst Masons upon this point. Some believe that the knowledge should only be communicated to qualified people (i.e. Masons) and that much of it is incommunicable anyway; while others, especially today, would be quite open to discuss Masonry with those outside it (although they are precluded from going public by the threat of retribution from their fellow brethren). The Masonic vows of secrecy are heavily incorporated into the degree rituals, and some would argue that such vows and pledges are out of touch with modern society; and with the threat of being branded a heretic and burnt at the stake gone, it could be argued that such oaths to fellow brothers merely provide a breeding ground for conspiracy. To what extent such views are correct or incorrect does not come within the parameters of this book. However, a balanced perspective of Masonry should include an appreciation of the charity work which they fund, which is invariably ignored in most literature concerning them.

There is yet another possible reason why Masonry's serious vows of secrecy have been maintained to the present day; that a preconceived notion of the degree procedures may destroy the possible experiences of those degrees for the candidate. It is still prevalent amongst Masons that the candidate must not know what he is about to experience within the lodge, before the ritual. As the reader will acknowledge later in this chapter, the degree rituals are carefully designed to create the right atmosphere and environment to facilitate the candidate's spiritual evolution. This involves stunning or more precisely surprising the candidate through the environment created to gain his attention absolutely so that he will be able to realise himself spiritually. If prior knowledge of the degree ceremonies would ruin the desired effects of those ceremonies, then it would indeed be a powerful motive for keeping the procedures of those ceremonies secret from prospective Freemasons and therefore the public at large. It is submitted that this is the most likely reason for Masons' sudden allergy to questions relating to their activities within the lodge. The spiritual change which many Masons profess to experience is explained below.

It is a perception widely held by Freemasons, that as a person advances through the three degrees he changes from being spiritually unconscious to being spiritually conscious, and most Masons believe that their spirits become resurrected so that even though they may die physically, their resurrected spirits or souls will live on forever within the universe or as they term it the 'Grand Lodge Above'. Such beliefs of physical and spiritual separation are not new, they form part of many (what we would regard as) primitive cultures of the world; such as the American Indians, Aborigines and Buddhists, to name a few. To Masons the existence of these beliefs in such ancient cultures, represents echoes of their Atlantean past. Even in the western world, the idea of a person's soul or spirit being capable of leaving the body is not uncommon. Such a phenomenon is known generally as 'astral projection' and the titles of numerous books concerning this subject can be found in most occult magazines. The significance to the Freemasons of the three degrees and the belief that their spirits eventually dwell amongst the stars above, is that it is supposed to immortalise their spirit, so that after death their souls will live on, everlasting in the universe as stars, or, as Freemasons refer to heaven, the 'Grand Lodge Above.' This concept of the immortality of the soul is stressed in the Fellowcraft degree:

Q. What were you next presented with?
A. Three precious jewels.
Q. What were they?
A. Faith, Hope, and Charity.
Q. What do they teach?
A. Faith in God, hope in immortality, and charity to all mankind.

The ideology or belief behind the three degrees may seem very strange to the reader at first, however the same sort of beliefs exist in almost all esoteric organisations (although their rituals are modified forms of those described here). These beliefs of the resurrected and enlightened spirit were, Masons believe, practised by the Egyptians and before this, too, in Atlantis. The degrees are probably the most fundamental aspect of Masonry and bring new experiences to the candidate while at the same time enforcing his duties with respect to Masonry and his obligations to his fellow brethren.

The first three degrees of Masonry, together with extracts from the Royal Arch and Mark Mason's degrees are documented below:

The First Degree - Entered Apprentice

The first degree candidate is taught that the first degree, also known as the Entered Apprentice degree, is in fact a preparation before advancing to higher states of spiritual consciousness. As far as the candidate is concerned it deals on a purely material level. The idea behind this, is that before a person can transcend spiritually, he must be raised from a firm material foundation. The candidate is made aware of the universe existing as a series of astral planes which are separated from each other by different rates of vibration. The candidate's spiritual advancement is actually said to coincide with his experience of passing through these vibrations and on to higher astral levels or planes.

The first degree is signified by the story of a candidate who takes a rough piece of ashlar from a quarry, which he prepares for the turning of the Fellowcraft (second degree). In the story, the candidate then enacts the moulding of the stone until its shape is perfect; and this is the method by which he prepares himself for acceptance to the Fellowcraft degree. In the first degree, masons do not believe that the actual physical moulding of the stone by the candidate is a prerequisite for spiritual advancement, however, the importance from the candidate's point of view is that he realises the symbolism behind the shaping of the perfect stone as the cornerstone from which the Temple is to be built. This, Masons believe, is the first stage in preparing the candidate for spiritual advancement. The candidate must realise his material being and seek to purify its constituents before he can begin to pass through the realms of spiritual liberation. The enactment of shaping the ashlar stone is an allegory for sending a message to the candidate's subconscious that he can only advance spiritually through the astral planes on solid material foundations, again this concept of communication through symbolism is very prevalent. The fact that the candidate is led through the ceremony being shown certain ancient building

tools and what they signify, is of significance to the candidate, primarily from a spiritual standpoint. If, early on in its
inception, Masonry would have chosen surgeons' instruments,
instead of ancient building tools with which to communicate
symbolism to induce a spiritual change, then these would
probably be used today instead of ancient building tools. It
is believed by esotericists, that the ancient Egyptians used the
symbolism of constructing boats as a medium through which
to communicate their esotericism.; also the concept of Alchemy
(the transmutation of base metals into gold), is an allegory
for spiritual enhancement, used many years ago by the
Rosicrusians. Before going any further, it is important that the
reader grasps that it is not the building tools in masonry
which are of prime significance, but how effectively they are
used in communicating the esoteric concepts for the candidate's spiritual development. This is succinctly described by
Berg in his *Kabbala for the Layman* (Kabbala is the Jewish
form of esotericism which uses the Torah through which to
communicate its esoteric meaning, and as one Masonic com-
mentator states "a strong element of which has been introduced into our Masonic system." [7]:

> . . . the tales and parables of the Torah are sym-
> bolic reflections of the inner metaphysical realm
> through which one could perceive the hidden, divine
> mysteries of our universe. [8]

Traditionally, the first degree candidate is kept in the dark
about what he is going to experience. Firstly, the candidate
is divested of any money and any metal objects which he
has on his person. He is dressed in loose white trousers
and a tunic, similar to those worn in martial arts. The left
side of the tunic is flapped over, exposing the left nipple
on the candidate's chest. The left trouser leg is also rolled
up exposing the left knee. On the left foot the candidate
wears a loosely fitting slipper. A hangman's noose, known
as a 'Cable tow', is placed around the candidates neck and

7. Wilmshurst, W. L., The Meaning of Masonry, p.24
8. Berg, P. S., Kabbalah for the Layman, p.65

he is blindfolded or hoodwinked before entering the Temple. The candidate is then questioned about his motives for joining the lodge of which (amongst other things), he must express a : "desire for knowledge, self improvement and a wish to be of service to his fellow man." The hilt of a sword is used to knock on the Temple door. The purpose behind the way the candidate is presented before entering the Temple is meant to signify how a medieval heretic would have looked and been treated as he faced the Inquisition, and to humble him to such an extent that he is able to realise his material being without distractions.

Inside the Temple, the point of a compass is pressed against the candidates chest. He is then asked (by the Worshipful Master), "Do you feel anything?" An answer is whispered to the candidate, "I do.", which he repeats out loud. The Worshipful Master then says to him , "Then let this be a sting to your conscience as well as instant death should you ever betray any of the secrets now about to be imparted to you."

It is important to note that the wording of the penalties for revealing the secrets, has, due to the public's aversion to them, been modified in recent years to ameliorate their public image. The candidate, up until recently, was also required to swear on the bible that "under no less a penalty . . . than that of having my throat cut across, my tongue torn out by the root, and buried in the sand of the sea at low water mark, or a cable's length from the shore . . . or the more effective punishment of being branded as a wilfully perjured individual, void of all moral worth, and totally unfit to be received into this worshipful Lodge, or any other warranted Lodge or society of men, who prize honour and virtue above the external advantages of rank and fortune. So help me God and keep me steadfast in this my Great and Solemn Obligation of an Entered Apprentice Mason."

The attitude which emanates from the first three degree rituals are typical of the above. After the candidate has recited the oath (the amended version which has been toned down from the original above), he is drawn closer to his brothers by being made to feel part of an elite and privileged brotherhood, he is also in a way warned, that if he does not strictly adhere to their policies of secrecy and obligation, he will be shunned by his fellow brothers and treated as an outcast. Again this language or communication tool comprised of ancient symbolism comes to the fore.

During the ritual the candidate is then asked if he is over twenty one years of age, and if he is prepared to serve his fellow creatures. The compass is now removed from the candidates chest and he is led around the Temple, while the Worshipful Master demonstrates the significance of the Masons' tools, as instruments of symbolism. Firstly to the east, to the cornerstone of the Temple which was the first stone of Solomon's Temple to be laid. After he has been led around the Temple three times he is asked , "Having been in a state of darkness, what is the predominant wish in your heart?" The word "light", is whispered into the candidate's ear which he repeats out loud. The blindfold is then removed and the candidate finds himself standing in front of the Worshipful Master. The candidate is then made aware, by the Worshipful Master, of the emblematic 'lights' of freemasonry: the Volume of the Sacred Law (to non Freemasons this is the Bible), and the square and compass.

The candidate is then required to recite certain passages which confirm his commitment to the lodge, his fellow brothers, and his adherence to his strict code of secrecy. For example:

I (candidate's name), of my own free will and accord, in the presence of Almighty God, and this Worshipful Lodge erected to Him and dedicated to the Holy Saint John, do hereby and hereon most sincerely promise and swear that I will always hail, ever conceal and never reveal, any of the arts, parts, or points of the hidden mysteries of ancient Free Masonry which may have been, or hereafter shall be, at this time, or any future period, communicated to me as such, to any person or persons whomever, except it be to a true and lawful brother Mason, or in a regularly constituted lodge of Masons; nor unto him or them until by strict trial, due examination, or lawful information I shall have found him, or them, as lawfully entitled to the same as I am myself. I furthermore promise and swear that I will not print, paint, stamp, stain, cut, carve, mark, or engrave them, to cause the same to be done on anything movable or immovable, capable of receiving the least impression of a word, syllable, letter, or character, whereby the same may become legible or intelligible to any person under the canopy of heaven, and the secrets of Masonry thereby unlawfully obtained through my unworthiness.

After this part of the degree ritual the candidate will be ranked as an entered apprentice Mason. The entered apprentice, having completed the ritual, is instructed about the significance of the left hand pillar in the Temple which is known as Boez. The word JACHIN is relayed to the candidate and he is told this is the secret password entrusted to entered apprentices for them to gain access to the Temple. The secret sign that an entered apprentice is taught, which is used in conjunction with the password, is shown in Plate 16. The right hand is held open, with the thumb protruding at right angles (representing the square), while being drawn across the thorax from left to right. This sign is meant to represent the way one of the three Juwes was killed as a penalty for murdering Solomon's principal architect. This story, which is described later, also provides the subject matter for the third degree ritual.

During the first degree ceremony various ancient building tools are demonstrated to the candidate as being useful to him, in the improvement and enrichment of his character, symbolism being a highly significant part of Masonic communication and indoctrination. The tools which are used in the ritual are demonstrated in conjunction with the story of the shaping of an ashlar stone, symbolising how, with the purity of character, the candidate can begin to shape his life for the advancement of his spiritual being. In Solomon's time the building of the Temple was closely associated with the degree rituals. Thus, Masonry would seem worlds away from such activities. However, many Masons would argue the end result is still the same, whether a candidate is actually building a temple or, whether he is merely enacting its construction. Masons believe that it is enough if the candidate applies the symbols of the ancient building tools and merely enacts the building of the Temple to progress his own character along its spiritual path.

Also during the first degree ceremony, the candidate is told that he must learn certain answers to certain questions before he will be allowed to go on to the second degree (Fellowcraft). The answers, as they appear in Masonic literature, are cryptic with only the first letter given to denote the word which the candidate must memorise and eventually recite. These questions and answers are given below, as it is believed that the reader will be interested in their content. Where one letter appears, the word which is meant appears in brackets after it, also note the candidate's answer to "what is Freemasonry?", the essence of which is emphasised throughout this book.

(Note that WM denotes Worshipful Master, and CAN denotes the Candidate).

W.M. (To Candidate). Where were you first prepared to be a Mason?
CAN. In my H.(Heart).
W.M. Where next?
CAN. In a convenient room adjoining the Lodge.
W.M. Describe the mode of your preparation?
CAN. I was divested of m...l.(metal) and h.(hood) w.(winked)., my r.(right)a.(arm), l.(left) b.(breast) and k.(knee) were made b. (bare), my r.(right) h.(heel) was

s.(slip)s.(shod), and a.(a) c.(cable) t.(tow) placed about my neck.

W.M.   Where were you made a Mason?

CAN.   In the body of a Lodge, just perfect and regular.

W.M.   And when?

CAN.   When the Sun was at its Meridian.

W.M.   In this country Freemasons' Lodges are usually held in the evening; how do you account for that, which at first view appears a paradox?

CAN.   The earth constantly revolving on its axis in its orbit around the sun, and freemasonry being universally spread over its surface, it necessarily follows that the sun must always be at its Meridian with respect to Freemasonry.

W.M.   What is Freemasonry?

CAN.   A peculiar system of Morality, veiled in Allegory, and illustrated by Symbols.

W.M.   Name the Grand principles on which the order is founded?

CAN.   Brotherly Love, Relief and Truth.

W.M.   Who are fit and proper persons to be made Masons?

CAN.   Just, upright and free men, of mature age, sound judgement and strict morals.

W.M.   How do you know yourself to be a Mason?

CAN.   By the regularity of my initiation, repeated trials and approbations, and a willingness at all times to undergo an examination when properly called on.

W.M.   How do you demonstrate the proof of your being a Mason to others?

CAN.   By Sns. (signs), Ts(tokens)., and the p......t(perfect) Ps (passwords). of my E(ear).

Normally, the time between a candidate's first degree and second is a couple of months; but before this it is required that the candidate take the above answers to memory.

The Second Degree - Fellowcraft

The second degree candidate is admitted into the Temple wearing an apron the same as everyone else in the Lodge who accompanies him into the Temple. The apron symbolises a builder of the Temple of Solomon, which the ancient builders of the Temple supposedly wore. The candidate is next subjected to the questions above, and will not pass beyond this stage until he answers the questions correctly. After this the candidate is led out of the Temple, and is told to dress in the same clothing as he wore in his first degree (to again symbolise the medieval heretic and to once again humble the candidate). At this point, the candidate's right leg, breast and foot are made bare. He is again hoodwinked, but this time the Cable tow is looped twice around the candidates neck. The candidate is led around the Temple by the deacons, who show him the usefulness of other tools and different parts of the Temple in more detail (remember this time that the candidate can see).

The purpose of the second degree is to bring to the attention of the candidate his emotional being. He is instructed about the importance of the ever present emotional energy which places the energies of the universe at his disposal. The candidate is taught the importance of firstly harnessing this energy, and secondly (but more importantly), controlling it through his everyday life. This power can also be dangerous to the candidate and he is told: "when this power is uncoordinated or perverted, it can induce people to murder." It is only when the candidate has full mastery of his emotional energies, that he can contemplate moving to a higher degree and a higher astral plane.

During the degree the candidate is shown the sign that Joshua made when he was praying for the sun to stay in the sky, until his enemies had been defeated. From Joshua 10:12 :

Sun stand still over Gibeon;
Moon, stop over Aijalon Valley.

The sun stood still and the moon did not move
until the nation had conquered its enemies . . . Never
before, and never since, has there been a day like
it, when the Lord obeyed a human being. The Lord
fought on Israel's side.

It would be hard for any reader (who is not a Mason), to
comprehend the significance of this Old Testament story to
modern day Freemasons. However, in chapter seven, the reader will realise the relevance of the Old Testament; which to
Freemasons are accounts of extraterrestrial involvement in the
shaping of mankind's evolution and society.

After being led around the temple and shown other
tools, he is once again presented before the altar. He is lowered onto his right knee and his right hand is placed upon
the square and compass which rest upon the Bible. The candidate's left arm is raised so that his forearm is vertical and
at right angles to his upper arm, symbolising the square. He
then repeats the Fellowcraft oath given to him by the
Worshipful Master:

I (candidate's name), of my own free will and accord,
in the presence of Almighty God and this Worshipful
Lodge of Fellowcraft Masons, erected to God and dedicated to the holy Saints John, do hereby and hereon
most solemnly promise and swear, in addition to my former obligation, that I will not give the secrets of the
degree of a Fellowcraft Mason to anyone of an inferior
degree, nor to any other being in the known world,
except it be to a true and lawful brother, or brethren
Fellowcraft Masons, or within the body of a just and lawfully constituted lodge of such . . . Furthermore do I
promise and swear that I will obey all regular signs and
summonses given, handed, sent, or thrown to me by the
hand of a brother Fellowcraft Mason, or from the body

of a just and lawfully constituted lodge of such; provided it be within the length of my cable-tow, or a square and angle of my work. Furthermore do I promise and swear that I will aid and assist all poor and penniless brethren Fellowcrafts, their widows and orphans, wheresoever disposed around the Globe, they applying to me as such, as far as in my power without injuring myself and family. To all of which I most solemnly and sincerely promise and swear without the least hesitation, mental reservation, or self evasion of mind in me whatever, binding myself under no less penalty than to have my breast torn open and my heart and vitals taken from thence and thrown over my left shoulder and carried into the valley of Jehosaphat, there to become a prey to the wild beasts of the field and the wild vultures of the air, if ever I should prove wilfully guilty of violating any part of this my solemn oath or obligation of a fellow craft Mason, so help me God, and keep me steadfast in the performance of the same.

The penalty for revealing the secrets, which fellowcrafts volunteer upon themselves, was derived centuries ago. It has now been toned down somewhat to reflect present day attitudes of Masons and the public at large, as aforementioned. In today's oaths, the candidate volunteers upon himself the wrath of his fellow brethren should he betray the secrets. However, the above oath is still of significance to masons as they are taught that: 'to have my breast torn open and my heart and vitals taken from thence', although a medieval penalty threatened upon masons for revealing the secrets, is strikingly similar to the ways in which 'Jack the Ripper's' victims were mutilated. This is further discussed in chapter six.

After the oath, the candidate is shown the secret grip of a Fellowcraft Mason; this involves shaking hands with another Mason, while placing the end of the thumb in between the knuckles of the index and middle fingers.

The candidate is then taught the significance of the left hand pillar in the Temple, known as Jachin which means 'to establish'. When the left and right hand pillars (Boez and Jachin), are united, they are said to form stability. The candidate is then told that 'SHIBBOLETH' is the secret password for the second degree. This word is derived from the Old Testament:

> The Gileadites captured the fords of the Jordan leading to Ephraim, and whenever a survivor of Ephraim said, "Let me cross over," the men of Gilead asked him, "Are you an Ephraimite?" If he replied, "No", they said, "All right, say 'Shibboleth'." If he said "Shibboleth", because he could not pronounce the word correctly, they seized him and killed him at the fords of the Jordan. [9]

This password should be used in conjunction with the sign shown in Plate 17. The secret sign which is shown to the Fellowcraft in conjunction with the password enables him to gain entrance into the Fellowcraft Lodge. The left forearm is held upright, at right angles to the upper arm, while the right hand is held over the Fellowcraft's heart with the thumb protruding at right angles to the index finger.

The Third Degree - Master Mason

The third degree enables the Fellowcraft mason to become a Master Mason, and therefore giving him the right to call himself a Freemason. This degree is the most serious and dramatic of the three. Freemasons believe that during this degree they become resurrected to a heavenly grand lodge which guarantees them an everlasting spiritual afterlife. The ritual in this degree comprises the enactment of the death of

9. Book of Judges 12:5

someone known as Hiram Abiff, who was the principle architect of Solomon during the time he was building the Temple.
By his death, the ancient building techniques of the Master
Mason were lost forever. In the degree the candidate enacts
the way he died, and also his rebirth from death by which
the candidate is supposed to release his soul from its physical dimension. This is known to freemasons as being raised
or resurrected, and after completing this ritual the Fellowcraft
may call himself a Master Mason.

It is important not to consider the third degree ritual
as unique, because notwithstanding the specifics of the story,
the concepts emanating from the story (death and rebirth) are
prevalent in many ancient cultures. In addition to the Osiris
story (as aforementioned), Hancock and Faiia comment on the
Aztecs that :

> This cult sought the spiritual transfiguration of its ini-
> tiates - a process of hard mental work and self- denial
> aimed at 'flaying away' attachments to the sense- world
> and thus releasing the soul, envisaged as 'a precious
> stone and a rich feather', from the encumbrance of
> matter. Part of the work appears to have involved the
> enactment of rituals in which the initiate would under-
> go a symbolic death and rebirth like the god
> Quetzalcoatl . . . [10]

As the reader will soon realise, these concepts of death and
rebirth are an inherent part of the third degree ritual.

The third degree ritual begins with the Fellowcraft entering the Temple with the other Masons in the Lodge. He is
then sent out of the Temple while the Temple is opened as
a Master Mason's Lodge. The candidate is then made ready
for his re-entry. This time his whole chest is exposed, he is
hoodwinked, and a cable tow is looped around his neck. The
candidate re-enters the Temple into an eerie darkness. In the
eastern corner of the Temple a candle provides a minimal
amount of light, which allows the candidate to see the

10. Hancock, G. and Faiia, S., Heavens Mirror, p.20

Worshipful Master directly behind it. The candidate is led to the altar and lowered onto his knees, with his palms placed upon the square and compass which rest upon the Bible. Again the candidate is required to repeat certain oaths after the Worshipful Master, but this time he repeats the oaths of a Master Mason:

I (candidate's name), of my own free will and accord, in the presence of Almighty God, and this worshipful lodge of Master Masons, dedicated to God and the holy Saints John, do hereby and hereon most solemnly and sincerely promise and swear, in addition to my former obligations, that I will not reveal the secrets of the Master Masons degree to anyone of inferior degree, nor to any other being in the whole world, except it be to a true and lawful brother or brethren Master Masons, within a body of a just and lawfully constituted lodge of such, and not unto him and them only whom I shall only hear so to be, but unto him and them only whom I shall prove so to be, after strict trial and due examination, or lawful information received.

Furthermore do I promise and swear that I will not give the Masters word which I shall Hereafter receive, neither in the lodge nor out of it, except it be on the five points of fellowship, and then not above my breath. Furthermore do I promise and swear that I will not give the Grand Hailing Sign of Distress except I am in real distress, or for the benefit of the Craft when at work, and should I ever see that sign given or the word accompanying it, and the person who gave it appearing to be in distress, I will fly to his relief at the risk of my life, should there be a greater probability of saving his life than losing my own.

Furthermore do I promise and swear that I will not be at the initiating, passing, or raising of a candidate in a clandestine lodge, I knowing it to be such. Furthermore do I promise and swear that I will not be at the initiating of an old man in his dotage, a young man in his nonage, an atheist, an irreligious libertine, an idiot, madman or woman. Furthermore do I promise and swear that I will not seek evil of a brother Master Mason, neither behind his back nor before his face, but will apprise him of all approaching danger, if in my power. Furthermore do I promise and swear that I will not have illegal carnal intercourse with a Master Mason's wife, mother, sister, or daughter, I knowing them to be such, nor suffer it to be done by others, if in my power to prevent it. Furthermore do I promise and swear that a Master Masons secrets, given to me as such, and I knowing them to be such, shall remain as secure and inviolable in my breast as in his own, when communicated to me, murder and treason excepted, and then they left to my own election.

Furthermore do I promise and swear that I will go on a Master Masons errand whenever required, even should I have to go bare-foot and bare-heared, if within the length of my cable tow. Furthermore do I promise and swear that I will always remember a brother Master Mason when on my knees offering up my devotions to Almighty God. Furthermore do I promise and swear that I will aid and assist all poor, indigent Master Masons, their wives and orphans, wheresoever disposed around the globe, as far as is in my power, without materially injuring myself or my family.

Furthermore do I promise and swear that if any part of my solemn oath of obligation be omitted at this time, I will hold myself amenable thereto whenever informed. To all of which I do most sincerely promise and swear, with a fixed and steady purpose of mind in me to keep and perform the same, binding myself under no less penalty than to have my body severed in twain and divided to

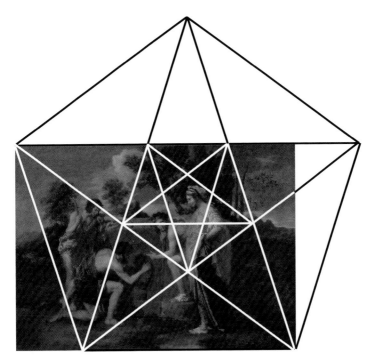

Plate 1.
Poussin's 'Shepherds of Arcadia' - showing the pentagonal geometry associated with the painting discovered by Henry Lincon and Professor Christopher Cornford.

Plate 2.
The Giza Pyramids - notice the difference between the three smaller pyramids at the front, and those behind them - is this testament to the depreciation in knowledge and building techniques since the Atlantis calamity?

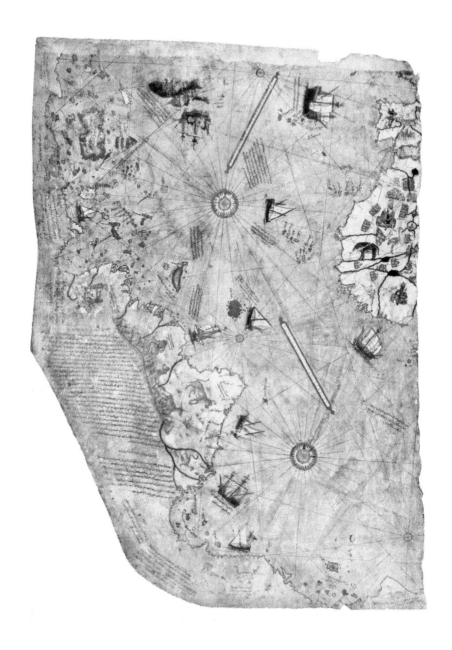

Plate 3.
 The Piri Reis Map - copied by Admiral Piri Reis in the 16th century from
a much more ancient map.

Plate 4.
The Sphinx at Giza - characteristic of a lion's body, drawing the inference that reference is being made to the star sign Leo. Also notice its condition - maybe the result of heavy weathering which occured at around 10,500 BC.

Plate 5.
The Great Pyramid at Giza - showing the sheer size of the pyramid contrasted with the size of man in the left hand side of the picture.

Plate 6.
Entrance to Karnak (Luxor) - the Ram's signify the precessional period of Aries.

Plate 7.
The base of the Menkaure pyramid Giza - the shaping and fitting of these huge granite blocks is yet another remarkable feat of the pyramid builders.

Above
Plate 8.
The quarry at Aswan - showing the uniform holes which
were bore into the rock. Dry
cedar wood was forced into
these holes - the expanding
force caused by the saturation
of the wood caused the rock
to split.

Right
Plate 9.
Cleopatras Kneedle (London) -
floated from Egypt in 1878 and
erected on the Thames
Embankment - which masons
believe was made possible
through the applicaton of their
knowledge

Left
Plate 10.
The Al Asqua
Mosque - home to the
Knights Templar for
seven years during
their excavations.

Below
Plate11.
The Temple Mount -
the base of King
Solomon's Temple -
was it underneath
here that the Templars
made their discovery?

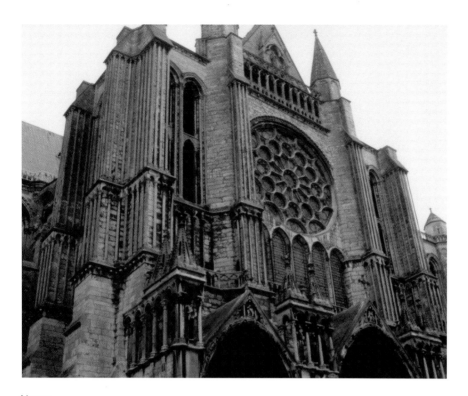

Above
Plate 12.
Chatres Cathedral - a great example of Gothic architecture which displays itself full of esoteric ideas and undertones

Left
Plate 13.
Templar graves at Kilmory, Argyllshire - the ships depicting their maritime pursuits and possibly how these Templars may have escaped from La Rochelle

Plate 14.
Inside Rosslyn Chapel - built on the proportions of Solomon's Temple - the highly decorated Boez and Jachin pillars can be seen either side of the altar

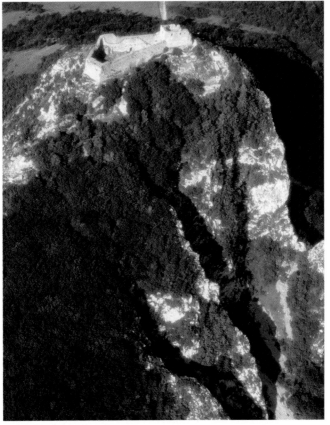

Left
Plate 15.
Montsegur - last stronghold of the Cathars - whose only crime was that they failed to be influenced by or adopt Catholicism

Plate 16.
First Degree sign (to be performed in conjunction with the password) - the thumb of the right hand is at right angles with the hand and is drawn from left to right accross the throat and then placed at the side - notice that for all three degree signs the heel of the right foot is placed into the arch of the left foot at an angle of 45 degrees

Plate 17.
The Second Degree sign (to be performed in conjunction with the password) - the left hand is first placed into position with the right hand following to the position above - the right hand is then drawn accross the chest to the right and then placed at the side, with the left arm then lowered and placed at the side

Plate 18.
The Third Degree sign (to be performed in conjunction with the password) - the thumb (positioned perpendicular to the hand) is drawn across
the abdomen from left to right and then back half way to the umbilicus
with slight pause before drawing the right hand to the left hand side of
the abdomen, where it is again drawn across to the right hand side of
the abdomen and placed at the side.

Plate 19.
Qumran next to the Dead Sea - these were the caves where the Dead Sea Scrolls (to some extent preserved in their clay pots) were hidden by the enigmatic Essene community, the same community in which many believe Jesus lived

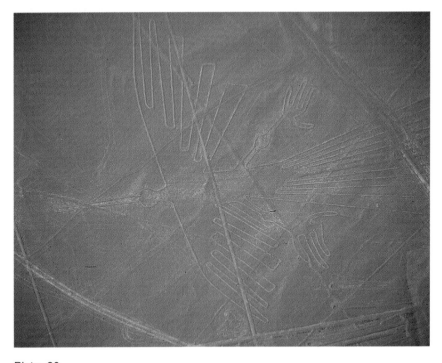

Plate 20.
The Hummingbird, Nazca - such precision in design over vast areas cannot be easily attributed to a primitive culture, but notwithstanding this - what created the impetus to create such images which could only be appreciated from a great height?

the north and south, my bowels burnt to ashes in the centre, and the ashes scattered before the four winds of heaven, that there might not the least track or trace of remembrance remain among men, or Masons, of so vile and perjured a wretch as I should be, were I ever to prove wilfully guilty of violating any part of this my solemn oath and obligation of a Master Mason. So help me God, and keep me steadfast in the due performance of the same.

The ritual thus begins, bringing out the importance of some of the aspects of masonry; such as brotherhood. The strong ideology of brotherhood which exists in Masonry is emphasised strongly in this degree:

. . . the third degree is the cement of the whole; it is calculated to bind men together by mystic points of fellowship, as in the bond of fraternal affection and brotherly love . . . when these bodies which have long been slumbering in the dust shall be awakened, reunited to their kindred spirit, and clothed in immortality . . .

The reference to 'slumbering in the dust', refers to the candidate before his resurrection: an unenlightened and unawakened spirit. However, once resurrected his spirit, they believe, is united with the metaphysical world above and will live on forever, in life or in death; in, what is known to Freemasons, as the Grand Lodge Above.

The resurrection which is the most important part of the ritual is, masons believe, a re-enactment of the death of Hiram Abiff, with the candidate acting Hiram's role. The story is in fact an allegory to enhance the candidates spiritual rebirth, and Masons believe that the stories of Isis and Osiris and other ancient legends from around the world where the hero or heroine comes back to life should not be taken literally, but are allegories too. The story, in general terms, concerns Hiram and three ruffians known as the Juwes, whose names were Jubela, Jubelo and Jubelum. The word Juwes is referred to later on in this book being what the masons believe was the incomprehensible word written on a wall in blood by Jack the Ripper. The story of these three Juwes tells that one day they cornered Hiram Abiff in Solomon's Temple and demanded that he tell them the secret signs and password of a Master Mason; thus allowing them to collect the wages of a Master Mason. Hiram replied unequivocally, that he would rather die than reveal the ancient building secrets to these three ruffians. The story continues in the ritual:

> The answer not proving satisfactory, the ruffian aimed a violent blow at our master's forehead, but startled by the firmness of his demeanour, it only glanced down his right temple. Yet with sufficient force to cause him to reel and sink to the ground on his left knee.

In the ritual, the Worshipful Master administers this blow, although with less force than when it supposedly originally occurred, and the candidate is guided down onto his left knee by the deacons around him. It is an interesting point to consider when or where these events occurred. Masonic teaching states categorically that the events occurred in Solomon's Temple, but there is no evidence to support this opinion. However, Knight and Lomas have presented evidence in the *Hiram Key,* that the story originally came from Egypt. If this is the case then it would seem to the reader that the basis for the third degree ritual concerning Solomon and his principal architect (Hiram Abiff) is nonsense. However, it is not so much the story's authenticity which is important to Freemasons, but the symbolism represented by the story itself and how it is imparted to the candidate to induce his spiritual realisation.

The ritual continues:

> Recovering himself from this situation (the candidate is brought up to his feet again), he rushed to the west gate where he stood opposed to the second ruffian, to whom he replied as before, yet with undiminished firmness when the ruffian, who was armed with a level struck a violent blow on the left temple which brought him to the ground on his right knee.

The Worshipful Master administers a second blow on the candidate's left temple, where he is guided down on his right knee. The candidate is then prepared for the final fatal blow:

> Finding all chances of escape in both these quarters curt off, our Master staggered, faint and bleeding, to the east gate where the third ruffian was posted and who, on receiving a similar reply to his insolent demand, for our Master remained true to his obligation even in this most trying moment, struck him a violent blow full in the centre of the forehead with a heavy stone maul, which laid him lifeless at his feet . . . Such was the manner of his death.

The Worshipful Master taps the candidate on the forehead at this point, and the candidate is lowered backwards onto a piece of cloth shaped like a coffin; some Lodges actually use a real coffin in the ritual, although most simply lay a black coffin shaped cloth on the temple floor. Some lodges in Scotland actually build a coffin shaped hole in the floor of the Temple from which to raise the candidate. The candidate is then wrapped in a shroud by the junior wardens. One of the Junior wardens then tries to raise the candidate using the entered apprentice grip, which slips from his grasp. Another junior warden then tries to raise the candidate up using the Fellowcraft grip which also fails. The Worshipful Master then attempts to raise the candidate by interlocking his hand over the wrist of the candidate. This hand grip proves to be successful and the candidate is raised to his feet with the help of the wardens around him, this is known as the resurrection. As he is raised to his feet the Worshipful Master whispers the words MAHHABONE MACBENACH to the candidate, which he is told are the sacred words of a Master Mason The Worshipful Master then places his right foot, knee and breast against the candidate while explaining to him the 'Five Points of Fellowship', and concludes by putting his left hand over the candidates back. As he does this the Worshipful Master says,

> "Hand to hand I greet you as a brother; foot to foot I will support you in all your undertakings; knee to knee, the posture of my daily supplications shall remind me of your wants; breast to breast, your lawful secrets when entrusted to me as such I will keep as my own; and hand over back, I will support your character in your absence as in your presence."

The candidate can now consider himself raised both physically, as performed in the ritual, and more importantly spiritually. It is believed by esotericists that this concept of spiritual enlightenment is contained in the Grail legends. Max Heindel believes that Wagner's operas exemplify man's struggle for spiritual enlightenment:

> And be it remembered that Faust's experience is not an isolated instance of what may happen under abnormal conditions. He is a symbol of the seeking soul. You and I are Fausts in a certain sense, for at some stage in our evolution we shall meet the Earth Spirit and realise the power of His name, properly uttered.[11]

The Master Mason's handshake consists of shaking a person's hand while pressing the thumb upon that person's middle

11. Heindel, M., Mysteries of the Great Operas, p.18

knuckle. Many Freemasons use this grip as a form of recognition in public life. This is probably because the Regulations of Freemasonry state that:

> No Brother shall appear clothed in any of the jewels, collars or badges of the Craft, in any procession, meeting or assemblage at which persons other than Masons are present, or in any place of public resort, unless the Grand Master or the Provincial Grand Master, as the case may be, shall have previously given a dispensation for Brethren to be there present in Masonic clothing. [12]

However Masons are allowed to wear very small badges on their lapels in public; these come in the form of the 'square and compass' or a 'forget me not'.

The ritual proceeds with the candidate being given the two words which make up the Master Masons password to enter the Temple: TUBAL CAIN. These words are also derived from the Old Testament, as the name of a worker of metal -"Zillah also had a son, Tubal Cain, who forged all kinds of tools out of bronze and iron." [13]

The newly qualified mason is also shown the secret sign of a Master Mason to go with the password, which is made by drawing the thumb of the right hand across the belly from left to right and the back to the umbilicus (belly button). As shown in the Plate 18, the thumb must be at right angles with the index finger (denoting the square). This sign is meant to represent the way in which one of the three Juwes is supposed to have died.

The Worshipful Master shows the now Master Mason a skull and two bones which lie to his right. He then shows him a glimmer of light in the east which indicates the 'morning star'. An analogy could be made here with the beliefs held by the ancients:

12. Grand Lodge, United Grand Lodge of England Contitutions (Supreme Grand Chapter Regulations- Article 178), p.110
13. Book of Genesis 4:22

Very much like the ancient Egyptians, the peoples of central America located their netherworld in a region of the sky through which ran the Milky Way. Another curious similarity is that both peoples appear to have believed that the gates of the afterlife realm swung open 'in the red glow of twilight which precedes the dawn'. What is most striking, however, is the extent to which both systems of initiation focused on astronomy, particularly upon an esoteric knowledge of the cycles of the heavens, and aspired to immortality amongst the stars.[14]

Such synergies are hard to dismiss as accident or mere coincidence, and add significant credence to the ancient authenticity of the Masonic rituals being derived from ancient times.
Many Masons claim to experience an out of body experience when they are playing the part of the dead Hiram Abiff i.e. that they can see their body from another position in the room. It is believed by many masons that the soul leaves the physical body of the person and then returns soon after. This method of projecting one's soul out of the physical body is recognised generally as astral projection, and (as mentioned previously) it is widely practised, especially amongst occultists. More importantly, the process of resurrecting someone without impaling them to a cross and killing them, is widely practised by other esoteric societies as well; including: the Ordo Templis Orientis (Alister Crowley groups), Klu Klux Klan, Rosicrucians, some American fraternities, and the Orange Order of Northern Ireland. The ideology behind this type of resurrection is that a person's soul becomes resurrected up to the stars so that their souls are reborn to a higher level of spiritual enlightenment, ensuring that the soul radiating the light of spirit becomes a living immortalised star. Many Freemasons today never pass beyond the third degree and see the lodge as an opportunity to socialise with their fellow brethren, rather than a place for learning the archaic symbolism and secrets of the Egyptians and Atlanteans.

14. Hancock, G., and Faiia, S., Heavens Mirror, p.23

As mentioned previously, many other esoteric societies practice similar rituals and possess much the same secrets that the Freemasons do, although the masons believe that they are only surpassed by the Templar Knights, with regard to possession of esoteric knowledge. The Templars, although few in number, are still in existence today and many esoteric societies maintain that they are the direct descendants of the Templars and their knowledge. Freemasons believe themselves to be the cream of nearly all the other esoteric societies in existence today.

With the mention of groups such as the Klu Klux Klan, many American Fraternities and the Orange Order of Northern Ireland, it is understandable if the reader may be slightly confused when attempting to rationalise the ideology of brotherhood and spiritual resurrection with some of the activities of such groups. The Grand Lodge is unequivocal about how Masons should conduct themselves:

> Therefore no private piques or quarrels must be brought within the door of the lodge, far less any quarrels about religion, or nations, or state policy, we being only, as masons, of the universal religion above-mentioned; we are also of all nations, tongues, kindreds, and languages, and are resolved against all politics, as what never yet conduced to the welfare of the lodge, nor ever will.[15]

It is difficult to rationalise such groups with the charitable and peace loving image that many may have of the Freemasons. But it is important to emphasise what the underlying purpose of Masonry is:

> This - the evolution of man into superman- was always the purpose of the ancient Mysteries, and the real purpose of modern Masonry is, not the social and charitable purposes to which so much attention is paid, but the expediting of the spiritual evolution

15. Grand Lodge, Uninted Grand Lodge of England Constitutions, Article 2, p.9

of those who aspire to perfect their own nature and transform it into a more god-like quality. [16]

This is further endorsed in John R. Bennett's *Origin of Freemasonry and Knights Templar*:

> The design of Freemasonry is neither charity nor alms-giving, nor the cultivation of social sentiments; for both of these are merely incidental to its organisation. But it is the search after truth, and that truth is the unity of God and the immortality of the soul. The various degrees or grades of initiation represent the various stages through which the human mind passes, and the many difficulties which men, individually and collectively, must encounter in their progress from ignorance to the acquisition of truth. [17]

This explains why freemasons refer to themselves as 'just men made perfect'; that their souls have been enlightened and they believe they follow a more perfect spiritual path. In contrast to other religions, esotericism has its roots set in the broadest sense. This is why esotericism has been vulnerable with respect to its adoption by many extreme groups merging their existing beliefs within it. Other religions are much more specific about presenting the attitudes and beliefs which should be adopted by their followers, for instance it would be very difficult to find any biblical justification for violent acts against other human beings from the teachings of the New Testament. Although there are some groups which have adopted esotericism whose ideologies and morals are suspect to say the least, the Freemasons themselves have not been without their critics in recent years. It is inevitable that there are some Freemasons who use the Lodge to simply further their own ends, and the ideology of brotherhood is inevitably abused by some of its proponents. Two exponents of such conspiracies were Stephen Knight (*The Brotherhood*) and Martin Short (*Inside the Brotherhood*) who exposed injustices which, they

16. Wilmshurst, W. L., The Meaning of Masonry, p.47
17. Bennett, J.R., Origins of Freemasonry and Knight Templar, p.109

endorsed, were a circumstance of either Masons or Masonry. However, there are many that maintain that although some Freemasons do conspire with each other within lodges, it is purely a circumstance of a group of men gathering together under the same roof. Although is it accepted that compared with fifty or a hundred years ago the impeccable standard set by Freemasons of the past has not been maintained by their Masonic descendants of today, and this is reflected in the numerous critics which they have attracted; this may simply be a case of a few bad apples within the Lodge and a reflection of a changing society. Opinions upon this issue are staunchly divided and thankfully such a debate is beyond the parameters of this book. After completing the three degrees, the master mason can choose, if invited, whether or not to follow higher degrees, up to thirty three if he so chooses. Extracts from two of these higher degrees are described below.

The Royal Arch Degree

It is estimated that only about two in every five Master Masons bother to carry out any further degrees. Most Masons wishing to progress further through the Masonic degrees will usually start with the Holy Royal Arch degree, commonly known to masons as the 'Chapter Degree'.

The degree revolves around three principal figures from the Old Testament : Zerubbabel, Haggai and Joshua. Before entering the temple, for the performance of the degree, the candidate must first of all be admitted. This requires him to repeat the Royal Arch passwords and their meaning, of which he has been instructed beforehand:

(N - Nehemiah, Z - Zerubbabel, Jan - Janitor)

N. Most Excellent, there is a report.
Z. Companion Scribe Nehemiah, who seeks admission.
N. (To Janitor) Whom have you there?

138

Jan. Bro (name of candidate), who has been regularly initiated into Freemasonry, passed to the Degree of a Fellow Craft, and in due time raised to the Sublime Degree of a Master Mason, in which capacity he has exercised himself for four weeks and upwards, and as a reward of merit has been entrusted with the pass words leading to this Supreme Degree to which he seeks to be admitted, and for which ceremony he is properly prepared.

N. How does he hope to obtain the privileges of this Supreme Degree?

Jan. By the assistance of the True and Living God Most High, the united aid of the Circle and Triangle, and the benefit of the passwords.

N. Is he in possession of the pass words?

Jan. Ask him.

N. (To candidate) Give me the passwords.

Can. 'Ammi Ruhamah.'.

N. The import of the words?

Can. 'My people have found mercy.'

N. Wait, while I report to the Most Excellent . . . he has been entrusted with the passwords leading to the Supreme Degree to which he seeks to be admitted, and for which ceremony he is properly prepared.

(The information is relayed to Zerubbabel)

Z. Is he in possession of the passwords?

N. He is Most Excellent.

Z. Admit him.

The candidate is then presented with a series of questions, relating to his desire to be admitted to the Supreme Degree.

Z. As you seek to participate in the light of our mysteries, we must call upon you to advance towards the Sacred Shrine, on which they are deposited, by seven steps, halting and bowing at the third, fifth, and seventh, for at each step you will approach nearer to the Sacred and Mysterious Name of the True and Living God Most High.

Having been led through the motions of climbing these steps, the candidate then comes upon a vault in which he has to enact being lowered into it. The surroundings of the vault are described to him, and a scroll is placed into his right hand:-

Can. It is found.
Z. What is found?
Can. Something like a scroll of vellum or parchment.
Z. What are its contents?
Can. For the want of Light I am unable to discover.
Z. Let the want of light remind you that man by nature is the child of ignorance and error, and would ever have remained in a state of darkness, had it not pleased the Almighty to call him to light and immortality by the revelations of His Holy Will and Word. Rise, wrench forth the Keystone, and prepare to receive the light of the Holy Word.

The candidate is raised from his kneeling position, and he is assisted in dislodging the keystone.

Z. Let the Candidate be again lowered into the Vault and attend to a portion of the writings of the Prophet Haggai.

A passage is now read from the Old Testament book of Haggai chapter 2: 1 - 9. The candidate now prepares himself for the 'Sacred and Solemn Obligation':-

Z. State your name at length, and say after me: Obligation.

Can. I (candidate's name), in the presence of the True and Living God Most High, and of this Holy Royal Arch Chapter, duly constituted, consecrated, and congregated, of my own free will and accord, do hereby and hereon most solemnly promise and swear that I will always hail, conceal, and never divulge any of the secrets or mysteries restricted to this Supreme Degree, denominated the Holy Royal Arch of Jerusalem, to anyone in the world, unless it be true and lawful Companion of the Order whom I shall find to be such after strict examination. I further solemnly promise that I will not dare to pronounce that Sacred and Mysterious Name of the True and Living God Most High, lightly or irreverently, nor to share it by syllables, unless in the presence and with the assistance of two or more Royal Arch Companions. All these points I solemnly swear to observe, without evasion, equivocation, or mental reservation of any kind, under no less a penalty, on the violation of any of them, than that of suffering loss of life by having my head struck off. So help me the True and Living God Most High, and keep me steadfast in this the Sacred and Solemn Obligation of a Royal Arch Mason.

Z. As a pledge of your fidelity, and to render what you have repeated a Solemn Obligation binding on you so long as you shall live, you will seal it with your lips four times on the Volume of the Sacred Law.

This degree, which is quite comprehensive, ends with a series of lectures upon the significance of the degree. They discuss the symbolic, historical, and mystical significance of the Royal Arch Degree.

Mark Mason Degree

The ideology behind this degree is that during the building of Solomon's Temple, each builder (or as the Masons refer to them : Master Masons) had their own individual mark which they placed on the particular stone they had shaped.

The degree includes two rituals which run concurrently called Mark Man and Mark Master Mason. These rituals are an enactment of a fictitious search for the most important stone in Solomon's Temple. Once the candidate has found the stone a passage is read to him from Revelation 2:17 :

> To him that overcometh will I give to eat of the hidden manna and I will give him a white stone and in the stone a new name written which no man knoweth saving he that receiveth it.

The candidate is required to make his own mark by conjoining his initials together, this mark is then entered into the Mark Masons' register. This part of the ritual is as follows:

> W.M. In former times it was the custom in all Fellow Craft Lodges for each Fellow Craft to choose a mark by which his work might be known to his Overseer, the mark selected being not one previously chosen by a brother of the same Lodge, and the triangle always excepted, that being the Mark Master's Mark of approval. He was at the same time taught how to present his Mark at the Warden's Wicket to receive his wages as a Mark Man. When you were passed to the degree of Fellow Craft, was such a Mark chosen by you?
> Can. It was not, Worshipful Master.
> W.M. Then the Senior Deacon will conduct you to the Registrar's table where that want shall be supplied. Senior Deacon, or Registrar of Marks, if present - (to Candidate) It is my duty to inform you that a copy of whatever Mark may be chosen by you will be inserted in the Register of this Lodge, and will be returned for registration in the books of the Grand Lodge and cannot afterwards be changed.

Here the candidate is given the opportunity to chose his Mark, made by combining his initials, thus forming his particular mark.

Later on in the degree the candidate is required to make a pledge of secrecy as a Mark Master Mason:

> I (candidate's name), in the presence of the Great Architect of the Universe, and of this worthy, worshipful, and regularly constituted Lodge of Mark Master Masons, do hereby and hereon sincerely and solemnly swear that I will never divulge any or either of the rituals or secrets pertaining to this degree to anyone in the world unless it be a true and regularly advanced Brother who, I shall have sufficient reason to believe, has come by them in as legal a manner as I am now about to do; or in the body of a regularly constituted and warranted Lodge of Mark Master Masons, consisting of three or more; that I will not unjustly use any Brother's Mark, but will receive it when presented to me, and grant his request, if just, and in my power, the same not being detrimental to myself or connections, but I shall not feel myself bound again to relieve him until he shall have redeemed his mark from its former obligation. All these points I solemnly engage myself to observe under no less a penalty on the violation of any or either of them than that having my right hand struck off, so help me, so that I can no longer mark, give the grip or reclaim the wages of a Mark Master Mason.

It must be emphasised again here that this story is of allegorical significance to Freemasons; there may be some truth within the story, however authenticity is not a precondition to the degree's importance and effectiveness to freemasons.

The Ideology of the Degrees

It is important for the reader to appreciate that the main purpose of the Masonic degrees is not simply to relay ancient stories of events gone by which constitute esoteric history, but to bring the candidate into new dimensions from a spiritual aspect through the use of these stories and their symbolism. While Masonic secrets are important to Masons, they alone do not constitute masonry or esotericism; as Schwaller de Lubicz notes, 'Esotericism cannot be written or spoken, and hence it cannot be betrayed.' [18] As Berg describes the Kabbalah (the Jewish form of esotericism) ' . . . and cannot therefore be described directly by means of the outer coverings with which we are familiar in this material world.' [19]

Many Masons maintain that the essence of Masonry is within the rituals and the effect they have on a Mason's personal evolution through the different dimensions of spiritual consciousness. By performing the rituals contained in the degrees the candidate, in many cases, actually believes that his spirit, advances through the higher stages of the astral plane - this is symbolised to masons as the rungs of Jacob's ladder. For further reading into the ideology and practice of esoteric rituals and their significance there are numerous books on astral projection. However, probably the most definitive, with respect to masonry (although not about Masonry), is *Maat Magick :A Guide to Self Initiation* by Nema. This book contains within it a series of steps which its author believes can lead to the reader's spiritual resurrection, without the requirement of performing rituals within an esoteric society. The book is of relevance because it has many parallels with the techniques used in Masonry, although the process of spiritual resurrection is spread over ten stages in the book instead of Masonry's three degrees.

It is hoped by now that the reader will have gained a greater insight into what actually goes on in Masonic lodges, but it must be stressed that the evenings Masons spend together are not purely ritualistic. After the rituals have been performed the Masons usually sit down to a meal and have a couple of drinks afterwards. This is how most masons account publicly for what goes on within the lodge, but as the reader will now appreciate there is much more to it than simply dining and socialising amongst themselves.

18. Lubicz , Schwaller de, Esoterism and Symbol, p.3
19. Berg, P. S., Kabbalah for the Layman, p.59

As well as all being brothers, the Masons also believe themselves to be the guardians of the ancient knowledge of Atlantis the keepers of the secrets which emanate from this knowledge. The Masons' belief that their knowledge was passed down from remote antiquity is echoed by Hancock and Faiia:

> In the mythology, traditions and scriptures of the countries through which we have travelled we have found ourselves repeatedly confronted by another shared system of ideas - the notion that the soul might be reborn down the ages, in different forms and circumstances, thus accumulating experiences and gradually progressing towards perfection. In all these cultures we also encountered the parallel notion that the task of perfecting the spirit was to be accomplished not only through good works and good thoughts but also through a ruthless stripping - away of all attachments to the material world and through mastery of an ancient system of spiritual knowledge.[20]

Having been given an account of the Masonic beliefs pertaining to their past and how they believe strands of this ancient knowledge have permeated into their modern day rituals, the reader may now be at liberty to decide for him or herself the validity of such perceptions. Much research still needs to be carried out in this area in order to properly clarify whether the form of the Masonic rituals are remnants of an ancient ritualistic system first initiated by a bygone civilisation in remote antiquity - possibly Atlantis.

Having understood the history of the esoteric phenomenon, as it has existed through the ages, it is now time to delve into what exactly the Masonic secrets are, and to attempt to rationalise how such beliefs can be held by thousands of men throughout the world, which in many respects are contrary to the founding principles upon which western society perceives history and the possible implications which emanate from such beliefs.

20. Hancock, G. and Faiia, S., Heavens Mirror, p.313

PART TWO

BELIEFS OF FREEMASONRY

Chapter Five

Jesus - the esoteric initiate

One letter in the early post is unlike any other. It is brief and startling and seems to be moving the story into a totally unlooked for direction. The writer is a retired Church of England vicar. "May I advise you," he states, baldly, "that the 'treasure' is not one of gold and precious stones, but a document containing incontrovertible evidence that Jesus was alive in the year 45 AD . . . This," he goes on to say, "would utterly destroy 'Christian' dogma." [1]

Up until recently, what was considered by some to be the true story of Jesus' life, was considered a well kept secret amongst many esoteric societies. This supposed secret knowledge pertaining to Jesus' life runs contrary to Christian accounts and if it were ever proved to be true, is enough to threaten the whole basis of the Christian faith. In medieval times a hint of such blasphemy would have been enough to

1. Lincon, H., Key to the Sacred Pattern, p.75

condemn any man to the gallows. However, in the past century glimpses of such beliefs and possible proof to substantiate them has emerged. Such beliefs could explain the Churchs' animosity towards esoteric groups, especially the Freemasons, and could also be used to explain the Papacy's attitude towards the Templars, and reasons behind the ferocity with which the Inquisition unleashed themselves upon the Cathars and the Templars. They would also explain why clergy today are instructed in no uncertain terms not to join the Freemasons. The idea that there might be a different version to Jesus' life than that which Christianity advocates, was first brought into the public limelight in the early 1980s through the publication of *The Holy Blood and the Holy Grail*, and the enigmatic actions of a French parish priest.

The Parish Priest

The story expounded by Baigent, Leigh and Lincoln in their highly explosive book *The Holy Blood and the Holy Grail*, was that of a parish priest residing in Southern France; who, while living on a meagre income of six pounds a year, had spent the equivalent of seven million pounds by the time of his death in 1917. Berenger Sauniere was appointed priest to the small parish of Rennes-le-Chateau on 1st June 1885. For a thirty-three year old priest this was certainly a step backwards in his clerical career, and it is likely that his appointment to the two-hundred-strong parish of Rennes-le-Chateau must have been prompted by something he had done to displease his superiors.

In 1891, Sauniere decided to carry out some restoration work on his village church. As he removed the altar stone, he found that one of the columns on which the altar stone rested was hollow. Inside the hollow cavity Sauniere found four wooden tubes, each containing a parchment inside. As the reader will already have noted, the Boez and Jachin pillars which once stood either side of the altar in Solomon's Temple were also rumoured to be hollow and containing parchments. It is also rumoured that the Boez and Jachin pillars which exist in Rosslyn Chapel (a scaled down replica of Solomon's Temple), contain ancient parchments found by the Templars under the Temple of Solomon; however this seems more like far fetched speculation than a theory worthy of any credibility.

As Sauniere was already familiar with ancient languages including Greek, Latin and Hebrew he was quite confident he would be able to translate the parchments. However, this was not to be the case, as most of the parchments were elaborately coded. Although most of the text contained in the parchments would have been discernible to him, it is believed unlikely, that he would have been able to crack the more elaborate codes. Whatever Sauniere managed to decipher, was enough to warrant immense interest in him and his discovery. The Bishop of Carcassonne immediately sent him to Paris, so that certain ecclesiastic authorities could learn of his discovery and study the parchments which he had found.

One man who scrutinised the parchments quite closely was Emile Hoffet, who was heavily involved in esoteric traditions at the time. Hoffet must have realised the importance of the parchments and immediately began introducing Sauniere to the upper class Paris society who were affiliated with esoteric groups. Sauniere must have been overwhelmed with the sudden change in the society with which he was now mixing, compared to his previous quiet, uneventful role as a village parish priest. He was now mixing freely amongst people such as Maurice Maeterlinck, Claude Debussy (A Templar Grand Master at the time), and Emma Calve - a famous singer who eventually became Sauniere's lover. It was evident that through his discovery, Sauniere had become a member of a very elite circle stretching throughout Europe. What information or knowledge did Sauniere discover, which elevated his importance to an unprecedented level (in the eyes of the esoteric masters around at the time), and provided him with what would seem to be an unlimited cash source.

As time went by, Sauniere made numerous trips to Paris and was spending thousands on projects such as the renovation of the Rennes-le-Chateau church, and the building of a large tower named the Tour Magdala. The Bishop soon got to hear of Sauniere's extravagant spending and immediately suspended him; this was however all in vain, as he was reinstated by the Bishops superiors. It would almost appear as though the Vatican itself, although outwardly displaying an aversion to esoteric societies, had been infiltrated by them. Or was it simply that the Vatican were afraid of Sauniere because he was in possession of particular parchments which could shatter the basis of the whole Catholic faith? For a clearer understanding of what Sauniere did find, it is necessary to first explain the history of the area around Rennes-le-Chateau and the people who once lived there, in particular the Cathars.

The Cathars

It is evident that around Rennes-le-Chateau and the whole of the old province of Languedoc in southern France, a strong Cathar influence has persisted through the centuries and Cathar beliefs and philosophy still persist there today. It is also evident that Sauniere immersed himself in Cathar history and tradition; but what of this connection with the Cathars, what relevance or bearing did it have on Berenger Sauniere, and what influence (if any) did the Cathars have on the Templars? On closer examination of the Cathars, it will become evident to the reader, that the Cathars' knowledge, influence and involvement in the legacy of Jesus and the Knights Templar can only be described as profound.

In 1209, Pope Innocent III issued a decree or Papal Bull which was in effect, an order to wipe out those heretics known as the Cathars, which constituted the majority of the population of Languedoc. Some 30,000 knights and soldiers joined in this internal Crusade, with the Templars abstaining, stressing that the real Crusade was in the Holy Land. What turned out as a crusade against the Cathars, turned into a mass genocide of those people who were unfortunate enough to be living in the Languedoc region. The command which emanated from Rome which dealt with how Cathars were to be distinguished from Catholics was "Kill them all, God will recognise his own." In many towns such as Beziers, Perpignan and Carcassonne, men, women and children were slaughtered indiscriminately. The thoroughness of the massacre was in part due to the zeal of the northern crusaders, who had for a long time wanted to pillage the wealth from the more prosperous Languedoc region.

To this day no satisfactory explanation has emerged for the reason behind such a brutal crusade being ordered against the Cathars of Europe. There is no evidence that the Cathars had done anything serious enough against Rome or to upset the Papacy enough to warrant their almost complete annihilation. It is true that the Catholic faith was particularly weak in the Cathar regions of France. Catholic churches in the region were much emptier than some churches today. At no point did the Cathars show any interest in or give any credence to the Catholic church or its beliefs. It was indeed strange that while the whole of Europe had embraced the Catholic faith, these simple people who lived in an enclave of southern France were immune from all propaganda and influence that the Catholic Church brought to bear.

Before the Cathar Crusade in 1209, the people who lived in the Languedoc region (mainly Cathars), were advanced in many areas, even by European standards. A large proportion of the population were literate and their beliefs were ultimately governed by a quest for knowledge. Both Templar and Masonic beliefs also revolve around a quest for knowledge in furtherance of their eventual enlightenment. The Cathars studied the ancient biblical languages of Greek,

Hebrew and Arabic; they were also renowned poets and highly accomplished philosophers. Although, probably the most
striking part of the Cathar way of life was that many studied the Cabala - an ancient Judaic tradition based upon esoteric ideology. Both Templar and Masonic beliefs are also inextricably linked to the Cabala, being the esoteric branch of
Judaism.

Cathars did not accept what they regarded as second
hand or impure faith, but claimed to experience a mystical
phenomenon which supposedly put them on first hand terms
with God himself. Could the Cathars be referring to the experience of the resurrection, as Freemasons claim to experience
when they are raised as described earlier in the third degree
ceremony. Indeed the Cathars also had initiation rituals and
believed in enlightenment through knowledge. Further evidence
linking the Cathars to the Templars and neo-Templar societies
is found within the idea of dualism. This is explained by
Morris:

> Many (Cathars), although not all, adherents believed
> in two equal and opposite principles of good and
> evil, and had thus abandoned the fundamental
> catholic idea of monotheism. In their own eyes,
> however, their religion appeared as a pure and orig-
> inal version of Christianity, cleansed from the dis-
> tortions introduced by the catholic clergy. [2]

The concept of dualism i.e. good versus evil, is mirrored in
many faiths, however the Cathars' sense of dualism was worlds
away from Catholic dualism. Cathar dualism centred upon the
cosmological struggles of the universe. The Cathars were keen
astrologers who believed that the movement of the stars was
in some way inextricably linked to the direction of their lives.
Astrology, in this context, is also studied avidly in Masonic
Lodges.

One of the main heresies which emanated from the
Cathars was that they saw Jesus as a prophet and a mortal

2. Morris, The Papal Monarchy- The Western Church from 1050-1250,
p.347

man, unlike the Christian notion of Jesus as the Son of God. Baigent, Leigh and Lincon explain that :

> The majority of Cathars seem to have regarded him as a prophet no different from any other - a mortal being who, on behalf of the principle of love, died on the cross. There was, in short, nothing mystical, nothing supernatural, nothing divine about the crucifixion - if, indeed, it was relevant at all, which many Cathars appear to have doubted. [3]

Such a belief, that Jesus was a mortal man, is echoed in the Islamic faith as well as again in Templar and Masonic ideology. Furthermore, the strict devotion of the Cathars to their faith and many other facets of their way of life such as travelling in pairs, comprise a large part of the Templar rule. Such synergyies can hardly be coincidental. Added to this is the fact that one of the parchments found by Berenger Sauniere in the church at Rennes-le-Chateau had (in addition to Templar references), a reference to the Cathars in the form of one of their sacred phrases, Rex Mundi. Cathar thought and tradition feature prominently in the Templar way of life, and it is quite probable that the Cathars were connected in some way to the creation of the Templar Order. Could it be that the Cathars, realising that Rome was losing patience with their growing popularity, initiated the creation of the Templar Order. Whoever the brain-child was or were behind the Templar Order they were certainly very astute; they realised that the safest guise under which a group (seeking to continue esoteric traditions), could operate, would be as part of an approved Order of the Papacy. An old Arab proverb says that to nullify your enemy's power against you, you must get close to him.

The Cathar crusade finally ended with the fall of the last Cathar stronghold, Montsegur (as shown in Plate 15) in 1244. It was rumoured at the time, that the Castle at Montsegur housed the Cathar treasure, which was thought to

3. Baigent, Leigh and Lincon, The Holy Blood and the Holy Grail, p.47

152

be extensive. Other rumours were also circulating at the time, that the treasure was not tangible but a mystical treasure which surpassed any other treasure before or since. Could the treasure be the supposed knowledge, contained in the parchments found by Sauniere and could these parchments have been related to this supposed secret Legacy of Jesus?

The Montsegur stronghold was built upon a mountain, with sheer cliffs on almost all sides. It could not be approached in sufficient numbers to launch a major attack so a siege transpired. During the siege there was much movement between those in the besieged castle and those who were sympathetic to them on the outside. Supplies were brought in on an almost regular basis, this was due in part to the undisciplined soldiers surrounding the castle and the difficulties of policing such a large area around the castle. It is believed that the Cathars material wealth was smuggled out of the castle; while their intangible wealth was smuggled out just before the siege ended, in an audacious escape by four Cathars and their guide. It is widely believed that these four Cathars perished soon after the siege in the caves at Ornolac. However, apart from the remains of some burnt bodies, nothing was ever found. It was rumoured that the Cathars did escape and hid themselves in caves near Rennes-le-Chateau. Were these Cathars given refuge by the knights Templar? Did they pass on their secret to the Templars? This would have been quite possible judging by the proximity of the Cathars and Templars in the Rennes-le-Chateau region and Languedoc as a whole. If something was passed on, was it what we know from legends as, the mystical and elusive Holy Grail?

What was so important to the Cathars, that they made so sure it did not fall into the hands of the crusaders? The material wealth was smuggled out before the siege ended, but why was the other part of their wealth (which may not have been material), only smuggled out after the siege? The Cathars of Montsegur knew they were going to die, but still made sure that their wealth (which must have been some sort of mystical object or secret knowledge), not only did not fall into the hands of the crusaders, but also survived. If it was simply some secret knowledge pertaining to Cathar beliefs, then it would not really have mattered if it fell into the hands of the crusaders as they were in essence wiped out anyway. However, if the Cathar treasure was, for instance, an ancient manuscript which gave undeniable proof of the life of Jesus, which was contrary to Christian accounts and the Catholic Church's view, then it would certainly be something worth preserving. It is quite possible that such a manuscript fell into the hands of the Templars who, as noted earlier, were closely affiliated to the Cathars in terms of beliefs, and also provided shelter for them during the crusade. In fact to this day thousands of people visit Montsegur claiming it to be a place of mystical value, the majority conjugating at the summer solstice.

It cannot be said, with certainty, that the Cathar treasure was in the form of ancient manuscripts which contained secret information upon the life of Jesus, but a number of factors may point to this being the case. To start with, the Cathars were initially denounced as heretics because they did not believe in many of the Bible's stories or Jesus being the 'son of God', which means that they must have had some powerful evidence to refute the Bible and the propaganda emanating from the Catholic Church. Another factor which adds to the inference that they were in possession of some kind of secret knowledge, was the fanatical zeal with which the Cathar crusade precipitated. Heretics were not in themselves any real danger to the Catholic or Christian institutions, but heretics which could prove certain knowledge certainly would have been.

The possibility of such proof existing also opens up another theory - that the secret manuscript relating to the life of Jesus or possibly, as some believe his descendants, did not fall into the hands of the Templars, but was hidden and found by Sauniere inside the altar pillar inside the church of Rennes-le-Chateau. If he had discovered such a manuscript, and used discretion and cunning in the way he dealt with it (i.e. he did not let it fall into anyone else's hands), then he would indeed have had tremendous bargaining power. He would also have needed an accomplice if he intended to use the threat of the manuscript's publication as a type of insurance policy. If he had of done this he could have bribed the Vatican, and also surprisingly enough, could have bribed the Templar or neo-Templar hierarchy. Most people would immediately assume that these esoteric societies would only be too glad for the truth, as they saw it, to come out. Especially if it went some way to avenge the Catholic Church's atrocities, committed against their fellow brethren - the Templars. However, their secrets are not meant for everyone's ears (maybe they feel the time is not yet right), but only those members worthy enough to be told the secrets - the initiates. This attitude is exemplified in a Masonic document known as Information for the Guidance of Members of the Craft :

> Masonic Secrets - In view of the increasing number of publications purporting or affecting to give particulars of the secrets and inner proceedings of the Craft, the Board desires to notify that the preparation, publication, sale or circulation of such works is a Masonic offence, and that when reported and proved, the offending Brother will be dealt with by disciplinary methods. The Board would add a strong warning to Brethren generally to be extremely cautious in any allusions, whether spoken, written or printed, to Masonic matters which may thus come into the possession of unqualified persons.

Also the Supreme Grand Chapter Regulations , Article 177 states that:

> No Brother shall publish or cause to be published anything which according to the established principles of masonry ought not to be published. . . No

Brother, without the consent of the Grand Master or the Provincial or District Grand Master as the case may be, shall publish or cause to be published the proceedings of any Lodge. [4]

Thus Sauniere could have been blackmailing the Catholic Church, and certain esotericists, or both, for it is unlikely that someone would have given him the present day equivalent of six million pounds, just for discovering an ancient manuscript; however, it is believed by some that the six million may have come from treasures which Sauniere unearthed in and around the Rennes-le-Cheteau region. Very few know the truth behind the riddle of Sauniere and Rennes-le-Chateau, but what can be assessed is the content of one of the manuscripts Sauniere found, which is explained in chapter six, and why it was so dangerous to some institutions, who may have allowed Sauniere to become a law unto himself. It is necessary to go back to the time of Jesus and contrast what the esotericists believe, as a possible motive for such historical enigmas and bloodbaths. However, let us begin with probably the earliest Christian movement as a marker from which explain these highly controversial issues and beliefs.

The Gnostics

Throughout the centuries many individuals and groups have been simply labelled as heretics. In the past their punishment had been either death, torture or at least some kind of public denouncement by the Catholic Church, under the veil of the Inquisition. One such group are known as Gnostics. As their name suggests (Gnostic is a Greek word meaning 'knowledge'), their beliefs revolve around the search for knowledge, and the true meaning of the Christian religion. The Gnostic church has even quoted passages from the New Testament as evidence to endorse that their beliefs relate to the true state of affairs, that Jesus led a secret esoteric life:

4. Grand Lodge, United Grand Lodge of England Constitutions, p.110

156

> To you it has been given to know the mysteries of the kingdom of heaven, but to them it has not been given. [5]

The impression of Jesus which emanates from the New Testament is of a remarkably influential character who performed numerous miracles. However, as Matthew quotes above, and in other parts of the Bible, there are numerous inconsistencies which in some ways hint at Jesus being a member an elite group which revolved around the Temple.

The Gnostics have always maintained that the origins of their beliefs came from the early Christian church, the Church as it existed in the times of Jesus and soon afterwards. They believe that Jesus was a mere mortal and not the 'Son of God'; they have never believed in the miracles he performed, and maintain that Jesus alluded to a secret tradition which was more ancient than the Pyramids themselves. But, such beliefs are nothing new. The Cathars believed almost the same thing, as did or do the Templars, and numerous esoteric societies which have come into existence since then. Furthermore this belief is actually contained in the Bible:

> My dear friends, do not believe all who claim to have the Spirit, but test them to find out if the spirit they have comes from God. For many false prophets have gone out everywhere. This is how you will be able to know whether it is God's spirit: anyone who acknowledges that Jesus Christ came as a human being has the Spirit who comes from God. But anyone who denies this about Jesus does not have the spirit from God. The spirit he has is from the Enemy of Christ; you heard that it would come, and now it is here in the world already. [6]

Many deceivers have gone out all over the world, people who do not acknowledge that Jesus Christ

5. Matthew 13:11
6. John's First Letter 4:1

came as a human being. Such a person is a deceiver and the Enemy of Christ. Be on your guard then, so that you will not lose what we have worked for but will receive your reward in full. [7]

I am sure that many readers, who are not familiar with the current literature which has accumulated in recent years purporting to give a very different story of Jesus' life from that contained in the new Testament, would be horrified at the mention of such 'blasphemy'. However, such beliefs about the life of Jesus, have been carried through the generations of secret societies for centuries. It is not the purpose of this book to become entangled in the religious arguments for or against what the true story of Jesus may be, but it is deemed necessary for the purposes of this book to give the reader some of the arguments which have, in the last few years, fuelled the belief that Jesus' life was different from that which it is portrayed in the New Testament. The reader is then at liberty to judge for himself whether or not to give any credence to the esoteric beliefs pertaining to Jesus' life.

The Nag Hamadi and Dead Sea Scrolls

Since the discovery of the Nag Hamadi and Dead Sea scrolls in 1945 and 1947 respectively, much debate has centred upon what kind of life Jesus actually lived. The Nag Hamadi scrolls found in the Egyptian desert stored in a number of pottery pots, were almost lost forever; as the boy who found them was at first using them to light his stove. Regardless of this, by 1977 all the Nag Hamadi codices (or what was left of them), had been published and they expounded some startling revelations concerning the life of Jesus. The Dead Sea Scrolls which were much more numerous, were discovered in a series of caves at Qumran some 20 miles east of Jerusalem, close to the Dead Sea (as shown in Plate 19).

7. John's Second Letter 7

By contrast to the Nag Hamadi Scrolls, the Dead Sea Scrolls have never been properly deciphered in their entirety and access to many of these documents has been very difficult to obtain for the last fifty years, although today access to the scrolls is much more freely available. There is evidence, in the case of the Dead Sea Scrolls, of a conspiracy to withhold the information contained in them. There is further evidence that attempts have been made to distort the origins of the scrolls and to obscure the era in which they were written. *The Dead Sea Scrolls Deception*, by Michael Beigent and Richard Leigh, presents evidence upon which one can only assume that a group of men, known as the 'International Team' or the 'Ecoli Biblique' (charged with the task deciphering the scrolls), have been intentionally suppressing their publication. The members of the International team are, surprisingly enough, affiliated to the Catholic Church. It is not difficult to imagine what knowledge the Dead Sea Scrolls may contain, or the motives behind the International Team's possible conspiracy to suppress the information contained in them.

The Nag Hamadi scrolls date from 400 AD, but they are copies of much earlier works and contain the earliest known account of the Gospel of St. Thomas. This account of the Gospel includes a passage in which Peter speaks to Mary Magdalene - 'Sister, we know that our saviour loved you more than the rest of other women.' Other references too would seem consistent with Mary Magdalene being the wife of Jesus; which is a belief held by the Christian Gnostics, Cathars, Templars and Masons of today. Funnily enough, the church at Rennes-le-Chateau is also known as the Church of the Magdalene, and Bergener Sauniere also built a tower near to Rennes-Le-Chateau naming it the Tour Magdala. It is strange that such reverence is given to the prostitute, who as described in the Bible tempted Jesus, however it would not have been strange to the Cathars and the Christian Gnostics, who believed she was Jesus' wife. It may not be strange either that the Cathars occupied the part of France, where it has been rumoured, Mary Magdalene eventually settled, with her children and where the legends of the mystical holy grail first emanated.

The Gospel of St. Thomas, contained in the Nag Hamadi scrolls, goes to state categorically that Jesus did not die on the Cross, but was substituted for by someone else :- "it was another Simon, who bore the cross on his shoulder." Again, such beliefs accord with Masonic beliefs that Jesus in some way survived the crucifixion. Their belief is that Jesus was resurrected, but not in the way that it is stated in the Bible. In the Gospel of Matthew, it urges people not to take the resurrection literally - 'Those who say they will die first and then rise are in error, they must receive the resurrection while they live.' [8]

Not only is this the view recanted by esoteric societies, but it also accords with the Gnostic views of a secret tradition existing within the early Christian Church. The reader will remember also that the third degree ceremony in Masonry revolves around the belief of being spiritually (not physically) resurrected to a higher astral plane so that the spirit may be immortalised forever. Masonic teachings endorse that the secret traditions which are hinted at in the Bible are the same as the Templar, neo-Templar and Masonic traditions of today i.e. that the New Testament is actually an esoteric work. Masons also believe that the Bible was not meant to be taken in its literal sense, as Christians believe it, but from an esoteric standpoint; that the stories and parables are of allegorical significance. Some freemasons also refer to their organisation as the 'higher church', obviously implying that they believe they are the closest to the true knowledge of the New Testament and purpose of Jesus' life. The Bible gives insufficient evidence on which to confirm or deny such an assumption, but the Dead Sea Scrolls (now that they have finally been authenticated), do.

The Dead Sea Scrolls were found at Qumran, next to the Dead Sea. They do not contain any of the Gospels, but were written on what has become known as the Qumran or Essene community. Contrary to Father de Vaux's (head of the

8. Knight, C. and Lomas, R., The Hiram Key, p.50

international team given the task of translating and, many believe, suppressing the publication of the scrolls), view that the scrolls were pre-Christian; it is widely accepted by scholars today that they date from the second century BC to 70 AD. Father de Vaux also claimed that the scrolls were of no real significance, as they did not refer or relate in any way to Jesus or the community in which he lived. Subsequent scholars staunchly disagree with this view, and it is now accepted by many people that the claims made by Father de Vaux, regarding the scrolls, were part of an on going conspiracy to suppress the insight that they contained.

There are too many parallels between the Qumran community in the Dead Sea Scrolls, and the way of life described in the New Testament, to be simply ignored. Both communities lived by a certain a code of rules which governed their daily lives. Numerous aspects of these rules were familiar to both societies: sharing amongst themselves, baptism, both adhered to the Law of Moses, both had a leader or Messiah, they both used the Temple as a place of worship, and both were at odds with their Roman occupiers (although this is played down somewhat in the New Testament). The Dead Sea Scrolls state that the council of the Qumran community was made up of twelve men; weren't these the twelve disciples of Jesus? Probably the most striking synergy of all, is the fact that both were imminently expecting a Messiah. Weren't both these communities one and the same? The International team had rebutted this suggestion by pointing to the difference in events which occurred in the two communities. However, might it not be the case that the events which transpired (assuming that the Qumran Scrolls were written about the community in which Jesus lived), contained in the Dead Sea Scrolls, are the true account of what actually occurred, and that the New Testament (as the Masons and other societies endorse), was misinterpreted by Paul who, as the Dead Sea Scrolls may testify, was at odds with the teachings of Jesus and the early Christian church. As mentioned previously, Masonic beliefs maintain that the 'true' meaning of the Bible was never meant to be taken literally, they also believe that the Romans used their interpretation of the Bible for their own ends to sustain their dominance over their established Empire. Masons believe that the New Testament is an esoteric manuscript, which when decoded, refers to an elite group of people (with Jesus as their leader), who were initiates of the Temple.

Biblical accounts tell us that Jesus was crucified upon the cross, and then rose again on the third day. However, the Dead Sea, Nag Hamadi Scrolls and Masonic accounts do not accord with these events. Their accounts endorse that Jesus was captured by the Romans, but did not die by crucifixion at the hands of the Romans. As the Nag Hamadi Scrolls reveal: ". . . since they nailed their man unto their death . . . It was another, their father, who drank the gall and the vinegar; it was not I." [9]

As noted earlier, Masonic thinking alludes to the idea that Paul and Rome orchestrated the interpretation of the New Testament for their own ends. Paul was the only one of the disciples who never personally knew Jesus, and the Bible hints that he was at times, at odds with the Temple's hierarchy. It is strange that the disciple who was the least connected to Jesus, has been relied upon (by clergy throughout the centuries), to form the foundation of the Catholic Church and the basis of its faith. Many believe Paul is also mentioned in the Dead Sea Scrolls, not expressly by name, but simply as- "the liar". If this is indeed correct then the Scrolls tell of him concocting lies about the early Christian church and the teachings of Jesus, to further his own position with Rome, and as retribution because he was never fully accepted into the council of Jesus' faith and society. Beignt and Leigh, who are the definitive authors for articles and books relating to this secret life of Jesus, sum up Paul in unmistakable terms:

> In all vissitudes that follow, it must be emphasised
> that Paul is in effect, the first Christian heretic, and
> that his teachings - which become the foundations

9. Baigent, Leigh and Lincon, The Holy Blood and the Holy Grail, p.403

of later Christianity - are a flagrant deviation from the 'original' or 'pure' form extolled by the leadership. [10]

Evidence that there existed an esoteric faith in ancient times has been endorsed by Hancock and Faiia, who have come to the conclusion that many of the faiths concerned with the worship of idols and sacrifice were deviations from the original beliefs, concerned with spiritual rebirth, held by the ancients. With regard to Masonry, the true state of affairs, for instance how they view religion and how they compare this to the superior beliefs which they pertain to, could be puzzling to the reader. The following extract from the 28th degree of Freemasonry (Knight of the Sun), should enlighten the reader into a greater understanding of these concepts:

> You must shake off the yoke of infant prejudice, concerning the mysteries of the reigning religion, which worship has been imaginary, and only founded on the spirit of pride, which envies to command and be distinguished, and to be at the head of the vulgar; in affecting an exterior purity, which characterises a false piety, joined to a desire of acquiring that which is not its own, and is always the subject of this exterior pride, and unalterable source of many disorders, which being joined to gluttonness, is the daughter of hypocrisy, and employs every matter to satisfy carnal desires, and raises to these predominant passions, altars, upon which she maintains, without ceasing, the light of iniquity, and sacrifices continually offerings to luxury, voluptuousness, hatred, envy, and perjury. Behold, my dear brother, what you must fight against, and destroy, before you can come to the knowledge of the true good and sovereign happiness! Behold this monster which you must conquer - a serpent which we detest as an idol, that is adored by the idiot and vulgar under the name of RELIGION !!!

10. Baigent, M. and Leigh, R., The Dead Sea Scolls Deception, p.266

Cathar, Templar and Masonic traditions are consistent with the belief that Jesus was a mortal man, who gained a following through his teachings, and did not perform the miracles which the New Testament describes. Knight and Lomas point out that there is strong evidence to suggest that the miracles contained in the New Testament are far too convenient to be true. The convenience they draw reference to is the fact that numerous miracles in the New Testament can be accounted for by other miracles that other Gods supposedly performed in other societies, some of which were at that time under Roman Rule. Many believed their particular Gods were born of a virgin. The most prominent cult in the Roman empire (at the time of Jesus), was known as Mithra, which was derived from the ancient cult of Zoroaster. The followers of this cult believed that their saviour was born of a virgin in a stable and was killed and subsequently rose again (similar to the story of Osiris from ancient Egypt). They also believed that their final judgement would determine whether they would go to heaven or hell. They believed in the resurrection, baptism and also a sacramental meal, very similar to the last supper. The Greeks, in Jesus' time, believed in a virgin born God called Dionysus, one of whose miracles was turning water into wine. It can hardly be coincidence that the miracles performed in the New Testament and story of Jesus which it portrays can be accounted for in this way, surely such synergies seriously undermine the authenticity of the Bible, in the context of it being a true account of what actually once occurred; as opposed to the miracles of the Bible being esoteric and of allegorical and metaphorical import.

The evidence which Knight and Lomas have uncovered with regard to the similarities between the New Testament miracles and the miracles contained in various other legends from different cultures is highly important. However, it must be borne in mind that Knight and Lomas are both Freemasons and that while they may bring evidence which undermines the Christian interpretation, that these miracles did actually once occur, they seem reluctant to explain the truer implications behind the evidence they have brought to light in the *Hiram Key*. The reader will already be aware that many believe the New Testament to be an esoteric document, whose miracles contained within it were not meant to be taken literally. But, what was their purpose, and why is it that many of the miracles in the New Testament are also prevalent in the legends of previous cultures? The Freemasons' explanation for this is that the stories and miracles of the New Testament are of allegorical significance, that their true import is esoteric and not literal. They also maintain that these stories and miracles of allegorical significance (contained in the New Testament), had been passed down from more ancient cultures:

> As Sejourne argues, their repressive political system 'was founded on a spiritual inheritance which it betrayed and transformed into a weapon of worldly power.' [11]

Surprisingly, Sejourne is not referring here to the Catholic church, but to the Aztecs which may demonstrate that history does repeat itself.

As aforementioned, esoteric candidates do not need to die physically only spiritually in order to achieve their initiation, and it is this which is the key to unlocking the mysteries of man's esoteric past. This is succinctly explained by John R. Bennet :

> The ritual of Freemasonry preserves, in its central circle, the leading features of the Dionysian institution. Hiram and Dionysus are names representing the illustrating in their history and experience the same ideas. The initiation was a symbolical progress, from the dark, dead and frigid north to the refulgent east - a pilgrimage. The moral teaching of these Mysteries was the same as that of the Mysteries of Osiris. [12]

11. Hancock G., and Faiia, S., Heavens Mirror, p.15
12. Bennet, John, R., Origins of Freemasonry and Knight Templar, p.12

It can be said that adopting, in its infancy, a religious document, such as the New Testament, which included different facets from many of the societies or cultures under Roman rule, served a very important purpose for the Roman Empire's continued existence. Both the Dead Sea and Nag Hamadi Scrolls speak of a revolt occurring against their Roman occupiers. The New Testament, however, portrays Jesus and his people as peaceful and apolitical who did not in any way revolt against the Roman occupation. If the New Testament was a carefully engineered religious document or if it was adopted by them and interpreted to perpetuate Rome's status quo, then the mere mention of the word revolt or any ideas connected with it, would have been kept out of the New Testament.

Another factor which lends itself to the idea of the New Testament's interpretation, by the Catholic Church, being a concoction of Roman propaganda, is the sheer lack of historical accounts relating to the New Testament's story, or for that matter the lack of any surviving historical accounts from that time. From the inception of Rome's adoption of Christianity, into which many believe were fused the cultures and religious cults of the countries under their dominance, many people were compelled into adopting this new Christian faith. Those who refused to adopt this new Christian faith, were persecuted and in many cases, condemned as heretics, and killed in the name of Christ. The Nag Hamadi Scrolls testify to this persecution of other religious freedoms. This suppression of all other non-Christian religions, was accompanied by the extirpation of all historical and religious literature which may have threatened Rome's source of control over its new Christian Empire. Indeed Christian Rome, from its inception, had to firmly stamp the authority of its interpretation on the New Testament and eradicate all dissenting opinions.

Furthermore there is an important point, which cannot be ignored, which adds credence to the above theory - The Book of Enoch. While being of great importance in Masonic tradition and beliefs, this Book along with many others are omitted from the Bible. In fact the Book of Enoch has had more influence on the New Testament than any other apocryphal work. This state of affairs arose in the 4th century when Pope Damasus commissioned the most learned Biblical scholar at the time, a man named Jerome, to prepare a standard Latin version of the Scriptures. These Books he decided to include are what comprises the Old Testament today. But on what authority can some books be included and others not? Are we to accept that the Bible is in its most complete form, by relying on the decision of the Church in the 4th century. Some of the books not included in the Old Testament have been published in what has become known as the Apocrypha, extracts of which are recited in the higher degrees of Freemasonry. It has been suggested that the reason these Books were not included in the Bible are that they are heretical i.e. they do not accord with the Church's version or interpretation of events. Another reason which has been suggested are that these Books : 'contain mysterious or esoteric lore, too profound to be communicated to any except the initiated.' [13] This seems to be further confirmed in the content of the Apocrypha :

> This is the dream that you saw, and this is its interpretation. And you alone were worthy to learn this secret of the Most High. Therefore write all these things that you have seen in a book, and put it in a hidden place; and you shall teach them to the wise among your people, whose hearts you know are able to comprehend and keep these secrets. [14]

> Make public the 24 books (of the Old Testament) that you wrote first and let the worthy and the unworthy read them; but keep the seventy that were written last, in order to give them to the wise among your people. For in them is the spring of

13. The Oxford Annotated Apocrypha 1977, p.xi
14. Apocrypha, Second Book of Esdras 12:35

understanding, and fountain of wisdom, and the
river of knowledge. [15]

It is not deemed necessary to explain the esoteric connota-
tions exemplified by the above extracts. The reader may now
be able to appreciate how such literature would be entirely
inappropriate, with regard to its inclusion in the Bible, and
its incompatibility with traditional Christian beliefs.

If by assuming, in all probability, that the Dead Sea
Scrolls, although written about the Qumran community, were
written about Jesus (referred to in the Scrolls as the:'Teacher
of Righteousness'), then the Qumran community and the community of Jesus described in the New Testament would be
one and the same. The Dead Sea and Nag Hamadi Scrolls
version of Jesus' life are consistent with Cathar, Templar and
Masonic beliefs. Furthermore, too many synergies occur
between references to the Temple in the New Testament, similar to Masonic traditions which also revolve around the
Temple. It would not be foolish, based upon the information
presented, to suggest that Jesus may have been the head of
a Temple hierarchy pertaining to ancient Hebrew and Egyptian
traditions, which are now in all probability being practised by
the Freemasons of today.

But, what of the Gospels? It has been established that
Paul and the Romans had strong motives for changing, amend-
ing or interpreting the Gospels to suit their own ends; but
how did they go about this? Were they rewritten by Paul?
This scenario seems unlikely because the Gospels are so different from one another. If Paul had rewritten them, he would
not have left such inconsistencies in the stories they tell. Paul
may not have needed to change the Gospels much (apart
from adding a bits here and there), he may only have needed to stamp his interpretation on them. Paul never knew Jesus
personally, but his interpretation of the Gospels has been
relied upon to form the basis of the Christian faith. Surely
his interpretation would be the last to be advocated in an
attempt to discover the precise meaning of the Gospels. It

15. Apocrypha, Second Book of Esdras 14:45

may be the case that perceptions have become more powerful than truth, when people begin to accept them as reality. For instance, Paul interprets the resurrection as a physical event, while many of the other Gospels give the impression of it being a purely spiritual phenomenon.

When read as a whole the New Testament displays itself to be full of inconsistencies which have never been properly explained, although many have stamped their various interpretations upon it. Many clergy maintain that different apostles, although witnessing the same events, interpreted them differently. But, under these circumstances, how can the clergy (who never witnessed any of the events in the New Testament) profess to give the correct interpretation of them to their congregation. While searching for an explanation for the Gospels' inconsistencies, it was thought necessary to re-evaluate the Mason's position upon this most controversial of topics.

The Masons are taught that the New Testament has only been changed in so far as people over the centuries have stamped Paul's interpretation upon it. As noted earlier, they believe that Rome and the subsequent Catholic Church have used the cryptic New Testament as a meal ticket to sustain their status quo through the centuries. However, they also believe that the reason for the Gospels' ambiguity is because they are in reality carefully coded, disguising the secret esoteric life of Jesus and his disciples. They believe that the New Testament, when deciphered, gives the true story of Jesus' life and the secret traditions of esotericism. The reasons why, they believe this information has been hidden, is because access to such revelations was meant to be known to those who had or have been initiated into the esoteric kingdom of God; another reason, although of less importance than the first, is that if the Gospels had expressly presented anything which hinted at being esoteric, they would have been immediately destroyed by the Romans and would not have survived the rigours of time; for instance, it was only through being carefully hidden in the caves at Qumran that the Dead Sea Scrolls survived.

Some allusions in the New Testament to Masonic traditions are demonstrated in Mark : 'And have ye not read this scripture; the stone which the builders rejected is become the lead of the corner.' [16] This is almost precisely the same sentence which appears in the Mark Mason degree of freemasonry, demonstrating that even today the Freemasons are still actively applying the esoterism which they believe is contained in the New Testament in their rituals. Masons believe that passages such as, for instance Luke, are a blatant endorsement that esoteric traditions are contained within the New Testament.

> "I assure you that there are some here who will not die until they have seen the Kingdom of God." [17]

If the Kingdom of God is interpreted as the Grand Lodge above, to which Freemasons believe their spirits become resurrected, then the passage makes sense. Masons believe they become resurrected to the grand lodge above, but they do not need to die physically (only spiritually) in order to achieve this. It is in this respect that Masons maintain that Jesus was a Freemason; or put more succinctly, practised esoteric traditions similar to those which the Freemasons practice today. Furthermore the New Testament may also refer to the immortality of the soul, a concept Masons believe is achieved through being raised spiritually in the third degree - 'I tell you the truth, if anyone keeps my word, he will never see death.' [18]

The greatest advocate and exponent of the belief that the New Testament is a carefully coded piece of literature is Barbara Thiering. In her best-seller *Jesus the Man*, she describes the code and its meaning, as well as bringing out an array of evidence suggesting that the Essene community at Qumran was the community in which Jesus and his disciples lived. Thiering, for instance, states that the word kittim in the New Testament means the Romans, and that the 'Word of

16. Mark 12:10
17. Luke 9:27
18. John 8:51

God' is a reference to Jesus. She describes the Community in which Jesus lived as hierarchical, in which the uninitiated are referred to in the New Testament as 'lepers', those in public disgrace as the 'sick, and those who did not follow the way of Jesus were known as the 'blind'. As Lawrence Gardner describes:

> Such information hidden in the New Testament was of considerable relevance when written, and it remains very important today. Methods of disguising the true meanings included allegory, symbolism, metaphor, simile, sectarian definition, and pseudonyms. The meanings were fully apparent, nonetheless, to 'those with ears to hear'. [19]

W. L. Wilmshurst explains that:

> The entire story is symbolical (story of Hiram Abiff) and was purposely invented for the symbolical purposes of our teaching. If you examine it closely you will perceive how obvious the correspondence is between this story and the story of the death of the Christian Master (Jesus) related in the Gospels; and it is needless to say that the Mason who realises the meaning of the latter will comprehend the former and the veiled allusion that is implied. [20]

This methodology of disguising meaning is highly similar, if not the same as the methodology employed by the Templars and the Freemasons, to hide their knowledge from the uninitiated. Only those with ears to hear may have access to its hidden meanings - 'he that hath ears to hear, let him hear.' [21]

A striking synergy between the practice of Freemasonry and the New Testament, is contained in the Gospel of St John.

> 'I am telling you the truth', replied Jesus. 'No one can enter the Kingdom of God unless he is born

19. Gardner, L., Bloodline of the Holy Grail, p.28
20. Wilmshurst, W.L., Meaning of Masonry, p.44
21. Mark 4:9

of water and the spirit. A person is born physically of human parents, but he is born spiritually of
the Spirit. Do not be surprised because I tell you
that you must all be born again. The wind blows
wherever it wishes; you hear the sound it makes,
but you do not know where it comes from or
where it is going. It is like that of everyone who
is born of the Spirit.' [22]

The above quotation can easily be taken both ways. The first,
that 'born again' is simply a figure of speech for the realisation of accepting Jesus as Lord, and turning yourself to God.
However, the second, and possibly more important, is that the
above passage could be interpreted as an account of the
Masons' third degree ritual - spiritual rebirth. The passage continues:-

'As Moses lifted up the bronze snake on a pole in
the desert, in the same way the Son of Man must
be lifted up, so that everyone who believes in him
may have eternal life.' [23]

The reference here to 'eternal life', could be referring to
immortalising the soul through being 'lifted up' or raised by
spiritual rebirth as in Masonry. Such a supposition cannot be
ruled out.

Having made a broad analysis of the validity of Masonic
beliefs concerning Jesus and his disciples, the reader is now
in a position to judge, for himself, whether he or she per-
cieves such beliefs to be ridiculous, unfounded, plausible or
whether they begin to reveal the truth about Jesus' life. The
purpose of this book is not to attempt to sway the reader
into believing one state of affairs or another, but simply to
state the beliefs held by Masonic and other esoteric societies,
and also to demonstrate that they are, in many cases, not
without foundation.

22. John 3:5
23. John 3:14

The following gives a summary of what the Freemasons believe to be the true story of Jesus; a knowledge which they practice and believe and was passed down to them via the Templars. These beliefs are as follows:

• Jesus was born out of wedlock, and this is why his birth is described as a virgin birth.

• Jesus married Mary Magdalene.

• He was the head of a group which practised esoteric traditions and revolved around the Temple.

• The group, although being esoteric, was very exclusive and only a select few were initiated into its higher levels.

• The uninitiated members of Jesus' community also used the Temple, but (although worshipping God), were as much in the dark as the Christians of today, and were not party to the hidden mysteries of the initiated few (similar to the initiated pharaos of Egypt).

• Jesus decided that it was unfair that only so few were given the privilege of being initiated and sought to change the situation, which marked a significant change in esoteric policy i.e. opening up esoteric doctrines to the many, rather than preserving them for a select few.

• Jesus' ambitions caused the displeasure of the Temple hierarchy, and this is the reason why throughout much of the Bible, Jesus was at odds with the Temple hierarchy.

• Jesus did not die upon the cross, but was saved at the last moment , however, the story of him dying and rising again on the third day is an allegory for spiritual rebirth.

• The miracles of the New Testament came from the legends of previous ancient cultures and are in fact allegories of esoteric traditions which have been passed down since Atlantean times.

• The New Testament is a coded esoteric or Masonic document and serves important functions by being so; its esoteric undertones can only be understood by the initiated (or particularly discerning readers who are aware of esoteric beliefs); the uninitiated it has been assumed will not be able to understand its true meaning, and such a cleverly disguised document was designed so, to pass beyond the scrutiny of their Roman occupiers - so much so that the Romans even adopted it for themselves by stamping their interpretation upon it.

• Jesus and Mary Magdalene had children whose bloodline continues to this day (this belief is discussed in the next chapter).

Jesus is an important figurehead in modern Masonry. He was the first to endeavour to open up esoteric mysteries to a much wider group of people. He is described by Masons as the father of Freemasonry, because if it were not for him it is possible that Freemasonry and other esoteric traditions would not have proliferated into the size and scope they are today. If the above beliefs regarding Jesus are true then it makes the arrests, torture and murder of so many Templars, in 1307, particularly ironic; they were persecuted by an organisation who took their authority from a book which their initiated brothers before them had written. This view is succinctly expressed in the 32nd degree of Freemasonry - 'Prince of the Royal Secret':

> It also calls to our rememberance the persecution
> of the Templars, and the situation of Jacques de
> Molay, who lying in irons nearly seven years, at

the end of which our worthy Grand Master was burnt alive with his four companions, on the eleventh of March, 1314, creating pity and tears in the people, who saw him die with firmness and heroic constancy, stealing his innocence with his blood. My brother, in passing to the degree of Perfect Master . . . has not your heart been led to revenge?

The reader must acknowledge that although the Masonic beliefs presented above are highly contentious they do warrant further research into the possibility that such beliefs may have been held by Jesus and his followers? It is not the intention of this publication to prove, one way or the other, which version of Jesus' life is correct (the Church's or the Freemason's), the purpose of this book lies solely with revealing Masonic beliefs and where possible finding evidence to attribute why they may foster such beliefs.

As noted above, in addition to their beliefs about Jesus' life the freemasons also believe that he had children by Mary Magdalene. This bloodline they believe continues to this day, and is discussed in the next chapter.

Chapter Six

The Holy Grail : Chalice or Bloodline?

The Scots descent traces further back through King Lucius of Siluria to Bran the Blessed and Joseph of Arimathea (St James the Just), while the Midi succession stems from the Merovingians' male ancestral line through the Fisher Kings to Jesus and Mary Magdalene. Conjoining the lines from their 1st - century points of departure, the descent is in the succession of the Royal House of Judah. This is a truly unique line of sovereign lineage from King David in one of the key descents which comprise the Bloodline of the Holy Grail." [1].

To understand the nature of the Holy Grail, its concepts and the beliefs connected with it from the Freemasons' perspective, it is necessary to be acquainted with their beliefs concerning Jesus and the Magdalene. Such concepts must be relayed as a continuum rather than a scattered array of

1. Gardner, L., Bloodline of the Holy Grail, p.345

unconnected ideas and beliefs, as is typical of some books dealing with Masonic concepts. It is granted that for those readers with strong Christian beliefs, the previous chapter may have contained concepts difficult to entertain. Both Christian and Masonic opinions would concur that Jesus through his endeavours left a legacy for generations to follow; although they would disagree as to the precise nature and meaning of this legacy. However, there is another legacy which Masons believe, was left by Jesus - a legacy not in written form or ideology, but in blood.

Jesus and the Magdalene

Christianity has always maintained that Jesus was a celibate man, unmarried and untouched by the temptations of mere mortals. Being, as Christianity maintains 'the Son of God', Jesus could not and did not produce any offspring. These assertions have been upheld by the Catholic church since its inception, heralding, as esotericists believe, the transition of the Roman Empire into the Byzantine. But, what if the Church is wrong? What if Jesus did have children? And what if any would be the significance of such a bloodline if it had survived through the centuries to the present day?

The birth of Jesus was a highly significant event. Firstly, and as the reader will become aware, because of the astrology - the stars heralding an important birth - and secondly because Jesus was directly descended from the Royal House of Judah - a descendant of King David. Although nearly all records of the Messianic legacy or kingship of Jesus were, Masons believe, systematically destroyed by the Romans, some survived namely the Dead Sea and Nag Hammadi scrolls. Masonic tradition also maintains that this concept of Messianic kingship is contained in the Gospels in coded form. However, the birth of Jesus was also prophesied in the Book of Esdras.

As was explained in the previous chapter, the Old Testament contains only those Books which the Church deemed prudent to include within it. However, the importance of these omitted works cannot be underestimated:

> And as for the lion whom you saw rousing up out of the forest and roaring and speaking to the eagle and reproving him for his unrighteousness and as for all his words that you have heard, this is the Messiah whom the Most High has kept until the end of days, who will arise from the posterity of David, and will come and speak to them . . . This is the dream you saw, and this is its interpretation. And you alone were worthy to learn this secret of the Most High. [2]

The Masonic teachings and beliefs relating to Jesus' life are that, although he was born out of wedlock (virgin birth), he had a kingly divine right to rule as a descendant of the Royal House of Judah. They also believe that he was married to Mary Magdalene and that she had three children by him, a bloodline which continues to this day. However, there are no references or hints to Jesus or the Magdalene having any children. Some esotericists believe that the Magdalene was three months pregnant with their first child when Jesus was crucified, and that by cunning deception he survived the crucifixion. The Bible recounts his coming back to life thus: 'and on the third day he rose again', which Masons believe should in this instance be taken literally as evidence that Jesus did not die on the cross. In defying death, he and the Magdalene reunited and conceived two more children after their first-born. It has been rumoured that these children were brought up in southern Gaul, the area were Sauniere found the parchments, and where the Cathars and Templars originated, and the Messianic bloodline (a closely guarded secret by those who knew) continued free from the attentions of the emerging Holy Roman Empire.

2. Apocrypha Second Book of Esdras 12:31

The Holy Grail

The elusive Holy Grail has sparked the imagination of millions for centuries. Numerous theories exist concerning whether or not the Grail existed and, if it exists today, where it might be. Beignt, Leigh and Lincon believe that the Holy Grail is purely a symbol for the bloodline of Christ, and that it does not exist in reality. Some startling revelations can be made by examining the Holy Grail (whatever it may be) and the concepts which emanate from it, against the backdrop of Masonic beliefs.

There is no firm agreement upon what the Grail (assuming it is a tangible object) was actually used for. The Grail is invariably depicted as a chalice, but was it the chalice from which Jesus and his disciples drank the wine at the last supper, or the chalice which collected the blood of Jesus at his crucifixion, or both? Its precise use has never been accurately ascertained; however, whichever belief a person adopts their symbolisms are quite poignant. If the Grail is the chalice from which Jesus drank the wine at the last supper, then this connection with wine, which is made from grapes connects the chalice with the grape vine - which symbolises lineage. Probably of greater symbolic importance is the Grail being considered as the chalice which collected the blood of Jesus during the crucifixion. By collecting the blood of Jesus it symbolises that which holds the blood of Christ - the bloodline of Christ. Masons are taught that the Grail was brought by Mary Magdalene to southern France, although many believe that the Grail was brought to Britain from the Holy Land by Joseph of Arimathea. Whatever the true state of affairs may be, Masons will not reveal to members of the public what the Grail actually is. Is it a chalice which once existed and still exists today, or a symbol of the bloodline of Christ, and never was a tangible object as some believe?

The Grail Symbolism

To attempt to establish what the Grail actually is, it is necessary to begin in medieval times when the Grail legends
such as those of Perceval and King Arthur, first started to
circulate.

The Grail Legends

The Arthurian Grail Legends are considered by most to be
unrealistic myths as opposed to true accounts of the life of
King Arthur. However, these legends were never meant to be
taken literally, but are esoterically coded in a language which
is devised in such a way that it may only be deciphered
and understood by esotericists. As the reader will recall, the
same is true of the Greek myths, Egyptian myths and many
others which have been passed down through antiquity. Those
outside the membership of esoteric organisations in existence
today cannot effectively relate to such myths, but to esotericists they are reminders of stories and events ingrained into
their esoteric beliefs, which hold the concepts upon which
their beliefs are founded. It is beyond the parameters of this
book to decipher all the hidden meanings within the Grail
legends, but those relevant to what lies behind the meaning
of the Grail are examined.
    One striking feature of the Grail legends are the prin-
ciples which they contain. These are moralistic principles
which emanate from the chivalry of the knights described.
These principles of knights helping each other, standing by
one another, and maintaining a strong sense of justice are
found in Masonry (known as Brotherhood). These elements
of chivalry and aiding fellow knights is known within Masonry
as the 'Grail Code', and their incorporation into Masonic ideology, such as their approach to charity and strong sense of
brotherhood is no coincidence. There is also another synergy
which can be made, connecting these legends with modern

day Freemasonry; as Pickett and Prince explain:

> In all stories, however, the quest for the Grail is an allegory of the hero's spiritual journey towards - and beyond - personal transformation. And as we have seen, one of the major motives of all serious alchemy was precisely that. [3]

Although there are numerous indications in the Grail legends connecting them with the notion of a spiritual quest which will equip the initiate for the afterlife, the principle of knighthood also exhibits another meaning. Examples of which are prevalent in *Parzival* (a story about a Grail knight by Wolfram von Eschenbach), as shown below:

> She ordered them all upon their life that they would never utter a sound about knights. 'If the love of my heart were to know what the life of a knight is, that would be great hardship to me. Now keep your wits about you and avoid all mention of knighthood.' [4]

In this context the meaning being applied to knighthood was something supposed to be kept secret. However its meaning is revealed when Perceval asks for directions into his uncles domain:

> 'You must direct me farther' (Fisherman answers Parzival) 'I shall take great care not to. The household is of such lineage that it would be a very great wrong if a lowborn man would ever come near them.' [5]

This concept of some special bloodline or kinship is further emphasised in King Arthur's legends:

3. Picknett, L. and Prince, C., The Templar Revelation, p.120
4. Eschenbach, W., Parzival, p.28
5. Ibid p.36

'Nay, my Lord Arthur . . . we are of no blood- kinship with thee, and little though I thought how high
thy kin might be, yet wast thou never more than
foster-child of mine.' [6]

This concept of some sort of supreme birthright is further
echoed in the degrees of Masonry:

You are to endeavour by every just means to regain
our rights, and to remember that we are joined by
a society of men, whose courage, merit, and good
conduct, hold out to us that rank that birth alone
gave to our ancestors. [7]

Thus you learn, my Most Illustrious brother how,
and by whom, Masonry has been transmitted to us.
You ought to see what it is, to enter to our lawful rights, which leads us to associate with men to
whom merit, bravery, and good manners, give titles,
which only birthright grants to the ancestors of the
Templars. [8]

In the 25th degree - 'Prince of Mercy', there appears a blatant reference to the 'blood of Jesus' :

Question : Are you a Prince of Mercy?
Answer : I have seen the great light, (Delta,) and
our Most Excellent, as well as yourself, in the 'Triple
Alliance' of the 'BLOOD OF JESUS CHRIST,' of
which you and I have the mark.

The passages from the Grail legends certainly point to a hidden lineage, a concept further endorsed in the degrees of
Freemasonry. Such a lineage kept secret, as it may have been
in jeopardy if it was ever disclosed to the wrong people.
However, it is to the Grail which we must turn if we wish
to discover further the implications of such a bloodline.

6. Knowles, J., The Legends of King Arthur and his Knights, p.17
7. Prince of the Royal Secret degree (32nd degree of Masonry)
8. Knight of Kadosh degree (30th degree of Masonry)

References to the Grail are few and far between even in the Grail legends, although it is spoken of quite blatantly in the Legends of King Arthur:

> . . . for in this castle and that chamber which thou didst defile was the blood of our lord Christ! and also the most holy cup - the Sangreal - of our Lord. Joseph of Arimathea brought it to this land, when first he came here to convert and save it. [9]

Here the Grail is referred to as a tangible object, although Merlin goes on to say:

> '. . . and by the loss and parting of the Sangreal the safety of this realm is put in peril, and its great happiness is gone for evermore.' [10]

It seems strange how the loss of a chalice could put the realm in danger, unless the grail he is referring to here is the secret of a special bloodline.

It is also important to note that Sangreal or San Greal means Holy Grail, but it may also stand for Sang Real which means Royal Blood.[11] This is further emphasised in King Arthur's Legends :

> 'I marvel . . . that ye thus chide so noble a knight, for truly I know none to match him; and be sure, that whatsoever he appeareth now, he will prove, at the end, of noble blood and royal lineage.' [12]

To Freemasons, the Holy Grail or Sangreal does symbolise a royal bloodline and hidden lineage which they believe is the descent from Jesus himself . Furthermore, within the 'Supreme Grand Chapter Regulations' special privileges are given to those referred to as a 'Prince of the Royal Blood':

9. Knowles, J., The Legends of King Arthur and his Knights, p.71
10. Ibid p.72
11. Gardner, L., Bloodline of the Holy Grail, p.3
12. Knowles, J., The Legends of King Arthur and his Knights, p.157

Should a Prince of the Blood Royal honour any private Lodge by accepting the office of Master, he
may appoint a Deputy Master . . . who shall be
regularly installed, and be entitled, when in office,
to all the privileges of Master, and, after he has
served his period of office, to those of Past Master.[13]

It is also stated in the Regulations that no brother shall continue master for more than two years, without the consent
of the Grand Master, however, article 115 states that:

This regulation shall not apply to a 'Prince of the
Blood Royal' who appoints a Deputy, but it shall
apply to the Deputy. [14]

This curious exemption from the regulations for a Prince of
the Blood Royal, could be indicative of Freemasons' reverence
to this special bloodline. Moreover the thirty third degree in
a branch of masonry known as 'Craft Masonry', is only accessible to royalty - the average mason not descended from royalty is excluded from performing this degree. The synergies
seem to be indicating significant connections between the Holy
Grail, a special bloodline, royalty and of course the
Freemasons.
     So, if the Grail is taken as a symbol of the bloodline
of Christ, and if Mary Magdalene and her children did indeed
travel to southern France, which is widely rumoured amongst
esotericists, then it can be said that the Magdalene brought
the Grail to France. But, what was or is the Grail, a tangible object passed down through the centuries, or a secret
bloodline from Jesus himself? Most people believe the Holy
Grail to be a chalice, however the Grail has also been
described in another form.

13. Grand Lodge, Uninted Grand lodge of England Constitutions article 72, p, 110
14. Ibid p.74

The Grail Stone

The Grail has also been referred to as a stone in Perceval, with immense power which can overcome the ageing process:

> It is well known to me that many a warlike knight lives at Munsalvaesche with the Grail. For the sake of adventure they always go on many travels, these same Templars, whether they are looking for care or praise: they endure it for their sins. There dwells a warlike host, I shall tell you about their food. They live off a stone. Its nature is very pure. If you have not recognised it, it will be named for you here: it is called lapsit exilis. Through that stone's power the phoenix burns up so that it turns to ashes, but those ashes bring life to it. Therefore the phoenix throws off its molt and gives off a very bright glow afterwards, so that it becomes more beautiful than before. Also, never did such illness overcome a man that if he sees that stone one day he cannot die during the week that comes soonest after it. Also, his colour never deteriorates. they must admit that his skin is of the same colour as when he saw the stone, man or woman, as if his or her best years had just begun. And if he were to see the stone for two hundred years, nothing would change, except that his hair might turn grey. Such power does the stone give to man that his flesh and bone receive youth without delay the stone is also called the grail. [15]

Although the above passage points to the Grail as being that which can give eternal life, Masons believe that this is simply a metaphor for immortalising the spirit through spiritual resurrection According to Gardner, author of *Bloodline of the Holy Grail*, this concept of the Grail being considered as that which can give life is also prevalent in the Welsh legend of

15. Eschenbach, W., Parzival p.124

Bran, in which his dead soldiers were brought back to life through being placed in a mystical cauldron. It must be considered a possibility that the stone referred to above may be a reference to the 'Stone of Scone', which is supposedly a sacred stone brought from ancient Israel. Also known as the 'Stone of Destiny', it was until recently kept under the coronation chair at Westminster Abbey. The location of the stone may be highly significant when the reader considers the Masons' belief about the link between the British Royal Family and the Grail.

The Holy Grail Chalice

As aforementioned, it is a widely held belief that Joseph of Arimathea brought the Grail from the Holy Land to Britain in about 73 AD. It is believed that he brought the Grail to Glastonbury and that since then it has been passed on by successive generations of his descendants, also known as Grail families, who have kept its whereabouts secret amongst themselves for centuries.

History tells us that the Templars were the guardians of the Grail. Taking into account the Templars' extensive resources and their reputation for seeking out knowledge, it is fair to assume that the whereabouts of such a chalice, so central to their beliefs, would possibly have been known to them. The Templars were also present in Britain, so they may well have guarded the Holy chalice, however, were they also guardians of the Grail in a different way? Within the order of Templar hierarchy, the highest ranks were conferred on those referred to as from Grail families i.e. those who were descended from Jesus and Joseph of Arimathea. In this way it can be said that the Templars were guardians of the Grail (as a symbol of the bloodline), by the inclusion of these descendants into their order. By being Templars, these people could be made to realise their birthright, and take action where necessary to preserve and continue this supposed bloodline of Christ.

Having explained the symbolism of the Grail, what of its existence as a chalice? Legend has it that Joseph of Arimathea brought the Grail to Glastonbury, and that it was there, upon Glastonbury Tor, that he stuck his staff into the soil, from which grew a Holy Thorn tree. In fact there is a thorn tree that stands alone on Glastonbury Tor today, of a species not native to Britain, but from a much warmer climate. Furthermore many believe that Joseph of Arimathea's remains are buried at Glastonbury Abbey, and some think this to be the whereabouts of the Grail chalice also. Although this theory warrants consideration, in recent years another theory has emerged.

Beignt and Leigh, and Lincon in their book *The Holy Blood and the Holy Grail,* draw attention to the fact that the Grail legends first began circulating in the 12 years between the discovery of the treasures of the Holy Land (by the Templars in 1128), and the removal of these treasures to Kilwinning - seat of the St Clair family in 1140. Knight and Lomas go further, maintaining that included amongst these treasures was the revered Holy Grail. They believe that there is a strong possibility that the Grail and other Templar treasures are now buried under the foundations of Rosslyn Chapel (as shown in figure 14 previously). This chapel, built in 1440 by Sir William St Clair, was built on the proportions of Solomon's Temple, although on a reduced scale. It is under the floor of this chapel that they believe the treasure lies. It is strange that Knight and Lomas hold such beliefs being, as they are, Freemasons. Masons are instructed that the Grail is located at Westminster Abbey. Placing the Grail in Westminster Abbey would seem to make a lot of sense. Firstly, judging by the Templars' and Freemasons' beliefs and attitudes concerning the basis of the Christian church, it is natural that they would not want to keep it on consecrated ground - Westminster Abbey is not consecrated. This would also seem to follow a pattern, as the supposed resting place of Joseph of Arimathea is Glastonbury Abbey, which is also not consecrated. Safety would also be another consideration as the

Church would dearly like to acquire such an item so close to their faith. But, what better hiding place than under the auspices of the Church itself. Many would look upon the location of such a hiding place as futile, but the concept behind this may be very clever, as it would be the last place the Church would look if it was searching for the Grail. The Abbey was originally converted from a Benedictine monastery in 1050-65, and was subsequently rebuilt from the 13th to 15th centuries - around the time of the Templars. Since William I up until 1760, it has served as the coronation church for most monarchs and most of these are buried within its walls, as well as many distinguished citizens which have risen to prominence throughout British history. It is the Masons' belief that one of the purest forms of the grail lineage is within the British Royal Family. If one is to accept this belief that the successive Royal families of Britain have each, to varying degrees, preserved amongst themselves a very pure bloodline from Jesus, then is it not fitting that many of these monarchs were crowned and eventually buried in the place which housed the ultimate symbol of their lineage - the Holy Grail. The true Templars in existence today, as opposed to Freemasons offered the title through the completion of certain degrees, are invariably from Grail descent and maintain absolute secrecy about their membership to the outside world. In fact one of the Templars forms of spoken recognition is: "In Arcadia habito" (in Arcadia I dwell) to which another Templar should respond "Flumen sacrum bene cognosco" (I recognize the sacred stream). It will not be difficult for the reader, after reading this chapter, to conceptualze the metaphoric meaning behind the 'stream'.

The Lineage

The importance of the lineage of Jesus to the Templars and Freemasons has been discussed, but if the lineage of Jesus is so special, what is its significance and appeal over other lineages? To answer this question it is necessary to go back further than Jesus and to consider his ancestors.

As previously mentioned, Jesus' ancestors date back into deepest antiquity. The Bible states that Jesus was descended from David on Joseph's side, and Aaron on Mary's side, which would have made him the Messiah for both lines of descent. However, the birth of Jesus does herald something more to Masons and esotericists alike. They believe in his kingly birth, i.e. king by divine right, but they also believe that the birth coincided with a great cosmic event and that it was foretold in the stars. The astrology at the time of Jesus' birth is explained in chapter eight, however a more detailed explanation can be found in Adrian Gilbert's *The Magi*.

Added to this idea - that the birth of Jesus and a kingly Messiah was foretold in the stars - the Masons further believe that his birth was imminent upon the change of constellation appearing over the horizon and moving into the ecliptic path of the sun. In Jesus' time this would have been a change from Aries to the constellation Pisces. A change in constellation appearing over the horizon occurs every 2000 years approximately, and is the result of the earth wobbling upon its axis, a process already discussed - precession. This concept, that a kingly messiah will be born when a new constellation appears over the horizon (about every 2000 years), is very difficult for anyone to accept; it is contrary to our perceptions and reasoning of the effects our universe has upon our lives. Furthermore it is more difficult to fathom that in conjunction with the above conditions, this Messiah will be born of a particular bloodline and descent.

Interestingly, the constellation Pisces is going to be superseded by Aquarius soon after the year 2000. Some esotericists believe that this change will bring with it a new Messiah, and this, they maintain, is confirmed in the Book of Revelation. Even Isaac Newton, who one would assume to be more logical and rational than the average person, believed in the second coming of Christ and the Day of Judgement referred to in the Book of Revelation. He estimated that the Day of Judgement and the New Messiah would come in the year 1948, however as time has shown he was obviously incorrect, but the point is that this man of science and logic believed in the second coming; although it must also borne in mind that he was a Grand Master.

The Day of Judgement and the coming of the second Messiah mentioned in Revelation, talks of the time when God will deal out justice upon the world. Many religious churches and groups now play upon this idea, in order to incite more members into the church. Some advertise that you can be saved by turning towards the church; saved from the Day of Judgement when God will pass judgement upon his flock. Contrary to these beliefs, esotericists maintain that when the Day of Judgement comes, the judgement and wrath of God will be upon the Catholic Church. The institution which they believe has corrupted the story of Christ to its own ends, and has for far too long, perpetuated a deception through the hearts and minds of innocent individuals, at the expense of the truth about Jesus' life.

Further evidence of this secret bloodline of Jesus has also been uncovered in relation to Sauniere and the Rennes-le-Chateau enigma. However before considering this there is another connection between what has been uncovered in Rennes-le-Chateau spanning from ancient times through to modern day occultism and Freemasonry. The main exponent of the mysteries emanating from the Rennes le Chateau village and surrounding region is Henry Lincon. It is interesting that he noticed that Poussin's Shepherds of Arcadia (mentioned cryptically in another parchment found by Sauniere, and supposedly depicting a nearby tomb) exhibited certain geometrical qualities. He engaged the services of Professor Christopher Cornford of the Royal College of Art to test his theory. As mentioned in chapter two, Cornford did find that the painting displayed pentagonal geometry cleverly hidden in its dimensions. The pentagonal dimensions of the Poussin painting are demonstrated in figure 1, as are the angles emanating from the pentogram on page fifty seven. Lincon also noticed that the staff in the painting is also carefully positioned at an angle of seventy-two degrees, an angle prevalent in pentagonal geometry. The reader may recall from chapter three that the Templar rule consisted of seventy-two articles. This number also curiously appears in the General Regulations of Royal Arch Masons:

> 48. According to ancient custom a complete Chapter of this Order of Freemasonry consists of the Three Principals who, when in Chapter assembled are to be considered conjointly as the Master, and each severally as a Master, two Scribes, a Treasurer, a Principal Sojourner, two Assistant Sojourners, and other companions, making up the number of 72 as a Council; and no regular Chapter can consist of more; but any number may be elected, exalted and received as Companions with all the privileges of membership save that they are not to hold the staff of office or to be considered as Councillors when more than seventy-two are present.

So, no more than seventy-two can be considered as the 'staff of office', this term obviously referring to the authority that Royal Arch Masons hold when seventy-two or less are present. A further curiosity is the staff in Poussin's Shepherds of Arcadia held at an angle of seventy two degrees; without drawing the inference that the word staff was purposefully incorporated into the above Royal Arch Regulation, the staff (as depicted in Poussin's Shepherd's of Arcadia) has through the centuries been considered as the symbol of authority. Even if such a connection cannot be reasonably entertained, the emphasis on the number seventy-two can hardly be ignored.

As previously described in chapter two, Hancock and Faiia found an array of longitudinal angles in the positioning of ancient sites around the world; these angles being 18, 36, 54, 72, 108 and 144. I challenge any reader to find an angle inside the pentagram ((p.57) apart from 90 degrees) which is not accounted for in the angles Hancock and Faiia have discovered. Then for the reader to ask him or herself how such correlations with the longitudinal angles (between sites of the ancient world) and the angles contained inside a pentagram could possibly be merely coincidental. It was expounded previously that by adding the digits of each angle inside a pentagram always produces the number 9. In fact Maurice Cotterell in *The Tutankhamun Prophecies* poses a very prudent question 'Why do they (the Freemasons) worship the number 9, the hexagon, the pentagon and the sun?' [16] Are we indeed witnessing proof which validates Masonry's claim, that inherent in Masonry are the remnants of an ancient legacy propagated over thousands of years capable of explaining the enigmas which exist in the ancient world?

The pentagram usually associated with the dark side of occult practices has always been an ancient mystical symbol. Lincon has also found pentagonal positioning between the villages of Rennes-le-Chateau, Blanchefort and Bezu, as well as supposed pentagonal and hexagonal relationships between the alignments of places around the Rennes-le-Chateau region.[17] Are all these angles emanating from pentagonal geometry, spanning through different epochs in time, the fingerprints of mans esoteric past? While considering the merits of such synergies all relating to the geometry of the pentagon, it would be prudent for the reader to consider the symbolism used in masonry to denote the position of Deputy Grand Master as shown below:

16. Cotterell, M., The Tutankhamun Prophecies, P.189
17. Lincon, H., Key to the Sacred Pattern, P. 133

In addition to the links found between the parchments supposedly found by Sauniere in Rennes-le-Chateau, they also testify to the possible existence of a bloodline from Dagobert II. It was Henry Lincon who first noticed that in one of the parchments (which was in fact an extract from the Gospel of St John) some of the letters were slightly raised above the rest. These letters, when arranged together, spelt out in French:

This treasure belongs to Dagobert II king and to Sion and he is there dead. [18]

According to Lawrence Gardner, Dagobert II was a direct descendant of the bloodline of Jesus.[19] His father, Dagobert I was murdered by assassins while hunting at Stenay - an act which was subsequently endorsed by the Church. Rumours circulated that the assassins had also murdered king Dagobert's kin but the burden of evidence is strongly in favour of the view that Dagobert II escaped. In all probability, the treasure referred to in Sauniere's parchment was Dagobert II's and Sion's legacy - the bloodline of Jesus, the Magdalene, and the Royal House of Judah.

In retrospect such a kinship would have had to remain secret, as the bloodline would have been a danger to other monarchs, if their descent were ever proved. If it is assumed that the Freemasons are correct in their beliefs relating to Jesus and his lineage, then such a knowledge if ever substantiated would be disasterous to the Church and the whole Christian faith. Imagine for instance the consequences of the public at large adopting the belief that the Church had attempted (on more than one occasion in the past), to exterminate this royal lineage and had used its own interpretation of the story of Jesus on which to build the foundations of the Catholic Church; such a scenario would make the Church's position untenable and would totally undermine the authenticity of the Christian faith. But assuming for a moment that these beliefs were true; wouldn't this explain why the

18. Lincon, H., Key to the Sacred Pattern, p.11
19. Gardner, L., Bloodline of the Holy Grail, p.222

Church and Rome have so feverently denounced all hints of heresy throughout the ages. If the foundations of the Church are firm, then why have they applied such strong measures, in the past, totally out of proportion and out of touch with the context of their faith. Put another way, it can be said that the Catholic Church has consistently and blatantly violated one of the ten commandments given by God to Moses which they profess to uphold : 'Thou shall not kill'. However, the Church is not the only institution over the centuries, which has abused its power by acting contrary to its principles. There is another story connected with the Grail which, although dating to over a century ago, keeps coming back to haunt people's perceptions of safely walking the streets at night - the unsolved Ripper murders.

Jack the Ripper

Many would argue that the identity of Jack the Ripper, and the circumstances surrounding his murders is one of the greatest crime enigmas in history. In 1976, Stephen Knight (famous for his book *The Brotherhood*), published *Jack the Ripper: The Final Solution* in which he relayed a story told to him by the son of Walter Sichert a famous painter. Walter Sichert's son claimed that his father together with Sir William Gall (at the time the Queen's Physician), conspired and carried out the Ripper murders. On its own the story would have simply been added to the numerous theories which exist, laying claim to the identity of Jack the Ripper. However, Knight's story also claims that these two men did not act alone, but were aided by a very powerful and influential organisation - the Freemasons. This theory that there was some Masonic involvement in the Ripper murders, although popular amongst the few, has never been seriously accepted, by the public at large, as a viable explanation to the Ripper enigma.

But when this story is considered in light of the issues previously discussed in this chapter, and in conjunction with Masonic beliefs, it overcomes much of the scrutiny that the above story alone is unable to withstand.

Within Masonry the story that there was Masonic involvement in the murders is relayed amongst Freemasons as authentic. But, they are not taught this theory (which many Masons believe to be true) in the context of Jack the Ripper's identity as a Freemason, or how he eluded capture. To many Freemasons such issues are incidental, the important issue to them involves the Grail, the hidden lineage, the bloodline of Christ and the preservation of this bloodline within the Royal Family.

The Masons believe that, while engaging the services of prostitutes, Albert, Prince of Wales at that time (1888), had made one of them pregnant. Considering the Masons' belief that the bloodline of Christ and the Royal House of Judah runs into the royal families of Europe and in particular the British royal family, such a state of affairs would have had disastrous consequences. The descendant of Jesus, the kingly blood, was now in the womb of a prostitute. Masonic beliefs endorse that a decision was made to find the prostitute and the unborn child and destroy them both before she could give birth. If it is assumed that the Freemasons did have a hand in the elimination of this prostitute and her Royal unborn, then in order to have mustered Masonic commitment to this end, the decision that the prostitute must die must have come from the senior ranks of the Masonic order. Even today the case facts still emanate numerous enigmas which it must be said are not typical of crimes committed by an individual acting alone.

What remains baffling to this day is how a man was able to brutally murder prostitutes, almost at will, and vanish as quickly as he appeared. How could a man bloodied by his butchery make his way through the streets of London, in the middle of the night, and not be seen by anyone? By adopting the theory that the Freemasons were involved in the Ripper murders, many of the enigmas which surround the case facts can be explained.

The Murders: brutal or precise?

All the Ripper victims were cut open around the abdominal area, and it was said that the incisions were made with 'surgical precision', implying that whoever the Ripper was, he had had some previous knowledge of surgery. This precision together with an eyewitness seeing a carriage bearing the royal crest raises questions of royal involvement and places suspicion upon Sir William Gall (the royal physician). However, possibly of more importance than this is the area of the victims' injuries - with each victim the abdomen was consistently a target for the Ripper. This fact fits perfectly into the Masons' belief, as it can be inferred that Jack the Ripper may have been searching for a foetus - possibly the unborn child of Prince Albert.

After the murder of Catherine Eddows, the Ripper wrote a message in chalk on the wall. As Stephen Knight explains:

> The message itself, according to a careful copy made by a conscientious PC who was at the scene early - which had been concealed in the Scotland Yard files on the case for nearly ninety years before I gained access to them - read: 'The Juwes are The Men That will not be blamed for nothing . . .' [20]

It has been suggested by criminologists that the Ripper meant to spell Jews, or that the Ripper misspelt his own name-James (James Madrick was a suspect in the case). But if he meant to write his own name, then such a sentence would not make much sense. No such word as Juwes exists in the Oxford English Dictionary, and this word has baffled nearly everyone except, as Masons believe, themselves. However, the word exists, and has meaning to Freemasons. The reader may recall that Juwes refers to the three most hated villains in Masonic tradition: Jubela, Jebelo and Jebelum which are prominent in the third degree ritual. This subtle clue, if it

20. Knight, S., The Brotherhood, p.54

was intended as such, would only have been discernible amongst Freemasons. In fact the way in which the Ripper victims were mutilated endorses that reference is being made to Juwes; as the way in which the three Juwes were supposed to have died, resembles the way in which the Ripper victims died, which seems more than merely coincidental. The manner in which the victims died and were mutilated is explained below:

Friday 31st August 1888 - Mary Ann Nickols : throat cut by two gashes, then two large incisions made from the abdomen - one across the groin, the other leading from the abdomen straight up to the chest.

Saturday 8th September 1888 - Annie Chapman : throat cut, abdomen sliced open, intestines severed from their mesenteric attachments and subsequently lifted out and placed over the left shoulder of the victim.

Sunday 30th September 1888 - Elisabeth Stride : throat cut - when the body was found it was still warm indicating that the Ripper was probably disturbed and made a quick get-away.

The bodies of Elisabeth Stride and Catherine Eddows were discovered within half an hour or each other - indicating that the Ripper must have struck again immediately after killing Elisabeth Stride.

Sunday 30th September 1888 - Catherine Eddows : throat cut, body ripped open from chest to abdomen, intestines ripped out and found lying over left shoulder of victim. Missing from Catherine Eddows body were her uterus and left kidney.

Friday 9th November 1888 - Mary Jane Kelly : throat cut, stripped of much of her flesh, abdomen slashed across and downwards, also uterus and other organs removed from the scene of the murder.

As the reader may recall from chapter four, the ways in which the victims died is similar to the ways the three Juwes died in Masonic tradition, as demonstrated through the secret signs a Mason has to show, in the first and third degree stages, before entering the Temple. The ways in which the Juwes died is further clarified as they are incorporated into the oaths of the first three degrees in the types of punishments a candidate invites upon himself, should he inadvertently reveal any Masonic secrets. The first degree candidate swears " . . . under no less a penalty than having my throat cut across . . .", all five of the Ripper victims had their throats cut. The second degree candidate swears " . . . under no less penalty than to have my left breast torn open and my heart and vitals taken from thence and thrown over my left shoulder . . ." In the mutilations of Annie Chapman and Catherine Eddows, their intestines were torn out and laid over their left shoulders. In the third degree the candidate invites upon himself "binding myself under no less a penalty than to have my body severed in twain and divided to the north and south . . ." Apart from Elisabeth Stride, the four other Ripper victims had had their abdomens torn open, this cannot be construed as an attempt to "sever the bodies in twain", but it may demonstrate that the Ripper was searching for something, and murdering in the same way as those which were murdered in Masonic tradition. The facts of the Ripper mutilations and the oaths of Masonic tradition have been presented to the reader in an unbiased way, and it is for him or her to draw conclusions as to the significance of the synergies which exist between the Masonic oaths and the types of mutilations.

In the cases of Cathrine Eddows and Mary Kelly, both uteri were removed. This fact adds further weight to Masonic claims that the Ripper was looking for a foetus. If this was his intention then it would be anticipated that he would

remove the uterus, and all evidence of a foetus ever existing. It may be argued also that the mutilations, if it is accepted that they were done in accordance with the Masonic oaths,
were performed to disguise his real intentions; fostering the
belief, amongst his pursuers, that he was a crazed brutal and
savage man, rather than one who may have calculated each
move very carefully.

The public outrage at the Ripper murders prompted a
demand for swift action in apprehending the Ripper, but he
was never caught. On the 31st of December (New Years Eve),
Montague Druitt was found floating in the Thames; another
suspect James Madrick died soon afterwards of arsenic poi-
soning for which his wife was hung while vehemently protest-
ing her innocence. These deaths may be construed as convenient. The deaths of these suspects have, to some extent,
given added assurance that the enigma of Jack the Rippers
identity would remain a mystery. If the motive behind the
Ripper murders was to preserve the Royal bloodline, and that
the Masons were the instigators of such a brutal plot, then
these deaths would have come as a blessing to those
involved; as they served to perpetuate the enigma of the
seemingly motiveless Jack the Ripper. The nature of the deaths
of these two suspects means that it cannot be said for certain whether they were killed or whether they died through
their own actions. Whether one believes that they were killed
as deaths of convenience, or their deaths were by misadven-
ture, will remain a matter of opinion. Although what is clear
are the beliefs held by Freemasons regarding the Ripper case
and the motives behind it; whilst the reader may also bear
in mind that the case of Jack the Ripper fits in well, almost
too well, to the Masonic version of events.

On 1st September 1908 came another twist to the Ripper
enigma, Sir Robert Anderson (at one time head of CID), was
interviewed by the Daily Chronicle, his admissions brought
great pressure to bear on the way the police handled the
case:

In two cases of that series there were distinct clues destroyed - wiped out absolutely - clues that might very easily have secured for us proof of the identity of the assassin. In one case it was a clay pipe. Before we could get to the scene of the murder the doctor had taken it up, thrown it into the fireplace and smashed it beyond recognition. In another case there was writing in chalk on the wall - a most valuable clue; handwriting that might have been recognised at once as belonging to a certain individual, but before we could secure a copy, or get it protected, it had been obliterated . . .

Stephen Knight was unequivocal in his opinion as to where the blame should lie:

The man actively responsible for concealing the truth behind the Ripper murders was Sir Charles Warren, Commissioner of the Metropolitan Police and one of the country's most eminent Freemasons. Warren impeded investigation of the murders at every turn, caused endless confusion and delays, and personally destroyed the only clue the Ripper ever left.[21] (This was the message in chalk perviously discussed)

The above extracts add further suspicion to the involvement of Freemasons in these brutal murders. If the Ripper murders were part of a Masonic conspiracy (as Stephen Knight concluded), then it is highly likely that they would have had Masons involved and working on the Ripper case, like Sir Charles Warren. If the above facts regarding the disappearance of evidence were attributed to the involvement of Freemasons, then wouldn't it explain why he was never caught. Whatever one may believe about the identity of Jack the Ripper, at the very least, it must be acknowledged that from the facts presented here and the synergies made with Masonic tradition,

21. Knight, S., The Brotherhood, p.53

the association between the Ripper murders and Masonic involvement becomes a real possibility.

The influence of the Grail this Century

In chapter one, it was mentioned that many of Wagner's opera's were based upon stories of Grail families. These operas were appreciated by no one more than Adolf Hitler, who, as an esotericist, would have known of the Grail descent and how it filtered through the families of Europe. Hitler also played upon the idea of his great Germanic empire descended from ancient times, and was obsessed with the thought that German people were superior to all other races because of their descent. Freemasons uphold that Hitler believed that the Grail bloodline had filtered into the German people, and because of this he believed his people were destined to rule the world. Masons also believe that he had obscured and misinterpreted, for his own ends, the meaning of Grail descent. Such contrasts of beliefs could explain Hitler's animosity towards Freemasons, for instance, while he was in power he banned the practice of Masonry. This issue is often used by Freemasons to defend their organisation, probably on the basis that if Hitler hated them, then they must be good; however, this is no argument at all, as both were initiates of esoteric doctrines and knowledge.

There is also an esoteric society, in existence today which, Freemasons will tell you, has also greatly obscured the meaning of esoteric ideology and Grail descent - the Ku Klux Klan. Founded in 1866 to deny rights to the black population after the American Civil war, it now boasts a membership of over four million. Being esoteric, they are heavily into symbolism and rituals as one would expect, also having their own form of third degree or resurrection ritual. They are also staunchly anti-Catholic, which is no surprise, and have extremist views concerning the preservation of Anglo-Saxon blood from other races, which they believe (due to their descent) are inferior to them. Although the Ku Klux Klan are principally a politically motivated organisation, unlike the Freemasons, they are also esoteric and use secret handgrips to denote their membership and to identify one another.

The Freemasons, while revering the Grail families of Britain and Europe (especially those of purest descent), have never adopted the extremist stance of some of their esoteric counterparts. Instead, there is a strong sense of equality amongst men engrained in Masonic ideology. In fact the Masonic toast consists of placing one glass over the other and vice versa while saying, "We're not above you, we're not below you, we are with you."

This concept of equality comes to the fore in the American constitution, in which nearly all those who drew up and signed the constitution were Freemasons. Masonic influence was, some Masons believe, also prevalent during the American War of Independence; as throughout the war, Americans maintained that they were not fighting against the British Crown, but against the British government for their rights to live as free citizens. Some Freemasons consider this exoneration or attempt to keep on good terms with the Crown, as an acknowledgement of the Royal family's Grail descent, being as the American hierarchy were, at that time, so Masonically orientated. Many also believe that this explains why the Orange Order remain such strong advocates of the Crown.

Within lodges today great reverence is given to the Royal Family, in the toasts and speeches which they perform. It is also of no coincidence that members of the Royal Family have served a traditional role as figure heads or Grand Masters of Freemasonry. However, Masons had not counted on the reluctance of Prince Charles to join the Masonic order:

> Great pressure was brought to bear on Charles when he was in his early mid - twenties to follow family tradition and become a Freemason. It was assumed by high Masons that when Charles reached his twenty - first birthday in 1969, he would be

initiated and take over from the Duke of Kent. He refused to be pressed into doing so, and when approached gave an emphatic 'No', adding, 'I do not want to join a secret society.' [22]

The reverence displayed by Masons to the Royal Family is obviously in accord with their beliefs concerning the Royal Family's Grail descent. Many of the Masonic secrets concerning the symbolism of the Holy Grail are contained in the 'Rose Croix' degree of Freemasonry, and it is hoped that by explaining Masonic beliefs regarding this subject matter that the reader will have grasped one of the most fundamental parts of Masonry.

Having dealt with these fundamentals, it is now possible to delve into other Masonic secrets and assess whether it is wise to give any credence to such beliefs - such as how they perceive the origins of man and God's identity in the Old Testament.

22. Knight, S., The Botherhood p.213

Chapter Seven

The Origins of Man and God

I remembered other strange Bible stories. There was Exodus's mighty words about "thunders and lightnings, and a thick cloud upon the mount . . . and Mount Sinai was altogether on a smoke, because the Lord descended upon it in fire." There was the good man Enoch who "walked with God" and was taken up by a "whirlwind" without having to die. There was Jonah, whose incredible sojourn in the belly of a whale might have been a trip in a submarine. There was the prophet Elijah, who heard a voice on Mount Horeb and departed from this earth riding in a "chariot of fire" which was "wrapped in a whirlwind." . . . How many of the myths of flight might some day turn out to be based on the other-worldly technology described in the Book of Ezekiel? [1]

In recent times much debate has centred on the types of beliefs held by the ancients, especially those relating to their so called gods. Von Daniken, Graham Hancock, Colin Wilson

1. Landsburg, A. and S., In Search of Ancient Mysteries, p.142

and Alan Alford (to name a few) have set imaginations afire with their conclusions concerning the ancients' beliefs of who their gods were. Mainstream Christianity advocates that there is one almighty and omnipotent God who serves the whole world through his son Jesus Christ. But how does this belief account for the powerful perceptions held by numerous ancient cultures which constructed paintings, statues and even mighty monuments of their supposed gods. Are we to accept that in all these ancient cultures people were influenced by someone who told others that there was a God and this is what he looked like? Could it be conceived that on such ill-founded endorsements these ancients, such as the Olmecs, Mayas and Egyptians, would have constructed such time con-suming and magnificent structures for them. It is on the basis of such unbalanced equations that some people today are beginning to adopt a more functionalist view of who these gods were; in contrast to God as a being which manifested himself purely through visions within people's minds.

It must be acknowledged that Christians do believe in the physical manifestations of God in the Old Testament. Masonic beliefs accord with Christian beliefs in many respects, for instance they believe in one almighty and omnipotent God who created the universe - although they refer to him as the 'Grand Architect Above'. Masons also believe in the physical manifestations of God as described in the Old Testament, but here their beliefs diverge immensely from Christian views; believing that God as referred to in the Old Testament was not God Almighty (or the Grand Architect Above), but took the form of an extraterrestrial being. This view, which many Masons say makes sense of the Old Testament, has been echoed in countless publications including Von Daniken's works and more recently by Alan Alford. Masons are taught these beliefs in conjunction with passages from the Old Testament, and closer analysis of the Old Testament brings forth a persuasive, although by no means conclusive, argu-ment that these perceptions are to some extent justifiable.

Extra Terrestrials ?

The public at large is finally beginning to consider at least the possibility of other life forms existing within our universe. However, many people will always remain sceptical for instance about UFO sightings, and even more sceptical about supposed extraterrestrial abductions. If a group of men were chosen at random and asked whether they believed in the existence of other life forms existing within our universe, it's guaranteed that opinions would be divided. However, the Chapter degree and other higher degrees of masonry teach Masons, not only that other life forms exist, but also that centuries ago their presence on earth was prevalent and that they meddled in mankind's past. Such beliefs may sound utterly preposterous to the reader, however there are many unexplained facts of history which may support or for some substantiate the belief that our planet was and possibly still is being visited by beings from other parts of the universe.

In the Chapter degree, Freemasons are taught not just the above beliefs, but they are also directed towards the evidence, which they believe is contained in the Old Testament. Furthermore, Masonic beliefs do not just end at the belief in extraterrestrials, but they go further, maintaining that mankind was in some way genetically engineered by them, either by purely scientific means, or by implanting their genes into ours, as they attempted to shape us both genetically and socially into a species worthy of existence. Probably the most prolific writer alluding to the possible influence of extraterrestrials in the past is Erik von Daniken and in his epic book *Chariots of the Gods* he states:

> The space men artificially fertilised some female members of this species (man), put them into a deep sleep, so ancient legends say, and then departed. Thousands of years later the space men returned

and found members of the genus homo sapiens. They repeated their breeding experiment several times until finally they produced a creature intelligent enough to have the rules of society imparted to it. [2]

In fact, if the word 'God' or 'the Lord', in the Old Testament, is replaced by the term 'alien' or 'extraterrestrial' then the stories contained within the Old Testament begin to look like a description of a social engineering project, in which those who did not follow the program, and refused to obey the word of the Lord or 'extraterrestrial', were simply killed or cast aside by the wrath of God. In order for the reader to judge the substance of such beliefs in extraterrestrials, it is necessary for the reader to make an attempt to think in terms of 'extraterrestrial' every time the word 'God' appears in the Old Testament; and it is to the ancient Biblical manuscripts which we must first turn for indications which may go some way to justify why Freemasons foster such beliefs.

The Old Testament tells us that God made man in his own image; that he created mankind. Furthermore:

Man was made like God, so whoever murders a man will himself be killed by his fellow man. [3]

When the Lord saw how wicked everyone on earth was and how evil their thoughts were all the time, he was sorry he had ever made them and put them on the earth. [4]

It cannot be proved conclusively whether or not mankind was a product of some sort of genetic engineering project, although science cannot as yet explain the enigmas surrounding mankind's evolution, and therefore the possibility of there being some kind of intervention in man's development cannot be ruled out. Indeed the science of genetic engineering has already advanced far enough to give man the ability to

2. Daniken, Erik von, Chariots of the Gods, p.69
3. Book of Genesis 9:6
4. Book of Genesis 6:5

clone a large variety of species, and to alter gene patterns for desired effects. Many people will have heard references to the 'missing link'; that there seems to be an unexplained jump in man's evolution which confounds scientists and Darwinian theorists alike. The rate of homo-sapian evolution through antiquity to the present should, as Darwinian theory dictates, be fairly linear. However unlike any other creature man's evolution over time seems to be exponential i.e. mans rate of evolution seems to have accelerated over time.

In Alan Alford's epic *Gods of the New Millennium*, he offers some very convincing arguments to support the theory that man was genetically engineered by some outside force. He draws reference to man's superior intelligence, which is above and beyond other animals upon the earth. It is a fact that man has over three hundred different physical traits which set him apart from his immediate cousins - homo erectus. Alford makes the point that homo sapiens or human beings have a bare minimum of bodily hair, he attributes this anomaly to the theory that we were genetically engineered. Alford also cites man's increase in intelligence and subsequent size of the head, which seems to have suddenly grown to its present size in a series of extraordinary leaps. The result of which could be an explanation to why childbirth is such a painful experience for women, and why it is fraught with numerous complications. In comparison to man's brain capacity, man's ways of using his brain potential has developed very slowly; according to Darwinian theory both should occur concurrently according to our evolutionary needs. When faced with the relative size of the human brain against his backdrop of theories, Darwin could only assume that there must have been a long struggle of man against man or tribe against tribe. However, as A. & S. Landsberg point out, "But archaeologists found little evidence of primate-verses-primate strife, and no human fossils showing gradual stages of evolution." [5]

Another unusual aspect of man or homo sapiens, is that the stage of infancy is extended beyond what could normally be expected compared with our evolving partners, the

5. Landsberg, A. & S., In Search of Ancient Mysteries, p.157

apes. Man is also a highly sexual being, compared with other
animals, we are highly sensual, able to mate all year round,
and designed to mate face to face which is almost unique.
In retrospect it can be said that man in some ways is an
evolutionary misfit whose facets cannot be explained using
Darwinian theory. Was God an extraterrestrial being, and did
he make man in his own image? These contentions would
certainly create a healthy debate especially where Masons are
concerned, as their teachings do allude to this theory of man
being the product of some sort of genetic engineering by an
extraterrestrial. Their beliefs however do not stop there; they
maintain that many of the stories of the Old Testament are
an account of extraterrestrial manifestations, attempting to instil
certain codes and morals into their creation - mankind.

After creating man, the first major action God takes is
drastic:

> "I will wipe out the people I have created, and
> also the animals and the birds, because I am sorry
> that I made any of them." But the Lord was pleased
> with Noah. [6]

> God said to Noah, "I have decided to put an end
> to all mankind, I will destroy them completely,
> because the world is full of their violent deeds." [7]

God sees that he has made a mistake in creating man, but
still keeps faith with one man:

> "Go into the boat with your whole family; I have
> found that you are the only one in the world who
> does what is right." [8]

After the Flood, God regrets what he has done. Does
this sound like the infallible God we are taught to worship
in Sunday School?

6. Book of Genesis 6:7
7. Ibid 6:13
8. Ibid 7:1

> Never again will I put the earth under a curse
> because of what man does; I know from the time
> he is young his thoughts are evil. Never again will
> I destroy all living beings, as I have done this time.
> As long as the world exists, there will be a time
> for planting and a time for harvest. There will
> always be cold and heat, summer and winter, day
> and night. [9]

Genesis 2:21 provides a basis on which to suggest that genetic engineering was involved in mankind's creation:

> Then the Lord God made man fall into a deep
> sleep, and while he was sleeping, he took out one
> of the man's ribs and closed up the flesh. He
> formed a woman out of the rib and brought her
> to him. Then the man said, "At last, here is one
> of my own kind, bone taken from my bone, and
> flesh taken from my flesh. Woman is her name
> because she was taken out of man."

The indications that man was created, rather than purely evolving into what he is today, are clearly evident in the Old Testament and also supported by the scientific evidence of man's evolution. In fact it was Darwin's contemporary, Alfred Russell Wallace, who described man's brain as: 'An instrument has been developed in advance of the needs of its possessor.' [10]

Whether or not God, as described in the Old Testament, was an extraterrestrial will always be, without firm evidence, a moot point. However, such a belief would rationalise and explain away many of the inconsistencies between our perceptions of an all perfect, omnipotent God which we are taught to believe in, and the fallible extraterrestrial God in the Old Testament that the above passages could be referring to.

9. Book of Genesis 8:21
10. Landsberg, A. & S., In Search of Ancient Mysteries, p.158

Ezekiel

The Old Testament story of Ezekiel is considered to be the most explicit of all biblical accounts in providing evidence of God's supposed form being an extraterrestrial. Throughout the degrees of Masonry, passages from the Old Testament, Book of Enoch and the Apocrypha are quoted at length and Masons are required to memorise and recite large sections from it. As Ezekiel recounts :

> I looked up and saw a storm coming from the north. Lightning was flashing from a huge cloud, and the sky around it was glowing. Where the lightening was flashing, something shone like bronze. At the centre of the storm, I saw what looked like four living creatures in human form, but each of them had four faces and four wings. [11]

Numerous inconsistencies emerge when attempting to reconcile this account and people's perceptions of God, and based upon this, how he would present himself to mankind. For instance:

> As I was looking at the four creatures, I saw four wheels touching the ground beside each of them. All four wheels were alike: each one shone like a precious stone, and each had another wheel intersecting it at right angles, so the wheels could move in any of the four directions. [12]

Based upon this account Josef Blumrich, highly renowned for his contributions to space exploration and a NASA engineer, decided to draw the type of object he believed Ezekiel was describing. The resulting drawing looked much like the UFO's we are accustomed to seeing in clamed UFO sightings; clearly raising questions as to the objectivity of the drawing. But this digresses from the point, which is - why would God need

11. Book of Ezekiel 1:4
12. Ibid 1:15

a machine or indeed any kind of contraption to announce his presence?

If the four creatures, referred to by Ezekiel, were Gods or angels then why would they need a vehicle which had four wheels and could move in any direction - why would they need anything to transport them at all? Was this passage simply an exaggeration by Ezekiel; if it was it is quite a detailed one. Why would gods, and what the Church would refer to as angels, appear with a contraption which had wheels on it? Ezekiel's account continues: 'Above the heads of the creatures there was something that looked like a dome of dazzling crystal. There under the dome stood the creatures . . .' [13] What need would the divine creatures have for such domes- decoration? It seems plausible that the need these creatures had for the domes they used, was the same need an astronaut would have for a space suit if he were on the moon.

The Lord or being/s then made Ezekiel his prophet so that he could speak to the people through him. But why would God the Almighty need a prophet at all? Couldn't he have spoken to the people simultaneously without the use of Ezekiel or for that matter any other prophet? Why is it that God, throughout the Old Testament, needed the use of a prophet through whom to communicate? On the one hand God (in the Old Testament), could muster immense powers of destruction at will, but on the other he needed a prophet through which to communicate to the people. If God was an extraterrestrial being, then it is quite possible that he could not speak at all - only communicate his thoughts to an individual. The being would also have been in possession of a craft (capable of travelling light years in space) which would definitely have been capable of the destruction described in the Old Testament.

Throughout Ezekiel's story there are accounts of him being taken to different lands by God:

13. Book of Exekiel 1:22

> I felt that powerful presence of the Lord and his spirit took me and set me down in a valley where the ground was covered with bones. [14]

> On that day I felt the powerful presence of the Lord, and he carried me away. [15]

Masonic opinion would probably advocate that Ezekiel was carried from place to place by some sort of space craft. It is a plausible explanation at least, or are we not to question the how's, if's and but's of Almighty God?

The Old Testament gives numerous accounts of mass murder and brutality carried out by the hands of God. Is this the same God who readily forgives us for our sins? Is this the same God who in one breath attempted to teach the ancient people about morality and then in another indiscriminately wipes out thousands. By taking a perspective of the subject matter presented, such actions by God seem more desperate than inconsistent. If God would have had all the time in the world to teach what he intended to the Israelites then he would obviously have used a much more subtle approach, and such huge demonstrations of power and destruction would not have been necessary. It is worrying to think that such destruction may have been manifestations of Gods own nature, and if (as Masons believe), we have been made in his own image this trait may be inherent within us - history would seem to uphold such a contention. If God in the Old Testament was really an extraterrestrial then it can be assumed that its time upon this planet would have been limited in some way (it may have needed supplies which were not readily available on this planet). This may not have given the extraterrestrial or extraterrestrials much time so educate its genetically engineered species; so the huge punishments many of which were so fatal and indiscriminate may be explained by God using the 'short sharp shock' treatment to achieve his aims. If Gods time upon this planet was limited then this

14. Book of Ezekiel 37:1
15. Ibid 40:1

would explain why he used such large demonstrations of power - such methods would have produced lasting symbolism in peoples minds for generations to come. Maybe God was hoping to impose enough fear into peoples minds to ensure that his indoctrination of morality and worship would last long after he was gone.

Moses and the Ark

The story of Moses contained in Exodus is also filled with anomalies. It does not make sense that God specifically chose the Israelites to be led out of Egypt, while protecting them against every other nation; are we not all equal under the eyes of God? The story of the Ark is also fascinating with regard to God's motives; why did God give Moses such specific instructions on how the Ark should be built? Why did God appear to Moses by descending upon Mount Sinai in a cloud of smoke : 'and the smoke thereof ascended to the smoke of a furnace, and the whole mount quaked greatly'.[16] Alan Alford makes the analogy with the smoke and vibration created if a Harrier Jump Jet attempted to land upon Mount Sinai. Although it is very easy to explain the Old Testament in terms of one Almighty and omnipotent God, God's actions and motives can, for many, be better explained by assuming that in the Old Testament God was some sort of extraterrestrial being who used a space craft to get from place to place.

To most people the Ark of the Covenant was a box lined with gold, which contained the ten commandments which God had given to Moses. However, there were many more facets to the Ark which seem to have by passed most peoples inquisitive imagination. For a start the Ark was described in the Old Testament as 'producing manna'; it then goes on to say that the manna provided the Israelites with sustenance. The Ark was also capable of wiping out all enemies before it. We are further told that the Ark's power

16. Book of Exodus 19:18

lasted for decades, and that anyone who went close to it became ill or simply died. The symptoms after getting too close to the Ark were hair loss and skin deformities - almost as if they had been scorched, but aren't these the symptoms of someone who has been exposed to high levels of radioactivity? If the Ark was radioactively powered then wouldn't this explain why its power lasted so long and how such a large amount of energy was contained in such a comparatively small box. Masonic beliefs do allude to the Ark being a functional device and they believe that the reason it was provided to the Israelites was for their survival in the harsh desert environment and also for protection from their enemies. But let's face it, if a person were going to spend years trying to socially engineer a certain group of a certain species of animal, wouldn't that person do everything that was within their power to preserve and protect such a group. Israelites are constantly referred to as the chosen people, but who were they chosen by, God or some extraterrestrial being?

Even though some factors point to God in the Old Testament being an extraterrestrial (and such a belief more easily explains it than a Sunday school interpretation), it may never be proved either way which is the correct interpretation of the accounts of the Old Testament. It is believed by some that the Ark of the Covenant still exists and is kept at Axum, Ethiopia, and is kept out of the reach of everyone except for the high priests which guard it. Graham Hancock's research and thoroughness contained in *The Sign and the Seal*, is a great endorsement of this being the case. It is unlikely that the ancient device or machine which may have been contained inside the Ark would still be there, but an examination of the Ark itself would surely provide some hints to the nature of what God placed into the Ark.

Although only two aspects of the Old Testament have been examined with regard to possible Extraterrestrial involvement (the Ark and Ezekiel's story), the whole of the Old Testament could be rewritten by replacing the word God with extraterrestrial. By doing this, many of the stories begin to make much more sense especially to a person who already possesses a belief in extraterrestrials. It makes the stories tangible enough for him or her to understand. However, many would argue that such beliefs, by, making the stories of the Old Testament more plausible, are far too convenient and themselves rest on the premise that there are other life forms existing within our universe.

Accounts of chariots and Gods descending to the earth from the heavens in clouds of smoke are not only exclusive to the Old Testament, but exist in numerous other ancient cultures. Von Daniken found synergies between flying Gods and catastrophes in the legends of the following ancient cultures: Indians (Mahabharata), Sumerian (Epic of Gilgamesh), Eskimo, Red Indians, Scandinavians and Tibetans.[17] It may be the case that God used to make his appearance by flying through the sky but, it is unrealistic to believe that the God we believe in, with all his power, would go to so much trouble. On the other hand sceptics may argue that the ancient legends which talk of flying Gods, which appear in cultures so diverse and far away from each other, are just exaggerated accounts or fantasies designed to foster a belief in gods within these cultures. The above belief may have developed into an accepted theory to explain away these ancient legends, if it were not for the fact that since Henrich Schleimmans discovery of the mythical Troy in Turkey, Arthur Evans' discovery of the Minoan civilisation at Knossos in Crete, and the tangible evidence which has been left from ancient times, such things cannot be so easily cast aside and do warrant further investigation.

Whether the Old Testament is or is not an account of extraterrestrial involvement in mans history, is a point which can always be argued over. Since no conclusive evidence has emerged to prove or disprove what actually happened in mans antiquity, Masonic beliefs will always remain a possible explanation of these past events and one which cannot be simply dismissed. When considering the Old Testament and the mistakes made by God (by his own admission), it may be

17. Daniken, Erik von, Chariots of the Gods, p.79

poignant for us to consider one of the phrases commonly used amongst people when they make mistakes- "I'm only human". There are also other enigmas which could point to there being some extraterrestrial involvement in mans past.

The Nazca Plain (Peru)

Near the ancient city of Nazca lies a vast plain thirty seven miles long and one mile wide. Seen from ground level the plain looks like a chaotic series of lines formed by the removal of stones exposing the darker earth underneath. When seen from a great height, the lines are no longer seen as a confused array, but become specific images representing creatures including various animals, birds and insects with numerous lines running in all directions. These images are not simply shown in straight line form (even though some of them run perfectly straight for up to 5 miles), but as the reader will appreciate from Plate 20, they are highly intricate lines on a massive scale demonstrating much greater knowledge and skill than archaeologists and anthropologists would attribute to the people at that time. The symmetry of these images which have been sculpted from the earth is remarkably accurate. It is another example of precision which is the hallmark of so many ancient cultures. The images at Nazca demonstrate their precision when intersected bi-symmetrically, many are near perfect mirror images.

The greatest exponent of the Nazca lines is surely Dr Maria Reiche, a German mathematician, who has spent almost her whole life studying and researching the intricacies of the lines. As she explains :

> Length and direction of every piece was carefully measured and taken note of. An approximate estimate of these would not have been enough to produce shapes, in which a deviation of a few inches would spoil the proportions, which, as we see them on aerial photographs are perfect. Those

acquainted with surveying techniques will best understand the accomplishments needed for such an undertaking. Ancient Peruvians must have had instruments and equipment which we ignore and which together with ancient knowledge were buried and hidden from the eyes on the conquerors as the one treasure which was not to be surrendered. [18]

That they can be seen from immense heights gives testimony to their size. However, there are no mountains around Nazca of sufficient height upon which to gaze down upon the images. At ground level the images represented by the lines cannot be made out at all. Why would an intelligent ancient people (we must assume that they were intelligent because of the precision and the feat of creating such images), put so much resources into constructing images in the earth which were useless to them in terms of appreciating the images themselves? Such questions can easily be dismissed by proposing that the culture in question believed in a God which was looking down upon them and that some enigmatic chief had claimed that God had spoken to him and instructed him to build the images. Such proposals are worthy of consideration, but it is probably more likely that there was a more tangible motivation for their construction. It is unlikely that people would spend considerable time and effort on a project whose benefits they could never fully appreciate, and for some God who might or might not exist and might or might not be looking down upon them anyway. The more likely proposition believed by some to explain the Nazca plain, assuming that it is accepted that extraterrestrials might exist, is that the ancient Nazca people had at least seen the God or Gods for which they built the images. And that it was this which prompted the images' construction, rather than basing their construction on a mere perception that there might be a God in the heavens watching them. Again no conclusive evidence, which is accepted by everyone, has so far come to light which can be used to prove or disprove

18. Hitching, F., World Atlas of Mysteries, p.71

outright the existence of extraterrestrial contact or involvement upon this planet. However, many other strange enigmas exist which could all be trying to tell us the same thing - that there was contact in ancient times between mankind and extraterrestrials, as the Masons believe.

As the reader may recall, the pyramids at Giza represent a celestial map of certain stars, which could only be appreciated by looking down upon them. In Uffington, England a horse 360 feet long and 130 feet high has, some time in the distant past, been carved out of the earth exposing the white chalk underneath. In Gorgia an eagle like figure which faces the sky, has been constructed of rocks by some distant peoples, the wingspan of which is 120 feet wide. In Ohio a Serpent represented by a lengthy mound was constructed at some time, which measures 125 feet in length. At Carnac, France, 3000 meinhers (long stones) have been positioned in rows along the ground. What was the purpose of these ancient constructions, the true form of which can only be seen from a great height? The question may be not, were these constructions built for some gods to appreciate (which seems self evident), but what type of gods were these constructions built for?

Another unexplicable facet of man's past was a piece of rock taken from a 2000 year old sunken vessel off the coast of Greece. By thorough analysis and through research with X rays, carried out by an American, Derek de Solla Price, he revealed that fused inside the rock was a series of cogs. Price reconstructed the device from the X rays and found it to contain an intricate system of gears (over 30 in fact), which it is believed represent the celestial movements within our solar system. No one knows how the device came into existence or how it was thought of all that time ago. If the device (referred to by some as the first computer) really does represent planetary movements within our solar system as many believe, then it is baffling where this knowledge came from. Again the possibility of extraterrestrial involvement cannot be ruled out, but neither can man's capacity for discovering this knowledge and constructing such a machine be ruled out either.

As mentioned previously, in Lubaatun, British Honduras in 1927 a skull (which has become known as 'the skull of doom'), was discovered in a 1000-year-old Mayan temple. So far no one has proposed any satisfactory explanation of how the skull was made in such times. It is carved from a piece of rare quartz and weighs over 11 and a half pounds. In the first place it is immensely difficult to carve the shape of a skull from such quartz, but the skull's most incredible feature is the hidden prisms in its base and eyes. When these prisms are combined with light passing through them, they reveal a startling array of luminescence. Whoever built the skull must have had a seriously advanced knowledge of optics and incredible lapidary skills. It is doubted today whether a similar piece of quartz could be carved out with the technology at our disposal, and it has been speculated by some that it was not carved out by man at all, but by more advanced beings. Two main trains of thought have emanated from the skull of doom. One is that at some point in time man possessed the knowledge to construct such a skull (possibly the Atlanteans), knowledge which has subsequently been lost through time. The other is that due to there being no other example or evidence of ancient precision optics anywhere around the world, then some other more advanced being must have constructed it. Whatever the opinions of people may be on the skull's origins, and other enigmas described previously, at the very least one would have to concede that 'There are more things in heaven and earth Horatio, than are dreamt of in your philosophy'. It is not the author's intention to sway the reader's opinion either way, but to attempt to provide some indications which may add some credence to Masonic beliefs.

The Dogon

Probably the most startling phenomenon to emerge concerning the possibility of extraterrestrial contact in the past, emerged from central Africa. The evidence is in the form of knowledge - the knowledge which the Dogon tribe from Mali possess. In the 1930's two eminent anthropologists Marcel Griaule and Germaine Dieterlen decided to study the Dogon tribe and resided with them for a number of years. Both men were eventually taken into the confidence of the high priests of the tribe who passed on the Dogons secret knowledge to them. This knowledge was published in their book, *Le Renard Pale* (*The Pale Fox*).

The Dogon claimed that the secret knowledge which had been passed down from generation to generation within their tribe over many thousands of years, referred not only to our solar system, but also to the star system Sirius. First of all they knew that: the planets revolved around the Sun, the earth spun on its axis, that Saturn is surrounded by rings, and they also had calendars based upon the Sun, Venus, Sirius and the moon. This information could be discovered through many years of study and as such is not that sensational. However, the Dogon also said that millions of years ago there used to be a planet in our solar system which revolved around the sun in between Mars and Jupiter, which is a belief held by many astronomers due to the asteroid belt between these two planets. There is no evidence to suggest that this primitive tribe had been taught such knowledge from other westeners. Griaule and Dieterlen are believed to have been the first to study the Dogon. What is more, they claimed that this knowledge was given to them by their ancestors who had had contact with extraterrestrials thousands of years previously.

Even more remarkable than the information previously discussed and disclosed by the Dogon was the place where they said, the extraterrestrials came from - a planet they called Digitaria, named after the smallest seed known to them; and which they said orbited the star Sirius. They added that Digitaria was very small and very heavy, and this is the exact description that astronomers have given to Digitaria or Sirius B - known to astronomers as a white dwarf. These extraterrestrials were called Nommo by the Dogon who also said that they taught their tribe (in ancient times) about Sirius B's elliptical orbit - that it does not orbit Sirius in a perfect circle, but has an elongated orbit with two foci (the two points which keep it in orbit). Also known to the Dogon was the relative positions and paths made by Sirius and Sirius B through the sky over a period of time. This information mirrors the scientific estimates of the relative positions of these celestial bodies over time

Although Sirius B cannot be seen through the human eye it was discovered at the turn of the century but, it was not until 1970 that it was successfully photographed. However, since then all the facts which have been discovered about Sirius B correlate accurately with the knowledge presented by the Dogon. For instance the following factors have been confirmed: that Sirius B revolves around Sirius every 50 years, Sirius B's elliptical orbit and also the weaving paths made by Sirius and Sirius B over time correlate with the information given by the Dogon, and also the dense and heavy characteristics of Sirius B described by the Dogon match what astronomers believe Sirius B to be - a white dwarf. How could the primitive Dogon without any instruments remotely as advanced as a telescope have known precise details of Sirius B which they could not possibly have seen or known about with their primitive resources? The Dogon have also disclosed other information relating to past astronomy, which has yet to be proved (if indeed such knowledge can be proved), that there existed a planet between Jupiter and Mars which was destroyed millions of years previously, and that it takes Sirius B one year to rotate upon its axis. What motivation would a tribe in central Africa have for believing in such astronomical trivia?

The immense astrological knowledge that the Dogon had gained could have possibly been derived from the beings they described - known to them as Nommo. It seems that such information, passed on through successive generations of Dogon could only have come from two sources. First, it may have been derived from an advanced ancient culture who had developed an instrument as powerful as a telescope for observing Sirius B and the four moons of Jupiter, or second, which some think is the more likely proposition, that extraterrestrials from Sirius B actually existed and initially left this knowledge, which has been passed down through the generations of Dogon.

The Dogons belief, that they were visited many thousands of years ago by extraterrestrials, is consistent with Masonic beliefs concerning extraterrestrials, although there is another consistency too. The account which the Dogons give, of what, as they call the being, Nommo did upon the earth does to some extent accord with Masonic beliefs relating to extraterrestrials possible involvement with man's development and evolution. 'When Nommo originally landed on earth he crushed the fox thus making his future domination over the earth which the fox had made.' [19]

It is not known for certain what the fox, which is referred to here specifically represents, but it seems to imply an evil or barbarous nature within man. If this is indeed the case, then what the Dogon are saying is that Nommo or the extraterrestrials landed upon earth and overcame the uncivilised element or elements of man's nature (maybe through genetic engineering), to 'make his future domination over the earth.' This 'future domination over the earth' could be referring to the fact that extraterrestrial genes were in some way imparted to us, or that our genes were somehow altered to become dominant over man's previous primitive nature.

The disclosures of the Dogon provide a powerful argument that they were visited by extraterrestrials at some time in the tribe's history. The Dogon tribe are also meant to have originated in Egypt, and they believe themselves to be the true descendants of the ancient Egyptians. Whether the reader believes that the Dogon were visited by extraterrestrials or

19. Temple, R., The Sirius Mystery, p.32

not, does not depend upon the information they disclosed (which has stood up to astronomical and scientific scrutiny), but whether they are telling the truth about their source. It is in some ways difficult to imagine what motives the Dogon would have for devising such a story, especially in light of their simple and, in the eyes of the western world, primitive background. For a more detailed insight into the Dogon and their beliefs, it is suggested that the reader should read *The Sirius Mystery* by Robert Temple.

The Dogon's beliefs seem to withstand many forms of scrutiny, and furthermore their beliefs seem to correlate with Masonic beliefs. On the American one dollar bill there appears a pyramid with an eye above it. To Masons this signifies a well known Masonic design: the pyramid relating to their eso-teric Egyptian legacy, and the eye often believed to represent Sirius, but to Masons it has in the past been used to sym-bolise many things, most notably the fact that there are other life forms which exist within our universe to which we are inextricably linked due to their involvement in man's past.

No one, it would seem, can prove the Dogons belief's, and no one for instance can come up with a viable alter-native theory to explain where the Dogon gained their knowl-edge. However, this book is not about resolving such enig-matic issues, but about relaying Masonic beliefs to the read-er and offering some insight into the factors which may endorse some of these beliefs. It is a difficult concept to embrace Masonic beliefs, especially concerning the existence of extraterrestrials and their involvement in shaping mans past. However, such beliefs have formed one of the cornerstones of Masonic beliefs, and it is difficult to entirely dismiss such beliefs. On the other hand Masons' beliefs may not rest upon the objectivity of the ideas relayed to them, but in the way these ideas are presented to Freemasons - in the dramatic atmosphere created through the performance of their rituals.

Another important aspect of Masonic rituals is the emphasis and numerous references to astrology. As discussed earlier, astrology was also a keen pursuit of the ancient

Egyptians and assuming Masonic endorsements (that their knowledge originally came from Egypt), it is no surprise that it has filtered into the Masonic pursuits of today, so much so that together with astronomy it has become incorporated into the degrees of Freemasonry.

Chapter Eight

Masonic Astrology

> . . .the Masonic tradition is but one of the numerous ancient allegories of the yearly passage of the personified Sun among the twelve constellations of the zodiac - being founded on a system of astronomical symbols and emblems employed for the purpose of teaching and illustrating the two great truths, of the being of One spiritual invisible, omnipresent, and omnipotent God, and the immortality of the soul. . . . these two great doctrines were also originally taught in all the ancient Mysteries, by the use of the same astronomical allegories and symbols, freemasonry alone retained its primitive truth and purity, while the others degenerated into a corrupt system of solar worship. [1]

The concept of astrology is taken very seriously amongst Freemasons and other esoteric societies. Masons are instructed at length about the constellations and planetary movements which they believe influences not only the lives of individuals but also events upon this planet. This belief rests upon the principle of cosmic harmony (as discussed in chapter one),

1. Brown, R. H., Stellar Theology and Masonic Astronomy, p.16

that what occurs above in the universe, is in tune with and effects what occurs below (upon the earth). Some esotericists believe, for instance, that the distance between planets can explain why we find the musical octave harmonious even though it is not made up of equal pitches. Masonic concepts of the universe and the idea of cosmic harmony are also closely connected with numerology which is another important aspect of masonry, for instance the harmonious nature of pentagonal numerology as previously discussed.

It has already been established that freemasons believe that their souls become resurrected or released, from its purely physical state, up to the universe above during the third degree ritual. Their interest in the stars and the sky however, does not stop there. Within lodges the masons study the constellations closely, as they are taught that celestial movements are inextricably linked to events which occur upon the earth. This concept known as dualism, as already discussed, is manifest amongst Cathar, Gnostic and Templar beliefs. This is an extension from the astrology we read in the papers every day, which only deals with the individual effects upon peoples lives. As was mentioned in chapter two, Enoch features quite prominently in Masonic tradition, as it was he that first documented the paths of celestial bodies:

> And in those days the angel Uriel answered and said to me : 'Behold, I have shown thee everything, Enoch, and I have revealed everything to thee that thou shouldest see this sun and this moon, and the leaders of the stars of the heaven and all those who turn them, their tasks and times and departures. [2]

> And the account thereof is accurate and the recorded reckoning thereof exact; for the luminaries, and months and festivals, and years and days, has Uriel shown and revealed to me, to whom the Lord of the whole creation of the world hath subjected the host of heaven. And he has power over night and day in

2. Book of Enoch 80:1

the heaven to cause the light to give light to men - sun, moon, stars, and all the powers of the heaven which revolve in their circular chariots. And these are the orders of the stars, which set in their places, and in their seasons and festivals and months. [3]

The zodiac and its constellations are a central feature of Masonic ideology, so much so that a degree is devoted to it (the Royal Arch degree) and the subject is prevalent throughout masonry as a whole.

In Egyptian, Greek, Mayan and Aztec mythology (to name a few), there are numerous stories of Gods and their interaction with man. Most people in the western world simply dismiss such myths and fables as misguided beliefs held by societies less advanced than our own. We would think it absurd if someone we knew suddenly started worshiping the God Horus or one of the Greek gods. However, in ancient times people were in all probability much less sceptical and clung to the beliefs and stories handed down from the high priests, the majority of these ancient people actually believed in the stories of these Gods and the things which they purportedly did. It would be naive of anyone to take all these myths at face value, however, as discussed in the previous chapter, masons do believe that many of these so called legends and myths actually refer to mans encounters with extraterrestrial beings. It is widely believed that there is more to many of these myths than they express at face value, and masonry advocates that it possesses the truest interpretation.

Masons and esoteric societies alike believe that many of the ancient legends and myths of Egypt and Greece for example, were cleverly designed stories of allegorical significance, only capable of being understood by those initiated into the higher degrees of esoteric mysteries. These legends also served an important part in the beliefs of the uninitiated, it gave them something to believe in as well as something to fear, ensuring that the initiated high priests of the

3. Book of Enoch 82:7

day would be able to maintain their dominance over the societies they ruled. This idea of coding information (in some cases celestial information) into legends or some other form exhibiting allegorical principles is not new. As the reader will recall, the Templars coded their esoteric knowledge into literature and gothic constructions. What to the lay man appears as a meaningless array of signs and symbols becomes a magnificent esoteric message to the initiated - capable of deciphering the symbols. Throughout this book many examples are given of coded esoteric knowledge which is only meant to be understood, and some would argue, is only capable of being understood by initiates. However, as noted in chapter five, this talent for concealing esoteric knowledge within a document can be a dangerous game, if (as the masons believe), it is left to the auspices and engineering of, let us say, a diminishing Roman Empire.

To give an example of how these ancient godly myths that masons believe, are coded into a form of celestial information, it is necessary firstly to take the most prevalent Egyptian story - that of Osiris. The story is quite simple, Osiris was slain by Typhon, and Isis searched for his body and raised him to life again. The ancient Egyptian initiates believed that Osiris represented the sun, Typhon darkness, and Isis represented the moon. One of Masonry's symbolic interpretations of this story is considered in terms of the yearly cycle of the sun. Firstly Osiris is slain, this signifies the end of the summer solstice where the sun appears for gradually decreasing periods during the day up until the winter solstice. After the winter solstice the sun is considered raised by the moon and begins to gradually appear for longer periods during the day - as Osiris was raised by Isis. The Egyptians also included Sirius in their myths - the star being identified with Sothis who signified the flooding of the Nile. The time of year which this occurred coincided with the rising of Sirius above the horizon.

Greek myths are also believed by esotericists to exhibit celestial significance. The story of the twelve labours of Hercules is, some maintain, an allegorical representation of the twelve signs of the Zodiac. In the legend of Jason and the Argonauts, Robert Temple maintains that the fifty argonauts (also featured in the Sumerian legend of Gilgamesh) represents the time it takes Sirius B to orbit Sirius - 50 years. It is worth mentioning here that the Order of the Golden Fleece, derives its name from the fleece for which Jason was searching in the legend. The Golden Fleece is also referred to in the first degree ritual as the candidate refers to the apron as being the:

> . . .badge of a Mason; that it had been worn by kings, princes, and potentates of the earth, who had never been ashamed to wear it; that it was more honourable than the diadems of kings, or pearls of princesses, when worthily worn; and more ancient than the Golden Fleece, or Roman Eagle; more honourable than the Star or Garter, or any other order that could be conferred upon me at that time.

Jesus also features crucially in Masonic tradition, and that it is no surprise that Masons view the birth of Jesus as an important example of the impact of celestial movements. Almost everyone is aware of the story of the three wise men, or Magi as they are known. As Matthew's gospel recounts, the three men came from the east guided by a star which lead them to the place of Jesus' birth. The gifts which the three wise men brought with them were, esoterists maintain, of symbolic significance, but the most important aspect of Jesus' birth to freemasons is its astrological significance. In Adrian Gilberts *The Magi*, it shows Jesus' horoscope at the time when, many esotericists believe Jesus was actually born - 29th July 7 BC. At this date Jupiter and Saturn are in conjunction forming a bright star, and, as Adrian Gilbert maintains, this conjunction occurring as it did in the constellation Pisces signified the "new age" of Pisces, i.e. when the constellation Pisces replaced the constellation Aries and entered the ecliptic path of the sun over the horizon. In astrological terms such an event is quite a rarity.

The Zodiac

Amongst the information which can be obtained from these ancient myths, is that which relates to the Zodiac which is probably the most prominent. For those unaware of the principals of astronomy, the Zodiac are the groups of constellations or clusters of stars which the yearly cycle of the sun passes through (although it is actually our planet which is moving and not the sun). Over the year the sun will have entered the twelve signs of the zodiac. Each constellation or cluster of stars have been named according to their resemblance to different creatures (the word zodiac means living creatures). The times when the sun is passing through these different constellations determines peoples birth signs i.e. Leo (July 24 - Aug 23), Virgo (Aug 24- Sept 23), Libra (Sept 24- Oct 23). The sun passes through each of the star signs in turn over the yearly cycle.

Symbolism is central to the communication of Masonic ideas and beliefs and these symbols have been used since Egyptian times and possibly before as a form of representing the different signs of the zodiac. John Dee who as a Templar Grand Master and astrologer to Elisabeth I's, used some of these signs in conjunction with each other to form the structure below:

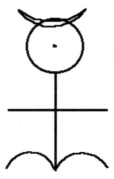

This structure appeared upon Dee's Monas Heiroglyphica and became a symbol which was printed upon Rosicrucian literature to indicate to its followers that the literature related to them. To anyone unaware of the different zodiac or planetary symbols, John Dee's and the Rosicrucian symbol is totally meaningless. The different symbols are shown below:

MOON   SUN   VENUS   ARIES

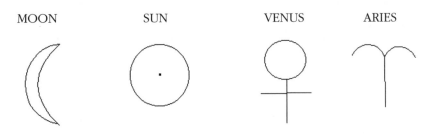

These symbols represent a very clever system of marking a particular epoch in time. The time which these signs refer to is the time when the sun, moon and Venus were simultaneously influencing the constellation Aries. Since, the moon, Venus and the sun's movements over time are all different from each other, this is a particularly prominent marker of time since the chances of this conjunction occurring are fairly remote.

The essence of astrology to most people is that it is method of determining a persons character from their birth sign and also a way determining future highs and lows of different aspects of that persons life, by planetary movements through the constellations (in astrology the sun and moon are considered as planets). The music from 'The Planets' by Gustav Holst is a good indication of the type of effect different planets have upon the zodiac. For example the passage describing Mars is very energetic, while that of Venus is very tranquil, mirroring the effects that these planets have upon the constellations and, many believe, our lives. In masonry, astrology is considered differently from that which appears in the tabloid press.

The Royal Arch Degree

To freemasons astrology is taken much more seriously, and an insight into the seriousness with which they consider the effects of celestial bodies can be gaged by extracts from the Royal Arch degree:

W.M. What does the word of an Entered Apprentice Mason signify?

Can. It has more than one collateral meaning, pronounced or written either forward or backward, but if divided into the radicals of which it is composed it will be found to signify the Fire God (the Sun).

W.M. What does the word of a Fellow Craft Mason signify?

Can. This word, if divided into its radicals, means the moon?

W.M. What does the word of a Master Mason signify?

Can. The roots of which it is composed signify the Benevolent God of Fire (the Sun); and, as it was by the aid of fire that metals were first brought into a state fit for use of man, this divinity was named Vulcan by the Romans, and worshipped by them.

W.M. What does the name of our Grand Master Hiram Abiff signify?

Can. It is derived from two roots, which signify the origin or manifestation of light; also he who was and is.

W.M. What, then, does the whole name signify?

Can. The source of eternal light (i.e. the sun) - taken as an emblem of Deity.

W.M. Whom, therefore, does our Grand Master Hiram Abiff represent?

Can. The great source of light- the Sun.

Symbolism within freemasonry is not as a rule confined to one particular aspect of it, but the same symbol or symbols may be applied to represent numerous Masonic concepts and beliefs. The reason for this is that while providing economy of symbolism, it leaves specific symbols from which all other Masonic beliefs may emanate, thus enhancing the symbols recognition and the beliefs connected to it. A good example of this, is the Boez and Jachin pillars and the keystone which is meant to link them together. These pillars are linked to a variety Masonic ideals such as: the three degrees, also to sig-nify wisdom, beauty and strength, the coming together of the priestly and kingly nature of Jesus, and of course the zodi-ac. This is exemplified in the Royal Arch:

W.M. Have all the ancient signs, symbols, emblems, and legends of the Mysteries, both ancient and modern, an astronomical allusion?

Can. They have. As the whole system has an ancient astronomical foundation, it could not be otherwise.

The pillars connection to the zodiac is demonstrated below:-

W.M. What is the Royal Arch?
Can. It may be defined in nearly the same words as the lodge, and is no less than the starry vault of heaven,

234

or great zodiacal arch, reaching from the vernal to the autumnal equinox.

W.M. How is the Royal Arch supported?

Can. By three of the cardinal points of the zodiac: being the equinoctial points at the base and solstitial point at the summit.

W.M. Of what are these three points emblematic?

Can. Like the three pillars of the lodge, they are emblematic of Wisdom, Strength and beauty. Dr Oliver, in his Dictionary of Symbolical Masonry, informs us that "the lodge is supported by three pillars, which are called Wisdom, Strength and Beauty; because no piece of architecture can be termed perfect unless it have wisdom to contrive, strength to support, and beauty to adorn."

The candidate then proceeds through the ritual by reciting a detailed account of the zodiac and making allegorical connections between the story of Hiram Abiff, the Royal Arch (zodiac) and other types of Masonic symbolism which is applied to the astronomical processes in an attempt to make sense of them.

The point where the sun advances through the zodiac at the summer solstice, is represented upon the Royal Arch as the Keystone. Through the process of symbolism, the royal arch candidate not only learns the importance of the zodiac as it effects peoples individual lives, but also the way in which the zodiac is affected through planetary movements.

As previously mentioned, John Dee (past grand master of the Templars) was a prevalent astrologer and applied this when choosing the most favourable date for Elisabeth I's coronation. This form of astrology, i.e. choosing the most favourable time for a particular event is known as electional astrology. It has been suggested in an article by Knight and

Lomas (co-authors of the *Hiram Key* and *The Second Messiah*), that Philip IV of France deliberately chose Friday 13 th October 1307, the time of the Templar arrests, through electional astrology. The astrological evidence today, achieved by simulating the celestial movements at that time would seem to support this. The positions of the Sun and Mars, it is claimed, signify a conquest over a mighty force, while the relative positions of the Moon and Saturn signifies a suppression of the population at large through a military force. Knight and Lomas' article adds that significantly the astrology at this date (13/10/1307) does herald, in astrological terms, a spiritual catastrophe. At 16.55 of this date a Lunar eclipse occurs on the same axis as it occurred, they claim, on April 3rd 33 AD, the day which it is believed that Jesus was crucified. This is significant because Jacques de Molay, Grand Master of the Templars at the time of the arrests was also crucified.

Astrology is an important feature of masonry, as it is another form of knowledge which was derived from the ancient Atlanteans. The emphasis placed on celestial bodies such as the sun and the moon and their cycles passages through the sky is typical of the knowledge emanating from the alignments of numerous ancient sites throughout the world. Although many frown upon the possible effects of celestial movements with scepticism, it is followed seriously by Freemasons and other esotericists. For instance many people who have left an indelible mark on history used to consult the Zodiac before making important decisions such as Adolf Hitler, John Dee, Ronald Regan, and many more esotericists, who would heartily deny such a practice publicly.

The final chapter of this book deals with a secret nearly all masons, or those which have knowledge of it, would deny ever existed - the 'Plan'.

Chapter IX

The Plan

Their agreement was this: First, that none of them should profess any other thing than to cure the sick, and the gratis. 2.
None of the posterity should be constrained to wear one certain kind of habit, but therein to follow the custom of the
country. 3. That every year upon the day C. they should meet
together in the house S. Spiritus, or write the cause of their
absence. 4. Every brother should look out for a worthy person, who, after his decease, might succeed him. 5. The word
C. R. should be their seal, mark, and character. 6. the fraternity should remain secret one hundred years. These six articles they bound themselves one to another to keep, and five
of the brethren departed, only the brethren B. and D.
remained with the father, Fra. R. C., a whole year; when these
likewise departed. [1]

The plan was first formulated by those Templars who escaped
the persecutions of Philip and the papacy. Its purpose was
the unification of certain parts of knowledge which when complete would ultimately lead to the discovery of an immense

1. Fama (Yates, F.A., The Rosicrucian Enlightenment, p.243)

power source involving lay lines. The existence of the plan is known amongst high ranking Freemason's, however, it is not known to what extent they or anyone else know the essential details of the plan; as throughout history parts of the plan have inevitably not survived. The Plan, as it is known, is probably the least plausible of all Masonic beliefs. It is believed that if its power was ever harnessed it may prove to have dire consequences. The plan touches upon some topics which have previously been covered in proceeding chapters, but rather than being a well kept secret of the past, it is in fact a well kept secret of a preconceived plan for the future - a future which as the reader will discover, is almost upon us.

Some of the details of this so called 'Plan' are contained in Umberto Eco's *Foucault's Pendulum* - supposedly a work of fiction. However, the book contains references from numerous pieces of literature, which by analysis have proven to be quite accurate. The authenticity of the story presented in Eco's book is questionable, however, the book does provide a good introduction into the form, purpose and outline of the plans content. Eco's story begins in 1894, when two dragoons decided to examine a tunnel complex under a large Gothic building in Provins (southern France) called the Grange-aux-Dimes (The reader will recall from chapter one who the Gothic architectures of Europe were). The two men, Chevalier Camille Laforge of Tours and Chevalier Edouard Ingolf of Petersburg, were accompanied by a caretaker who informed them that there were many more subterranean chambers further under. The dragoons proceeded deeper and deeper into the tunnel complex until they arrived at a large chamber with a well in its centre. Ingolf was lowered into the well and after some time climbed out telling his companion that the chamber was empty. In fact Ingolf had found something and as the story recounts, something which was to cost him his life.

Provins is famous for its extensive network of tunnels which date from the time of the Cathars. What is known is that the Cathars used these tunnels while hiding from the Romans, and Cathar insignia can still be seen today on the walls of the tunnel complex. The Templars also used these tunnels for the same purpose, during the time that other Templars were being arrested the most notable in Provins, according to Eco, was Raynard de Provins. Eco emphasises that it was important that he be arrested so that the French king would believe that Provins was cleared of Templars and would not have suspicions of finding any more in the area. It is possible and may not be surprising if the Templar submission to the arrests on Friday 13th 1307 were done to preserve their knowledge of the 'Plan' i.e. that members were deliberately sacrificed so that others may perpetuate the knowledge contained in the 'Plan'. Provins would have been an ideal place for many of the Templar fugitives to hide. In the eleventh century, it was the seat of the Comte de Champagne, where no official French body could gain unconditional access. Provins was a place the Templars knew well and knew where they could hide.

The story continues that after the death of Ingolf it became clear that he did find something in the well he was lowered into. He had the opportunity to conceal something quite small from his partner. According to Eco what he found was a small case which was studded with jewels. Although the case was of some value, Ingolf soon realised that the true prize was the small parchment inside containing a coded message. Ingolf, as the story goes, then spent the next 30 years of his life as a recluse examining and researching the consequences of the message he had found. It could not have taken him long to decipher the message; the key to the code was to take the first letter of every word, and replace it with its preceding letter in the alphabet (S becomes R, D becomes C, etc. with A becoming Z). It was the content of the information contained in the parchment which would have taken up Ingolf's time to understand its meaning. The deciphered parchment which appears in *Foucault's Pendulum* is shown below:

On the Night of Saint John
36 Years beyond the Hay Wain
6 Sealed messages intact with Seal
For the Knights with the White Cloaks
Relapsed of Provins for Vengeance
6 times in 6 places
20 years each time for 120 Years
This is the Plan
The first to the Castle
Again after 120 years to those who ate the bread
Again to the Refuge
Again to our Lady beyond the River
Again to the hostel of the Popelicans
Again to the Stone
3 times 6 (666) before the Feast of the Great Whore[2]

Simplified the plan reads:

    On the knight of Saint Johns Eve (24th June), which as the reader will have noted before is a very significant date for the Templars (St John is also the patron Saint of Masonry). Thirty six years post the Hay Wain; the Hay Wain was the means of escape for the Templars who left the Paris perceptory before the Templar arrests. At first glance the year of the Hay wain would seem to be 1307, however as Eco clarifies, because each year was taken from one Easter to the next and that when references were made to years in those days, it was the date at the end of a year which denoted that year. This meant that the date for the Hay Wain was 1308; if 36 years are added to this it makes 1344.

The Meaning of the plan

The plan refers to six messages for the knights with the white cloaks, which is obviously referring to the Templars. Six times in six places; it is important to note that six, along with 3 and 9 were treated as mystical numbers by the Templars (the

Tempar's like their descendants the Masons believe that their is a magical significance associated with certain numbers, for example they believe the figure 1746 represents the celestial fusion between the earth and the stars). 20 year each time for a total of 120 years. This is the plan. The plan mentions 6 knights appearing 6 times in 6 places, each knight carrying a sealed message which was to be opened at 20 year intervals for a total of 120 years. By 120 years the six sealed messages will have been opened (6 x 20 = 120), and the group of 6 would meet another group of 6, with the process starting again with the next group etc.. This would last until all six groups (every 120 years) had achieved their purpose. So, with 6 groups two of which would meet up together every 120 years at the cryptic locations given in the plan, the meeting were to be completed by: 5(meetings) x 120 = 600 years, 1344 + 600 = 1944 .

The final line is again pedantic in its numerology. Three times six before the Feast of the Great Whore. Three sixes or 666, added to 1344 makes the year 2000. The year 2000 is further confirmed by the plans reference to the Feast of the Great Whore, which is obviously a reference to the Great Whore of Babylon mentioned in Saint John's Apocalypse (which is supposed to occur in the year 2000):

> Then an angel carried me away in the Spirit into a desert. There I saw a woman sitting on a scarlet breast that was covered with blasphemous names and had seven heads and ten horns. . . . She held a golden cup in her hand, filled with abominable things and the filth of her adulteries. This title was written of her forehead: Mystery Babylon the Great The Mother of Prostitutes and of the Abominations of the Earth. I saw that the woman was drunk with the blood of the saints, the blood of those who bore testimony to Jesus. [3]

3. Book of Revelation 17:3

The reader knows by now that, according to Eco, the plans meetings were to conclude in 1944, and that the plan is to be carried out in the year 2000, but what of the significance of the Plan, in fact why have a plan at all? The plan may have been designed to avenge the death of Jacques de Molay and the other Templars who were persecuted and killed after their arrests, which were ultimately attributed to King Philip and the Papacy. The completion of the plan is supposed to signify the beginning of a New World Order, a World where the Templars will never again be branded as heretics and the Catholic church will be punished for its deceptions through the ages and for their persecution of the Templar Order and suppression of the truer knowledge. According to the original Templars, it will be the coming of a New earthly Jerusalem where justice will conquer all. This view is contained in the Confessio (as previously mentioned, one of the manifestos which triggered the creation of the Rosicrucians and as many believe were prompted to unite the people with knowledge of the plan):

> We ought therefore here to observe well, and make it known to everyone, that God hath certainly and most concluded to send and grant to the world before her end, which presently thereupon shall ensue, such a truth, light life and glory, as the first man Adam had, which he lost in Paradise, after which his successors were put and driven, with him, to misery . . . All the which, when it shall once be abolished and removed, and instead thereof a right and true rule instituted, then there will remain thanks unto them which have taken pains therein.[4]

Although Eco's plan could in all probability have been contrived on a knowledge of the plan's existence, however, there exist too many synergy's confirming the existence of such a plan for it to be simply dismissed as mere fantasy. Eco's plan even accords consistently with the historical evidence

4. Confessio (Yates, F.A. The Rosicrucian Enlightenment, p.256)

concerning the Templars. For instance Eco's plan refers to the first at the castle, for anyone who does not have a skilled knowledge of the Templars it would be very difficult for someone to find which castle they meant (if it was a castle at all), through conjecture. The Castle represents the Castle at Tomar - Portugal, as already noted was a safe haven for the Templars fleeing from Europe via Spain. Then to those who ate the Bread. On 1st of May each year a festival is held in Scotland called the Night of Beltane Fires, which is celebrated by the eating of bread; so, the second place must be Scotland. The refuge refers to the Paris perceptory, this was the last place the Templars left before their arrests. Our Lady beyond the River denotes Marienburg in Germany. This town was the stronghold for the Teutonic Knights, an order many Templars assimilated into after their dissolution. Again to the Hostel of the Popelicans is Bulgaria(these were the Cathars of Bulgaria); and again to the stone, which through the century's was mistakenly believed to be Jerusalem or even Stonehenge, but is according to Eco is actually Alamut - Azebaijan.

According to Eco, the meetings between the French and the English Templars failed to take place in 1584. It was shortly after this time that numerous pieces of literature began appearing, leading to the creation of the Rosicrucians, however the Fama testifies to another possible motive for the appearance of these enigmatic manifestos:

> And although at this time we make no mention of either names or meetings, yet nevertheless everyone's opinion shall assuredly come to our hands, in what language so ever it may be; nor anybody shall fail, who so gives his name, but to speak to some of us, either by word of mouth, or else, if there be some let, in writing. [5]

The English and French meeting was interrupted by the Gregorian reform Calendar, this meeting between the English

5. Fama (Yates, F.A. The Rosicrucian Enlightenment, p.251)

and French Grand Masters failed to take place because the French had adopted the Gregorian Calendar in 1583 (a year before the meeting was supposed to take place). This meant that because the English had not adopted the Calendar (until 1752), the French, working on the Gregorian Calendar, would be 10 days ahead of the equivalent date in England. So, when the French arrived for their meeting with the English on 24th June (Saint Johns day) 1584, it would have been the 13 th June in England. The French Grand Master may have waited for the English for a few days, but did not wait for 10, for on the 10th day the English Grand Master would have arrived, at which point it would have been the 13th July in France. The English Grand Master, John Dee, would soon have realised his mistake, but what could he do, without knowing how to contact his French counterpart there was nothing he could do immediately.

A year before the fated meeting which never materialised, it is known that John Dee had been residing in Trebona ,Bohemia; there he had been busy making contact with numerous alchemists, Templars and other neo-Templar societies. It is unusual that he was in Bohemia before the meeting with the French. Could it have been that he was seeking the German part of the plan before he received the French part? Did he want the plan for himself? The answers to these questions will probably be left unanswered, but what is of more concern is what he did in Bohemia from 1583 to 1589.

It is probable that Dee had turned his attentions to finding the German part of the plan. He created a massive following in both Bohemia and Germany, which were tolerant to other religious and esoteric activities. Dee was already renowned as a respected author and his works were easily available in the more liberal countries of Europe. Apart from Dee's literature, he was also very accomplished in the field of public relations. It was he who instigated the Royal wedding between Fredrick V, Elector Palentine and Elisabeth, daughter of James I, in 1613.

The manifestos

It is also believed that Dee's influence was also prevalent in the creation of the two manifestos published not long after the wedding, which as was mentioned in chapter one and can only be described as an esoteric publications. The *Fama* (1614) and *Confessio* (1615), who some believe, written by Johann Valentin Andreae (subsequent Grand Master of the Prieure de Sion - another neo-Templar order), seems a clear and unambiguous message to the Templars in possession of the German part of the plan to come forward and join the English keepers of the plan. They may not have been total-ly convinced that the English keepers of the plan were request-ing them to come forward, but John Dee's *Monas Hieroglyphica* and the many references to Templar traditions in the mani-festo, would have assured the German keepers of the plan that it was not some Catholic conspiracy. Although the man-ifestos would not have been explicit to most lay people, they did prompt an overwhelming response from esoteric organi-sations and the German public. So much so, that Robert Fludd, the English Grand Masters successor to John Dee, pub-lished some works which intended to clarify the exact mean-ing of the Manifestos.

These manifestos were really an appeal to the keep-ers of their part of the plan to come and meet up with other keepers. This is exemplified in the *Fama*:

> After the death of J.O., brother R.C. rested not, but as soon as he could, called the rest together (and as we suppose) then his grave was made. Although hitherto we (who were the latest) did not know when our loving father R.C. died, and had no more than the bare names of the beginners, and all their successors, to us, yet there came into our memory a secret, which through dark and hidden words, and

speeches of the 100 years, brother A., the successor of D.(who was the last and second row of succession, and had lived amongst many of us) did impart unto us of the third row of succession. . . . It shall be declared hereafter to the gentle Reader, not only what we have heard of the burial of R.C., but also made manifest publicly by the foresight, sufferance, and commandment of God, whom we most faithfully obey, that if we shall be answered discreetly and Christian-like, we will not be afraid to set forth publicly in print our names and surnames, our meetings, or anything else that may be required at our hands. [6]

It is no coincidence that the same author who wrote the manifestos, also wrote *The Chemical Wedding of Christian Roseencreuts* - a significant piece of Roseicrucian literature. The public response to the manifestos was so overwhelming that further literature attempted to refine the meaning of the manifestos and direct its appeal to the few with knowledge rather than the inquisitive many. Esotericists' also believe that at this time Francis Bacon was busy writing the Shakespearean plays and sonnets. The Shakespearean plays, apart from being possibly the greatest works of British literature ever written, contain a mass of information which, some believe is elaborately disguised through its esoteric nature, and some believe that it makes reference to the plan. According to Foaucaults Pendulum, when Fredrick V was defeated by Spain with the fall of Heidelburg, the English Templars turned their attention to the French (for their part of the plan), and similar literature to that circulated in Germany was circulated in France; which is exactly what occurred.

With the amount of literature being churned out over Europe at this time, it was inevitable that in attempting to reach the few who had knowledge of the plan, many other peoples interests would be aroused too. Some of these may have wanted the parts of the plan for themselves, or others

6. Fama (Yates, F.A., The Rosicrucian Enlightenment, p.244)

may have wanted to prevent the plan from ever reaching fruition. While this was going on, attitudes towards the plan also changed; in the past it was considered, by the few Templars who knew, exclusive knowledge which only they should discover and utilise. However with hints of knowledge of the plan now extending to other groups, emphasis on discovering the contents of the plan and utilising its power had now changed to a from a Templar to a nationalistic pursuit. This further hindered French, German and English Templars from coming together. Not only had the creators of the plan failed to account for possible changes in calendar cycles, but they had also failed to anticipate how the virtues of nationalism might override the virtues of Templar brotherhood. In *Naometria* (1605) Simon Studion's apocalyptic work, it mentions a tripartite alliance between Henry King of France, James I of England, and Fredrick of Germany; if there was such an alliance, could it possibly have been prompted by knowledge of the plans existence.

But, what is or what was the plan, and why has it generated so much latent literature? First of all in Eco's plan, each part of the six messages held by the Templars in different countries when put together form part of a single message, which can only be deciphered with the six messages together; this much accords with esotericists knowledge of the subject. Once deciphered the coded messages would reveal the location and the type of map to be used in determining the location of an incredible power source. The map, whose location would be indicated in the message (and the message should have been complete by 1944), would then be placed under Faucaults Pendulum (Conservatoire des Arts et Metiers-Paris) on Saint Johns Day (24 th June), and a beam of light should indicate the location of the power source on the map. Whether the plan concerns reference to a type of map to be used, has yet to be ascertained, however, it is known that John Dee held a keen interest in cartography (map making). It is possible that by missing the date of the meeting with the French he may have tried, in conjunction with searching for the French Templars, to discover the secret location of the power source without the six complete messages.

The power source which the plan is concerned with is subterranean; it is at a point where the Telluric currents under the earth's crust converge. These telluric currents are commonly known as lay lines which feature quite prominently in this book, for instance, it is believed that the pyramid builders harnessed their energies and that the Gothic churches, which were built by Templars, were built upon and map out lay lines; the consequence of which gave the buildings divine properties. It is believed in some esoteric circles that control of the power of the lay lines would result in the control of sea levels, tides, currents and the resulting weather that a change in these factors would produce all over the world. Many esotericists believe that the ancient people of Atlantis (Atlanteans) had discovered it, but whether through foul play or through one of their experiments with it going wrong, the result was the destruction of their civilisation, as referred through history as the Great Flood, and all traces of its existence. The Templars called the point which these lay lines or telluric currents converge, the Umbilicus Telluris or the Navel of the World. Furthermore, as previously explained, Hancock and Faiia have discovered a connection in the longitudinal positioning of sites known as 'Navel's of the World' - the longitudinal angles between these sites all being linked to pentagonal geometry and the number nine. It will probably be difficult for the reader to imagine a power source considerably more powerful than any nuclear bomb, and which is supposedly capable of shifting continents, and causing all kinds of adverse catastrophes on a global scale.

Knowledge alone, of the location of the convergence of these subterranean lay lines, which are meant to be so vital to the stability of the world environment is not enough. Why were the six messages only to be brought together in 1944 and the plan completed in the year 2000? Why were 600 years meant to pass before the Templars were allowed to know where these lay lines converged? According to Eco, the reason for this is that the plan had to be sufficiently staggered so that mankind could become technologically advanced enough to construct some sort of valve device which could control these currents. The Templars knew that we would again reach a stage of technology in which, like the Atlanteans, we would be able to harness the power of the worlds telluric currents. The Templars also designed the time between the discovery of the location (1944), and the harnessing of its power in the year 2000, to allow time for the construction of such a machine able to control the Umbilicus Telluris. But what would be the point or purpose of controlling such a power source? Would it be to create mass destruction, to hold the world to ransom, or would it be used for constructional purposes? If such a power source does exist then who can know how it will he harnessed when discovered?

The Protocols of Zion

At the turn of the last century a piece of literature was circulated around Europe known as *The Protocols of the Learned Elders of Zion*. In it were contained a series of twenty four declarations which were attributed to the Elders of Zion - who it said were the heads of the Jewish communities around the world. The Protocols spoke of a Jewish plot to take over the world through methods such as: the suppression of the working classes, producing arms and supporting revolutions where they occurred. It is submitted that these methods through which the Jews were supposedly going to achieve world domination, were the result of some writers vivid imagination. Notice, the word author is not used here - because esotericists maintain that the original author of the Protocols did not mention Jews at all, but was writing about the Templars or Neo Templars, and according to Baigent and Leigh and also Stephen Knight the original Protocols originated from a masonically orientated society. The Protocols of the Elders of Zion still include many parts of the original Protocols and with just a few changes, the Protocols of Zion it is believed, can be almost converted into their original form. If the words tunnel network under the Metro are replaced by the tunnel network under Provins, and every time the word Jew appears it is changed into Templar, and also if the Elders of Zion was replaced with the Templar hierarchy or Grand Masters which were supposed to bring together the parts of the plan; the work, as many esotericists would maintain, almost reverts back to its original. After these changes to the Protocols are made, they could easily be mistaken for the plan itself. It is not in doubt that the Protocols of Zion had a profound effect in how Jews were treated and perceived in Europe and beyond. It has been said that it was the Protocols which motivated Hitler and Stalin to exterminate the millions of Jews they did, however, with regard to Hitler (although he incited his followers to read the Protocols), it is necessary to view his motivations from a deeper perspective.

At the end of the nineteenth century the 'Order of the new Templars' was established in Austria and Germany, which boasted of links with the Rosicrucians, Cathars, Templars and an ancient wisdom, but what was more striking was its emblem - the swastika.[7] In 1918 an another esoteric Order was formed, called the Thule Gesellschaft which was connected to the Order of the New Templars. Among the first members to join this secret society, were Rudolf Hess, Rosenburg and Adolf Hitler. The esoteric indoctrination of this group must have had a deep influence on Hitler, who became obsessed with the Grail. A testament to his esoteric tendencies lies in the fact that throughout the war he never made any important decisions without conducting his horoscope; many of his other staff exhibited occultist or esoteric tendencies too. Another prominent member of Hitler's staff was Heinrich Himmler, who was fascinated by the Grail legends and imparticular, Otto Rahn's *Kreuzzug gregn den Gral* (*Crusade against the Grail*). Himler even commissioned a book, *Court of Lucifer*, in which Montsegur was established as the

7. Baigent, M. Leigh, R., and Lincon, H., The Holy Blood and the Holy Grail p.77

Grail itself. He also commissioned a history of the brotherhood and also organised a group researchers within his for-
eign intelligence department to study the Cathars,
Rosicrucianism and Freemasonry[8] and also to seek out the
supposed ancient esoteric societies of the Thule in Iceland
and Tibet. Some people even go so far as to attribute Hitler's
sweeping moves across Europe to his search for the six messages which make up the plan: Paris (where the pendulum is
kept), Russia and the Balkans (popelican territory), attack on
Britain (British part of message). Hitler also began two sweeping moves, one in North Africa and the other in Southern
Russia; it was his intention that these two armies would eventually meet, therefore taking Palestine which is where many
believed the last meeting place of the plan was to be held
(the stone -Jerusalem). This line of argument, that Hitler moved
his armies to obtain the different parts of the message, is by
no means a strong theory capable of withstanding much scrutiny. Many other theories exist to explain Hitler's moves during the War which are much more plausible, for instance the
search for oil and raw materials. However, if it is assumed
that Hitler intended to reach Jerusalem and that he was in
search of the messages of the plan, this would explain why
he ploughed so much of his military resource into North
Africa and Sourthen Russia, leaving the door agar for a
Russian counter offensive on his Eastern Front. Most historians will agree that although a brilliant orator, many of Hitler's
military strategies can be described as flawed to say the
least; but, was this man a megalomaniac, or was he conducting his military strategies in a frenzied desperate attempt
to find the plan, knowing when he did find it he would
be assured of dominance? Was Hitler indeed searching for different parts of the plan, wouldn't this explain his military tactics during the War, and wouldn't it explain why he still
believed he was going to win the war even when the might
of the Russian and allied forces were all set to crush what
was left of a crippled Germany?

8. McIntosh, C., The Rosy Cross Unveiled, p.22

If Hitler did believe that the Jews held a part of the plan which he sought, it could explain the way in which he dealt with them during the war. All Jewish clothing and belongings were meticulously searched through by the Nazis, as were their bodies after they had been sent to the gas chambers. Also, use was made of their bodies which would of enhanced the screening process further e.g. gold teeth were removed, as was artificial limbs, hair, and even sometimes skin. Doesn't such fanaticism in the way the Nazis sifted through every item of Jewish belongings raise the possibility that they might have been searching for more than just the effective recycling of their possessions and property. Another factor which would enforce this theory, is the fact that the gas chambers were designed to make the Jewish people believe they were entering showers - rather than the place where they were to be exterminated. Everything was constructed so that the people would not know what was going to happen to them. It has often been maintained that the concentration camps were designed in this way so as not to cause panic and prevent the Jews revolting. But also, on the other hand, it can still be argued that by not knowing their fate the Jews who had on their person vital knowledge, would not have the opportunity to rid themselves of it.

By 1943 it is believed by numerous esotericists that Hitler had collected four parts of the six part plan. The parts which eluded him could have been the Poplicans part (which no one knew if it still existed or not), and the last part as the reader will recall which according to Eco was meant to be handed over in 1944 at the stone. In 1944, Hitler sent an envoy to Britain offering an alliance, the man he sent was one of his most trusted - Rudolph Hess. Hess may have been instructed to let those in Britain (who understood the immense consequences of knowing the location of the Umbilicus Telluris) know that Germany had in her possession four sixths of the plan. He flew his meshashmit to Scotland and was immediately imprisoned where he was more or less kept for the rest of his life (apart from the times he spent attending the Nuremberg trials). It seems strange though that he was not moved to somewhere in England, even London. Rumours had it that he had in his possession a secret which could severely disrupt if not shatter the western world (so much so that it prompted a film to be made - Wild Geese II). It was as if his seclusion served a purpose to the British, or were they were also afraid of him speaking to anyone. In fact, one of the surgeons who treated Hess in Spandau wrote a book claiming that the man he was treating had none of the scars purportedly aquired by Hess in World War I, and therefore was not Hess. While Hess was kept at Spandau, he was also treated by the Americans and Russians, who took turns in attending to his welfare. Could it be that another was put in his place, for fear of what he might disclose to the Russians; as the seeds of the 'Cold War' had already begun to germanate?

The final meeting place for the last part of the plan to be exchanged was, according to Eco at Alamut- Azebaijan, with the Arabs. The Templars, although fighting against them for possession of the Holy Land, made strong links with them as their interests in gnostic religion and ancient mysteries coincided. If this last part of the message is known to people, then it is more than likely that someone or maybe by now many people know at least five sixths of the plan. So, these modern day Templars that may be missing one message of the plan, may know the location of Umbilicus telluris, may be close to knowing, or maybe have no idea at all because they are unable in some way to calibrate the map without this message. However, assuming that such a power source exists upon the earth, there could be an easier way of finding where the worlds subterranean Telluric currents converge, because if the Atlanteans found the place, then isn't it possible that with today's technology, and if such a place really exists, we could find the Unbilicus Telluris.

In nearly all peoples minds, we are taught to believe that we are more advanced than any society which has existed before us on this earth, however this may not necessarily be true. It would be difficult to imagine people from ancient times being able to produce micro chips, but at the same time its difficult to imagine how we would build a pyramid of Egyptian size and precision. So, although we consider ourselves advanced today, we may in some respects be less advanced than those in very ancient times. This may prevent us from finding the Umbilicus Telluris geologically, but the possibility is wide open and may of already been found by someone using this method.

Originally, after the six messages were unified, the plan was meant to be used to avenge the deaths of Jacques de Molay, to avenge the dissolution and persecution of the Templars by the Catholic church. However, it seems a distant possibility that such motivations, of things which occurred hundreds of years ago, still exist today. The people involved in these events , Clement V, Philip of France and members of the Inquisition have all passed away, and although the Catholic institution still exists today it is much more refined and less ruthless than it was in the days of Molay and does not really pose a threat to the institution of Masonry. The designers of the plan must have believed either that the Catholic church was going to reach an unprecedented position of power across the world, or what is more likely, that they had intentions that these Neo-Templars could formulate some kind of New World Order, to perpetuate the esoteric coninuum.

The reader will already have understood, through reading this book, that Masonic institutions are already very prevalent across the world. The reader must also concede that it is very possible that esoterism, as it has existed through history, may have had a profound effect on the shaping of history and the direction of mankind's development. Mankind may also be greatly indebted to esoteric societies for providing insights into mans subconscious nature which may not have been realised otherwise. However, with such powerful esoteric beliefs also comes great responsibility, and these beliefs should not be amplified to the extent of causing conflict, as is typical of some esoteric societies, but should be extenuated to more accurately reflect the whole ethos of esoteric knowledge and the purpose for which it was designed.

Select Bibliography

Ahmad, S.H., *The Hidden Mysteries of Numbers*, Kessinger Publishing, 1912

Alford, Alan, *Gods of the New Millenium*, Hodder and Stoughton, 1997

Andrews, Richard, and Schellenberger, Paul, *The Tomb of God*, Warner Books, 1997

Bacon, Francis, *The Advancement of Learning*, Kessinger Publishing, 1621

Bauval, Robert, and Gilbert Adrian, *The Orion Mystery*, Heinemann, 1994

Bauval, Robert, and Hancock, Graham, *Keeper of Genesis*, Mandarin, 1997

Baigent, Leigh, and Lincon, *The Holy Blood and The Holy Grail*, Arrow, 1996

Baigent, Michael, and Leigh, Richard, The Temple and the Lodge, Corgi, 1990

Baigent, Michael, Leigh, Richard, and Lincon, Henry, *The Messianic Legacy*, Corgi, 1991

Baigent, Michael, and Leigh, Richard, *The Dead Sea Scrolls Deception*, Corgi, 1992

Baigent, Michael, and Leigh, Richard, *The Exilir and the Stone*, Viking, 1997

Begg, Paul, Fido, Martin, and Skinner, Keith, *Jack the Ripper A to Z*, Headline, 1991

Bennett, John, *Origin of Freemasonry and Knight Templar,* Kessinger Publishing, 1907

Berg, Philip S., *Kabbalah for the Layman,* Research Centre of Kabbalah, 1981

Bernard, David, *Light on Masonry*, Kessinger Publishing, 1829

Bible, *The Apocrypha*, Oxford University Press, 1965

Capra, Fritjof, *The Tao of Physics,* Flamingo, 1983

Carey, M.F., *Freemasonry in all Ages,* Kessinger Publishing, 1896

Collins, Andrew, *Gods of Eden,* Headline, 1998

Conway, David, *Secret Wisdom,* Jonathan Cape, 1987

Cotterell, Maurice, *The Tutankhamun Prophecies*, Headline, 1999

Cox, George, and Jones, Eustace, *Arthurian Legends of the Middle Ages,* Senate, 1995

Daniken, Erich Von, *Chariots of the Gods,* Souvenir Press, 1969

Daniken, Erich Von, *Signs of the Gods*, Souvenir Press, 1980

Edwards, I.E.S., *The Pyramids of Egypt,* Penguin, 1947

Eschenbach, Wolfram von, *Parzival*, Continuum, 1991

G.J., *Mahhabone: The Grand Lodge Door Opened*, Poemandres Press, 1996

Gilbert, Adrian and Catterell, Maurice, *The Mayan Prophecies*, Element, 1995

Graves, Robert, *The Greek Myths:1*, Pelican Books, 1980

Freemasons Hall, *Uninted Grand Lodge Constitutions and Regulations*, Uninted Grand Lodge, 1995

Galanopoulous, A., and Bacon, E., *Atlantis: the Truth Behind the Legend,* Nelson, 1969

Goodwin, Joscelyn (translation), *The Chemical Wedding of Christian Rosenkreutz*, Magnum Opus, 1991

Gurdjieff, George, *All is Everything*, Routledge, 1950

Hall, Manly, *America's Assignment with Destiny*, The Philosophical Research Society, 1979

Hall, Manly, *The Lost Keys of Freemasonry*, The Philosophical Research Society, 1976

Hancock, Graham, *The Sign and the Seal*, Heinemann, 1992

Hancock, Graham, *Fingerprints of the Gods*, Heinemann, 1992

Hancock, Graham, and Faiia, Santha, *Heaven's Mirror*, Michael Joseph, 1998

Harris, Melvin, *The True Face of Jack the Ripper*, Michael O'Mara Books, 1995

Heindel, Max, *Mysteries of the Great Operas*, The Rosicrucian Fellowship, 1921

James, Peter, *The Sunken Kingdom,* Pimlico, 1996

Jowett, p., *The Dialogues of Plato*, Clarendon Press, 1892

Knight, Christopher, and Lomas, Robert, *The Hiram Key*, Arrow,

1997

Knight, Stephen, *Jack the Ripper: The Final Solution*, Treasure Press, 1984

Knowles, Sir James, *The Legends of King Arthur and his Knights*, Senate, 1997

Landsburg, A. and S., *In Search of Ancient Mysteries,* Corgi, 1974

Lawrence, T. E., *Seven Pillars of Wisdom,* Penguin, 1973

Lincon, Henry, *Key to the Sacred Pattern,* Windrush Press, 1997

Lubicz, Schwaller de, *Sacred Science,* Inner Traditions International, 1982

Lubicz, Schwaller de, *Esoterism and Symbol,* Inner Traditions International, 1985

Lubicz, Schwaller de, *A Study of Numbers*, Inner Traditions International, 1986

MacHuisdean, Hamish, *The Great Law,* Erlestroke Press, 1937

MacKey, Albert G., *Encyclopedia of Freemasonry*, Kessinger Publishing, 1904

McIntosh, Christopher, *The Rosy Cross Unveiled,* Aquarian Press, 1980

Mavor, J., *Voyage to Atlantis*, Souvenir Press, 1969

Murphy-O'Connor, *The Holy Land*, Oxford University Press, 1998

Nema, *Maat Magick*, Weiser, 1995

Petrie, N.w. Flinders, *The Pyramids and Temples of Gizeh*, London, 1990

Randall - Stevens, H.C., *Atlantis to the Latter Days*, The Knight Templars of Aquarius, 1957

Renfrew, Colin, *Before Civilization*, Penguin, 1990

Roquebert, Michel, *Cathar Religion,* Editions Loubtieres, 1997

Short, Martin, *Inside the Brotherhood,* Grafton Books, 1989

Singer, Andre and Lynette, *Divine Magic*, Boxtree, 1995

Stewart, Basil, and Davidson, D., *The Great Pyramid*, Kessinger Publishing, 1927

Tedlock, Dennis, *Popol Vuh,* Simon and Schuster, 1985

Temple, Robert, *The Sirius Mystery*, Destiny, 1976

Thiering, Barbara, *Jesus the Man*, Corgi, 1993

Waite, Arthur Edward, *A New Encyclopaedia of Freemasonry*, Wings Books, 1996

West, John Anthony, *Serpent in the Sky*, Wildwood House, 1979

Wigston, W.F.C., *Bacon Shakespeare and the Rosicrucians*, Kessinger Publishing, 1923

Wilmshurst, Walter, *The Meaning of Masonry*, Gramercy Books, 1995

Wilson, Colin, *From Atlantis to the Sphinx*, Virgin, 1997

Yates, Frances A., The Rosicrucian Enlightenment, Routledge, 1996

Index